IMAGES
of America

DELTA MUSIC AND FILM

JEFFERSON COUNTY AND THE LOWLANDS

On the Cover: Big Bill Broonzy (right), a Jefferson County blues pioneer, member of the Blues Hall of Fame, and Grammy nominee, stands with Memphis Slim (left) and Little Bill Gaither (back page) around 1940. Broonzy's filmography includes over 20 credits in documentaries, movies, and television shows. (Courtesy of Frank Driggs Collection.)

IMAGES
of America

Delta Music and Film

Jefferson County and the Lowlands

Jimmy Cunningham Jr. and Donna Cunningham

ARCADIA
PUBLISHING

ISBN 978-1-4671-1395-3

Published by Arcadia Publishing
Charleston, South Carolina

Printed in the United States of America

Library of Congress Control Number: 2014954489

For all general information, please contact Arcadia Publishing:
Telephone 843-853-2070
Fax 843-853-0044
E-mail sales@arcadiapublishing.com
For customer service and orders:
Toll-Free 1-888-313-2665

Visit us on the Internet at www.arcadiapublishing.com

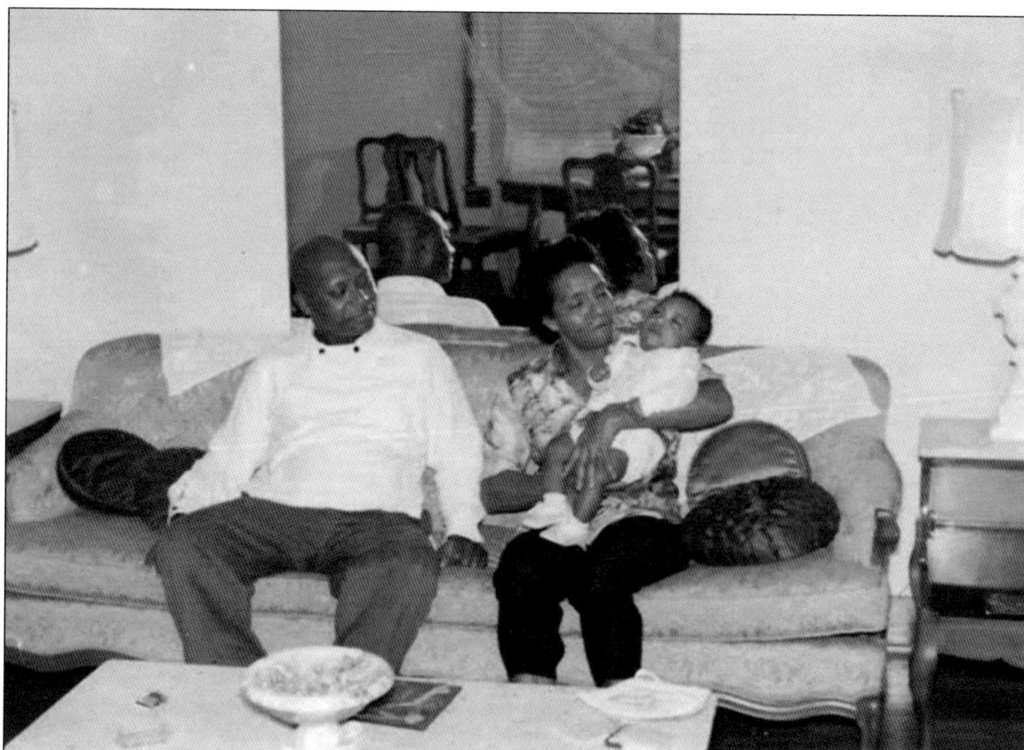

This book is dedicated to Geraldine Smith (shown holding her grandson, Jimmy Cunningham Jr., and seated next to her husband, Mark Smith), who often admonished her daughter, Donna Cunningham, in the 1950s about listening to Howlin' Wolf, John Lee Hooker, Muddy Waters, and other bluesmen. She derisively called their music "that ole gut-bucket blues." We hope for her sake that Z.Z. Hill is not in heaven playing "Down Home Blues" too loudly. (Courtesy of Donna Cunningham.)

Contents

Acknowledgments 6

Introduction 7

1. Early Entertainment Influences in the Delta Lowlands 9
2. Music Legends of the Delta Lowlands 21
3. Songs Connected to the Delta Lowlands 37
4. The UAPB/Delta Lowlands Music Connection 53
5. Jefferson County Juke Joints, Honky-Tonks, and Nickelodeons 61
6. Lesser-Known Music Greats of the Delta Lowlands 75
7. Select Gospel Quartets and Groups in the Delta Lowlands 95
8. Film and Television in the Delta Lowlands 101

Acknowledgments

It has been a great experience to write about what few others have, regarding our part of the Delta. However, none of this would have been possible without the many folks who kindly contributed to this project. Mucho shout-outs and appreciation go to the following: Greg Johnson and the Special Collections Department of the University of Mississippi (awesome assistance!), Jim O'Neal (what a pleasure to correspond with a Blues Hall of Famer who granted us use of a wagonload of pictures), Maxine Brown, Morris Hayes, Larry Braggs, Garnett Brown (great conversations and great pictures), Katherine Gogel, James Leary, Rob Morrison, James Fraher, the Arkansas History Commission, Karen Wolfe, Dave Cooper, Joe Pitts, Jocelyn Richez, the *Pine Bluff Commercial*, Ray Hagen, Kenneth Johnson, Journeyman Pictures, Toby Byron, Don Sepulvado, Devlon Chandler, Shola Lynch, the Racy Brothers, Henry Hackett, Carol Williams Rankin, Paul Perdue, Mike Boulan, the Kinsmen, Wanda Ficklin Walker, Colette Ficklin, Naomi LaVeaux Summerville, Dedrick Jones, Earl Gober, Steven Braud, Karen Wolfe, Dornetta Hobbs, Zac Ray, Mike Holcomb, Mae Francis Price, Walter Witherspoon, Ruth Ward Rice, Vernell and Vicky Racy, University of Arkansas at Pine Bluff (UAPB), Henri Linton, Juanita Currie, Mary Greenlee Jones-Wood, University of Arkansas at Little Rock Center for Arkansas History and Culture, and the Special Collections Department, University of Arkansas Libraries.

Many talented groups and artists were not included in this book because of space constraints. However, several of these artists have helped keep music traditions alive in the Delta Lowlands and beyond. We salute them, especially those organizers of events with live music such as Pine Bluff's Music on Main Street, Wabbaseka's Scatterfest, Altheimer's Bluesfest, Dumas's Ding Dong Days Festival, Dermott's Crawfish Festival, the Lake Chicot Fall Festival in Lake Village, and many others.

Also, the intellectual tools to write this and our previous book, *African Americans of Pine Bluff and Jefferson County*, were developed in us by special people. Those master teachers whose English, American history, and theater instruction helped lay the foundation for this publication include Dr. Virelene J. Coleman, Dr. Carolyn Blakely, Frances Johnson Evans, Wade Hall, Dr. Betty Williams, Dr. Juanita Torrence, Gardenia Ambler, and Dr. K.D. Godwin. You all are *always* with us in our writing and research!

Finally, we thank God for blessing us with another opportunity to write a testimony of the Delta's genius. With supportive family members like Alicia Cunningham, Alvin Starks, and Camuriel and Marc Cunningham, God has surrounded us with an army of the best "go-to" people ever. Also, we thank our little family cheerleaders in Kai O'Neal and Sean Carter Jr.

INTRODUCTION

Colossally talented. Woefully ignored. Scarcely researched. These phrases apply to one of America's most unheralded, yet important, regions in music and film production and innovation: the Arkansas River Lowlands, colloquially called the Delta Lowlands. A narrow subsection of the Arkansas Delta, it includes all or portions of Lonoke, Jefferson, Lincoln, Desha, and Chicot Counties, along with tiny segments of Pulaski and Drew Counties.

While most people know of the Delta's rich music heritage, many do not associate the Lowlands with that rich culture. Typically, that designation is reserved for all of Mississippi's Delta and portions of the Arkansas Delta, from areas near Helena to Blytheville. In film, almost no distinctive association is made with any part of the Delta.

Are we then exaggerating the Delta Lowlands' creative importance? The reader can be the judge. In music, the region boasts ties to the following persons: a former resident known by many scholars as the "Father of Delta Blues;" the person credited with writing the first song using a boogie-woogie bass line, effectively revolutionizing 20th-century popular music; one of the first artists with large record sales, who helped launch America's fascination with recorded popular music; the artist who popularized the electric bass; the first African American record producer for a major label and the first major producer of blues; the writer of the first commercially recorded country music song; the person credited with introducing the blues to Europe; the first blues performer to be the subject of a written biography; one of the most recorded artists in the history of jazz; a rock 'n' roll legend who learned his inimitable piano style while in Pine Bluff; and one of the earliest disc jockeys in the nation to play rock 'n' roll daily on the radio. The Delta Lowlands is also the place where iconic artists like Miles Davis, Bobby Rush, and Sam Cooke, among others, had critical formative experiences.

In film, radio, and television, the distinctions continue. The area has ties to the following: the person first credited with synchronizing sound with motion pictures, developing the first slow-motion camera images, developing the Nielsen Ratings, and producing over 11,000 inventions in film and photography; the person who became America's first Western genre movie star and who costarred in one of America's earliest blockbuster movies; the first female television heroine and the first female to star in a Western television program; the first African American woman to sign a contract with NBC television; the producer and writer of three of the most popular television series of the 1970s and 1980s; the screenwriter of one of the most well-known sci-fi movies; and an actor who costarred in a 1960s television series that became one of the most famous television/movie franchises ever. The area is home to the first radio station to broadcast in Arkansas, the first VHF television station to broadcast in Arkansas, the first African American–owned radio station in the state, and the broadcast tower that was the second-tallest man-made structure in the world when it was built.

This book's eight chapters chronicle key aspects of the Delta Lowlands' music and film story. Considering the overabundance of area talent, specific criteria were used to objectively choose artists for inclusion. Hence, we determined that a musical act had to have recorded its work, as well as meeting one of four other criteria: membership in a regional or national hall of fame; inclusion in a published encyclopedia or compendium of music; placement of a song on a national music chart; or, recipient of a major national award (Grammy, Stellar, or Dove, for example) in music.

Interestingly, after applying the criteria, the list produced unexpected results. It was no surprise that the largest number of artists meeting the criteria worked in the blues genre, because of the area's Delta roots. However, it was surprising that so few gospel artists met the criteria, especially considering the profound history of gospel quartets in the area. Hence, it was decided to include a chapter devoted to a small sampling of gospel groups that may not have met the formal criteria (the exception was the Racy Brothers), but who were, nonetheless, representative of the region's talent.

The chapter dedicated to film is the largest single unit in this book. Despite the use of the term "film" in the book's title, television and radio are also included. The selection criterion was simple; the persons or productions included had to be listed in the Internet Movie Database (IMDB), an authoritative online repository of entertainment industry information.

Our sincerest desire is that this book will inform people all over the world about this region's awesome musical and film legacy. More important, we hope that it will serve to guide a regional strategy highlighting the area's contributions as sources for heritage tourism.

One

Early Entertainment Influences in the Delta Lowlands

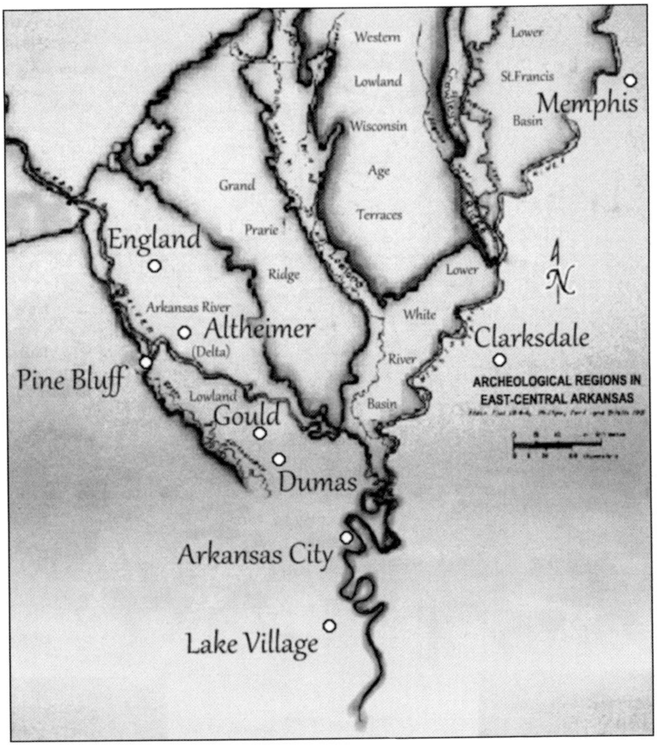

This map shows the five subregions of the Arkansas Delta, including the area listed formally as the Arkansas River Lowlands. This area, running north and south, includes communities in or around Scott (Pulaski County), England (Lonoke County), Pine Bluff/Altheimer/Wabbaseka (Jefferson County), Grady/Gould (Lincoln County), Dumas/Arkansas City/McGehee (Desha County) Dermott/Lake Village/Eudora (Chicot County), and Jerome (Drew County). The colloquial term "Delta Lowlands" is used throughout the book to eliminate confusion for readers, particularly those outside of Arkansas, as there is a region in the state of Kansas also known as the Arkansas River Lowlands. (Courtesy of UAPB Research Station and Zac Ray.)

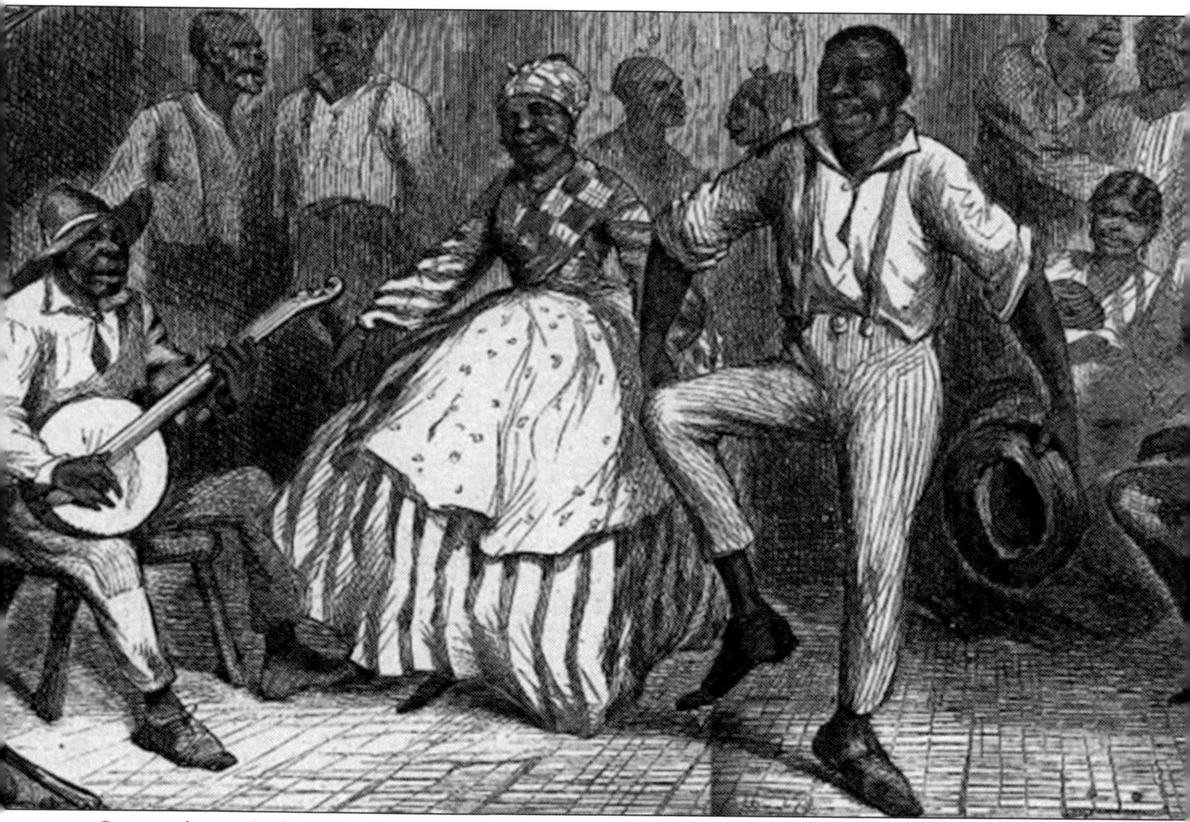

Spirituals, work songs, and field hollers shaped early-1800s music for slaves in the Delta Lowlands. Former Pine Bluff slave Jim Davis recalled: "I used to be a banjo picker in Civil War times. I could pick a church song as good as I could reel. Some of 'em I used to pick was 'Amazing Grace' and 'Old Dan Tucker.' I could pick anything." Banjos, which are widely referenced in Delta Lowlands slave narratives, were originally more popular among slaves, possibly because of their West African origins. The predecessors to the banjo were the *akonting* and the *ngoni* in Africa and the *banjar* in the Caribbean. Fiddles, in contrast, shared equal popularity among whites and blacks. (Courtesy of *Harper's Weekly*.)

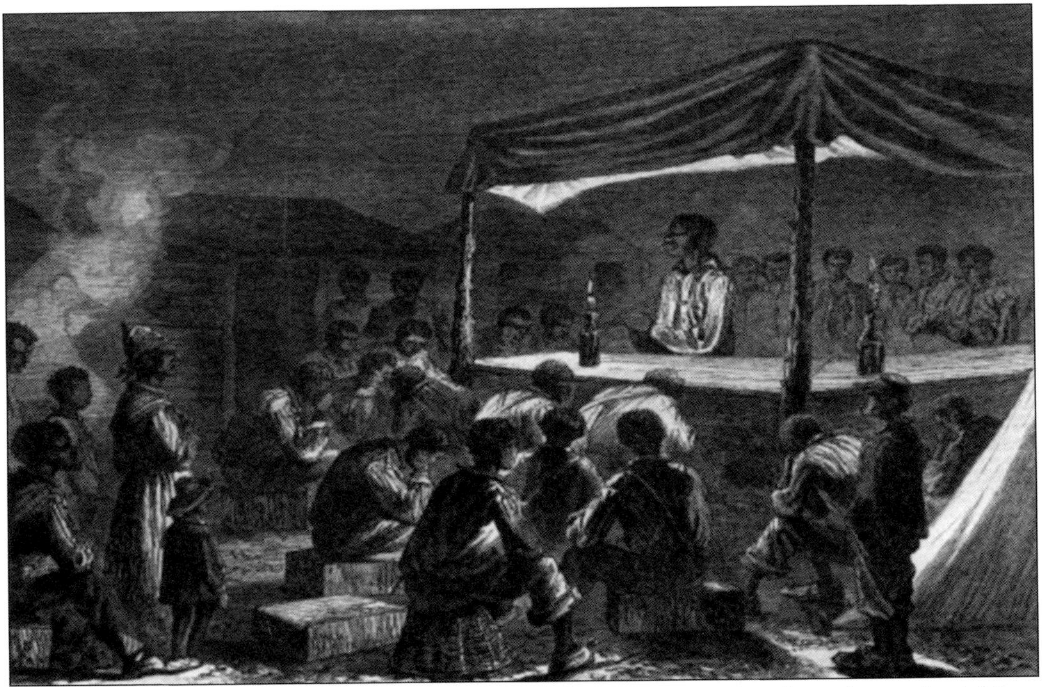

During slavery, secret night worship, which included singing, was often the only way for African Americans to meet spiritual needs. However, worship without the oversight of whites brought high risks, particularly in two of Arkansas's three largest slaveholding counties, Jefferson and Chicot. Former slave Stephen McCray relates: "We had church, but iffen the white folks caught you at it, you was beat most nigh to death. We used a big pot turned down to keep our voices down. . . . I was baptized in Pine Bluff, Arkansas. Our baptizing song was 'Hark from the Tomb.' " Chicot County former slave Lucretia Alexander remembered how slaves would "sing [church] songs in a whisper." (Courtesy of the Gilder Lehrman Collection.)

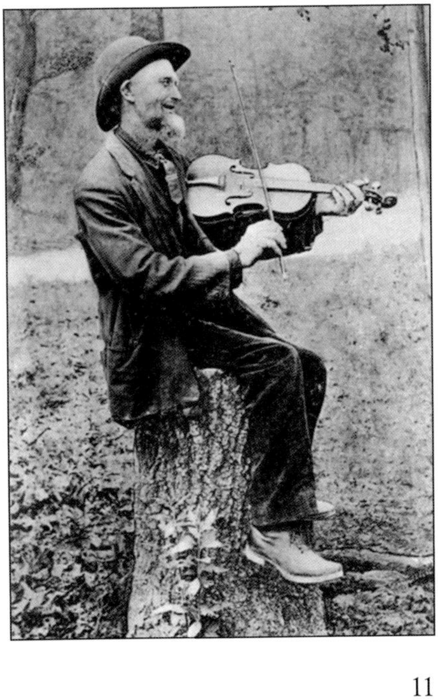

An unknown Arkansas man plays fiddle around 1910. The lyrics for one of the nation's most popular fiddle songs, "The Arkansas Traveler," are attributed to Kentucky transplant and Chicot County planter Sanford Faulkner, who wrote it after an 1840 encounter with a quirky backwoodsman. The origins of the actual tune are unclear, though some credit Faulkner also. The song quickly became one of the most recognizable fiddle songs of the South. In 1922, Arkansas-born Eck Robertson's recording of the song became the first country music commercial recording ever released, according to the *Encyclopedia of Great Popular Song Recordings Volume 2*. The song also served as Arkansas's state song from 1949 to 1963. (Courtesy of Shiloh Museum of Ozark History)

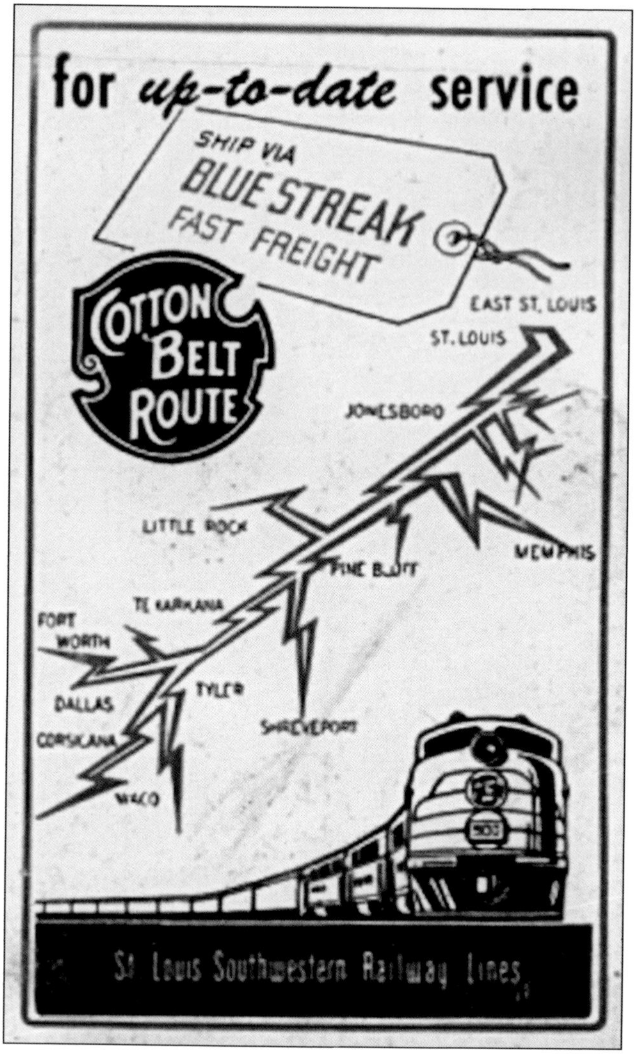

Delta Lowlands entertainment benefited immensely from the presence of the Cotton Belt train route and US Highway 65. While a means of cargo transport, the Cotton Belt also provided passenger transportation for singers, musicians, circuses, and shows, especially from the 1880s to the 1930s. Lowlands communities in and around Pine Bluff, a major transportation and cotton export hub because of the confluence of trains, highways, and the Arkansas River, had prime exposure to this entertainment. By the late 1930s, highways began displacing rail as the preferred mode of passenger travel. The "chitlin' circuit," an informal network of performance venues for African American artists during segregation, particularly in the South, thrived in areas connected by highways. Of Arkansas's three main chitlin' circuit highways, two intersected in the Delta Lowlands, US Highway 79 and US Highway 65. These roads facilitated major travel for artists in subsequent decades, primarily between the Delta and the Southwest and through the Deep South. They also facilitated touring by national acts. Consequently, numerous major entertainers came through the Lowlands, performing at its small clubs, juke joints, and theaters. Places like Eudora, Dumas, Arkansas City, and others benefited from their proximity to Highway 65; acts headed to Pine Bluff and Little Rock often performed in these smaller towns. The constant exposure of Delta Lowlands residents to the best in music, film, and theater entertainment contributed to the development of keen homegrown talent. (Courtesy of City of Tyler, Texas.)

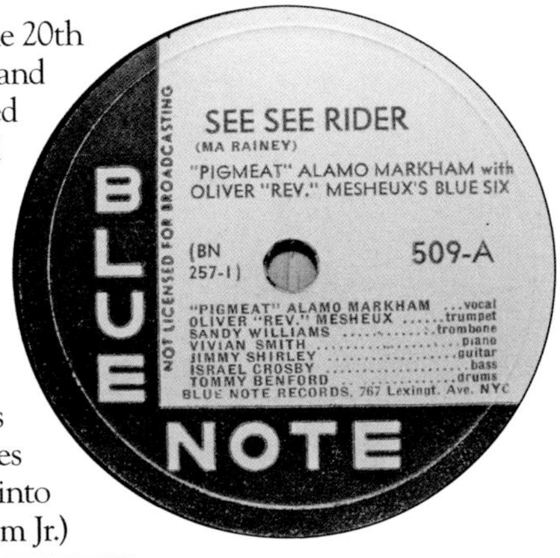

"See See Rider," one of the most influential blues songs of the 20th century according to allmusic.com, was reportedly written and sung by an itinerant former slave of the same name who lived in Jefferson County, just off the Arkansas River. Blues legend Big Bill Broonzy first heard it there around 1908, according to his biography. This date makes it the earliest reference to blues in any written record in Arkansas. See See Rider, who played a homemade guitar, bass, and fiddle, was a popular traveling songster. He introduced Broonzy to the new genre of blues, as Broonzy explained to researcher Alan Lomax. The song "See See Rider" was first recorded in 1924 by blues icon Getrude "Ma" Rainey, and it has been covered by scores of major artists. In 2004, the original recording was inducted into the Grammy Hall of Fame. (Courtesy of Jimmy Cunningham Jr.)

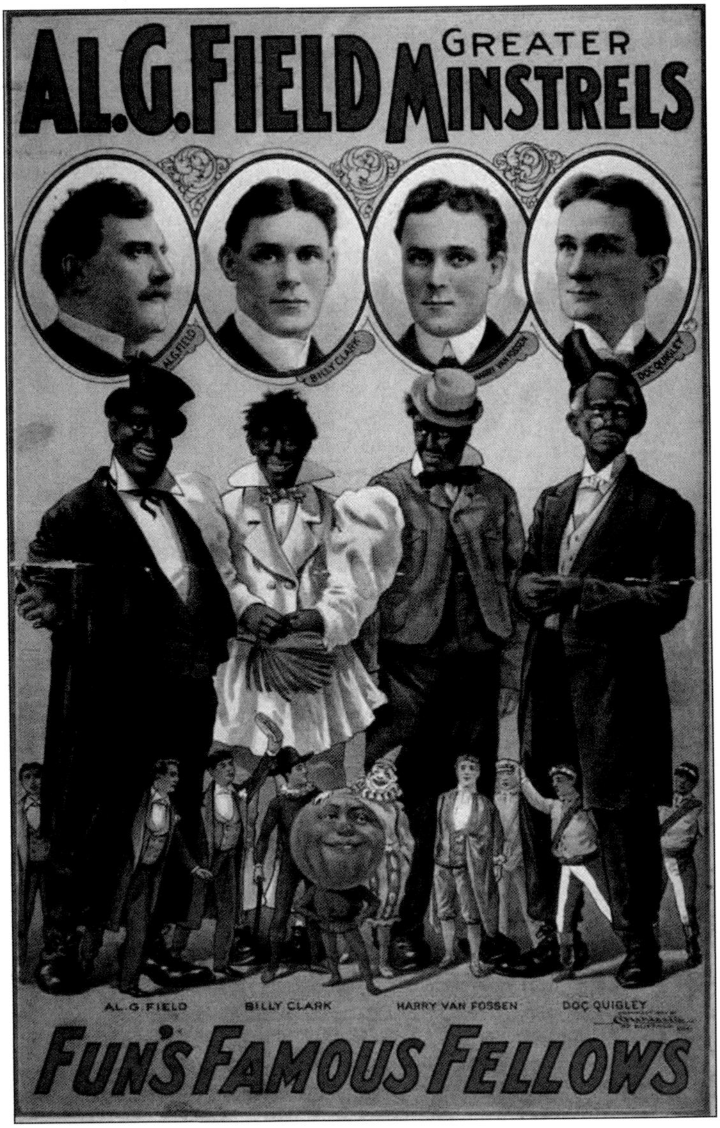

Minstrel shows, which often featured white performers in blackface, came to the Delta Lowlands frequently. The Al G. Field Minstrel Show came annually on its national tour and featured Pine Bluff's very own Dolf Kastor, a popular lead vocalist. When the act performed at the Saenger Theater in 1924, the local newspaper headline read, "Dolph Kastor came home yesterday and brought the Al G. Field Minstrels with him." (Courtesy of Library of Congress.)

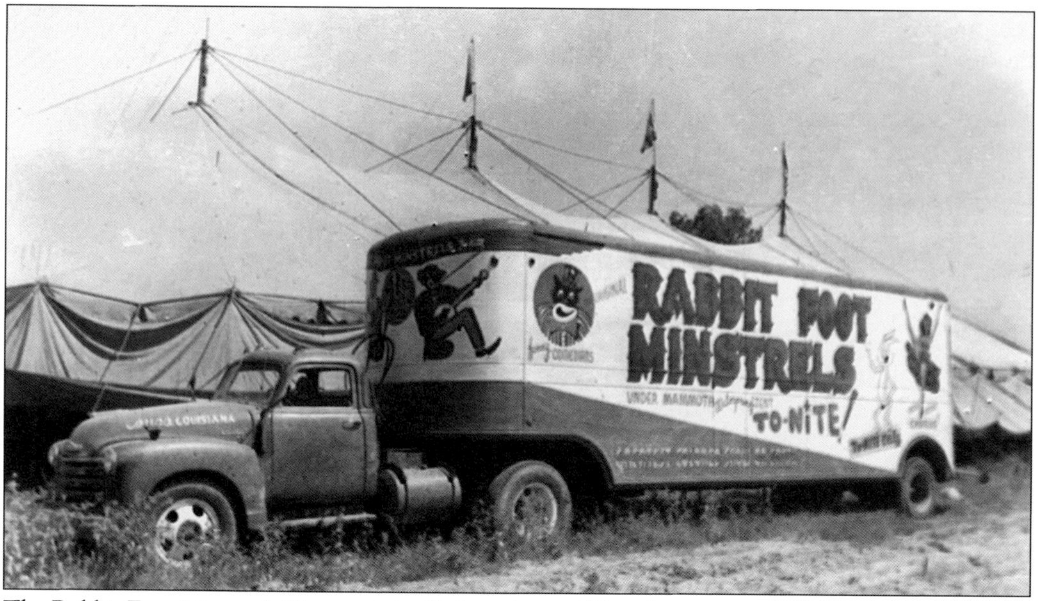

The Rabbit Foot Minstrels Show, originally based out of Florida, was composed of black performers who entertained throughout the South beginning in the early 1900s. Leon "Pee Wee" Whittaker, raised in part in Lake Village (childhood home of bluesmen "Po" Bob Woodfork and Robert Lee "Smokey" Wilson), was a member, as were blues legends Louis Jordan and Ma Rainey. The show toured the Delta Lowlands consistently. Its 1957 schedule in *Billboard* magazine underscored the chitlin' circuit's route through Highway 65, announcing stops in Lake Village, Eudora, Dermott, Dumas, and Pine Bluff. (Courtesy of William H.B. Jones.)

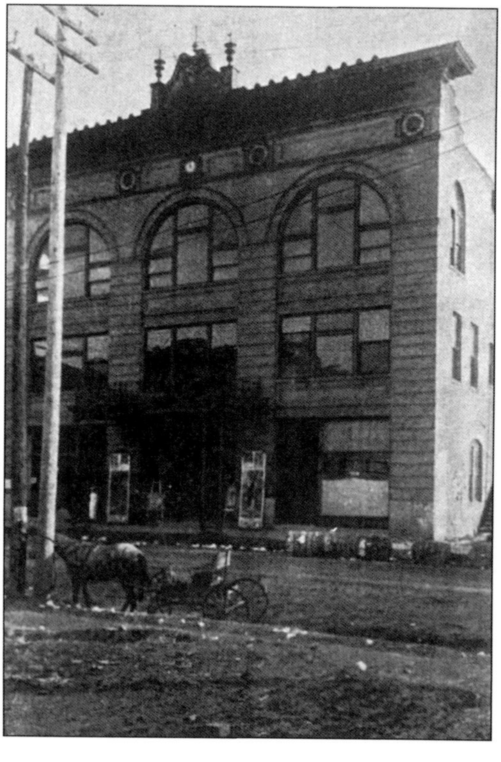

In January 1907, the Elks Theater was the first place in Pine Bluff, and possibly in the Delta Lowlands, to show a movie. The city opened several movie theaters thereafter, providing opportunities for people like film innovator Freeman H. Owens, who worked at the Elks Theater as a youth. By 1912, the Lowlands region boasted several theaters, in Dermott (Electric Theater), Arkansas City (the Lyrie), Lonoke (Magnet Theater), Lake Village (Star Theater), Eudora (Crystal Theater), and others. (Courtesy of Rotary Club of West Pine Bluff.)

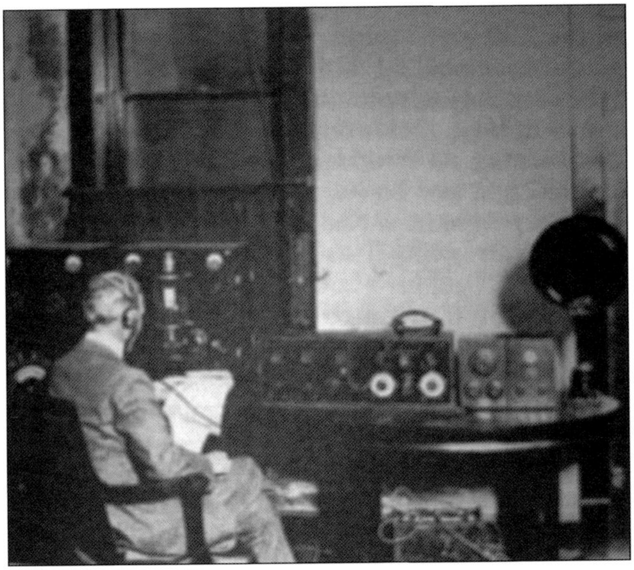

An announcer works in 1922 at the first radio station to broadcast in Arkansas, Pine Bluff's WOK. Started by Arkansas Power & Light founder Harvey Couch, the station went on the air for the first time on February 18, 1922. Broadcasts were on Tuesdays and Fridays for one hour. The area's bountiful talent of musicians, bands, and orchestras played during the station's yearlong run. In 1981, Elmer Dancy's KYDE-AM in Pine Bluff became the first black-owned radio station in Arkansas. The next year, Wayman Dun II's KWDT in Lonoke became the first black-owned FM radio station in the state. (Courtesy of James Leslie Collection.)

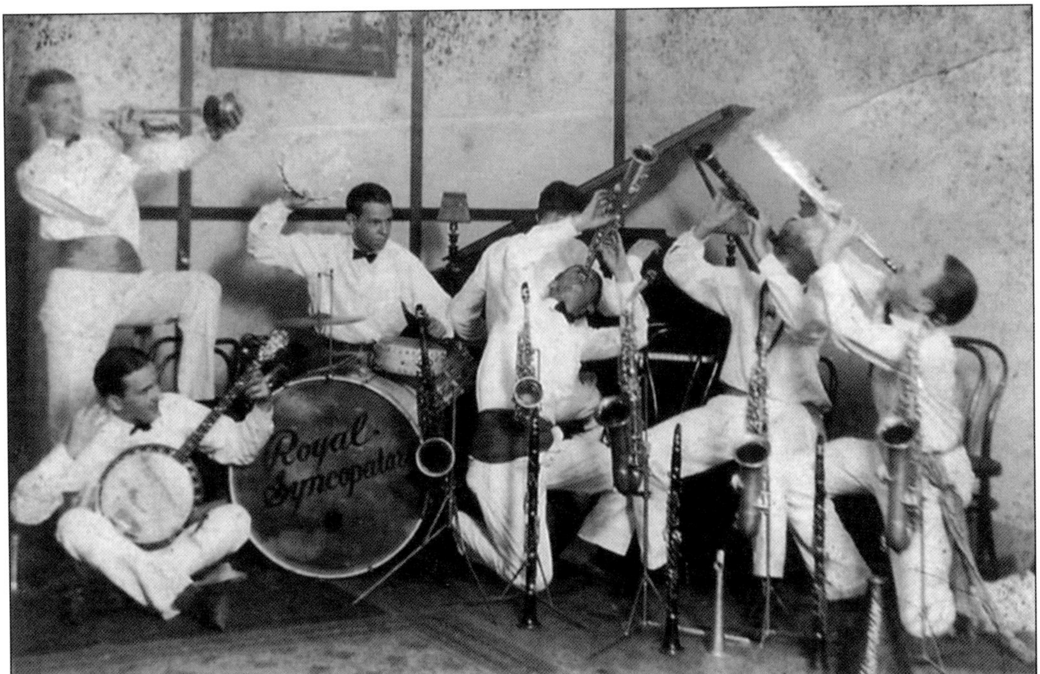

The Royal Syncopators of Pine Bluff was a 1920s jazz group. While the Lowlands produced many blues artists because of its Delta roots, jazz also had an important presence. The genre developed because of the area's proximity to the larger markets of St. Louis, Kansas City, Dallas, and New Orleans, where it flourished. Many big-name jazz artists came through the Lowlands' chitlin' circuit on their way to performances in larger markets. (Courtesy of Paul Perdue.)

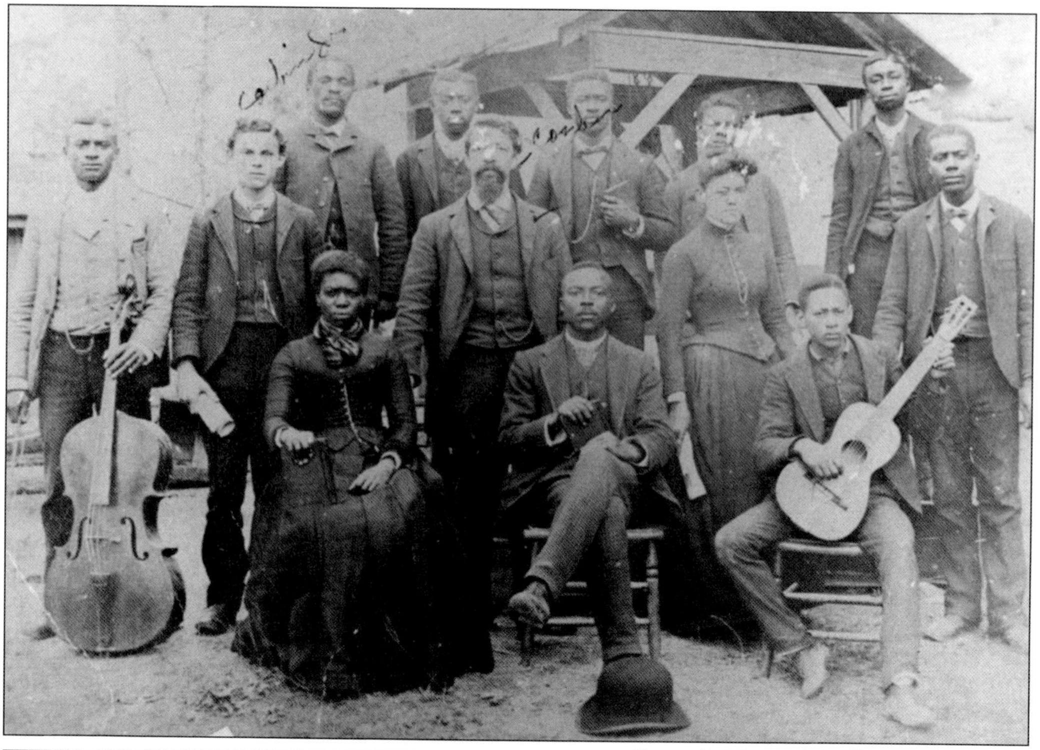

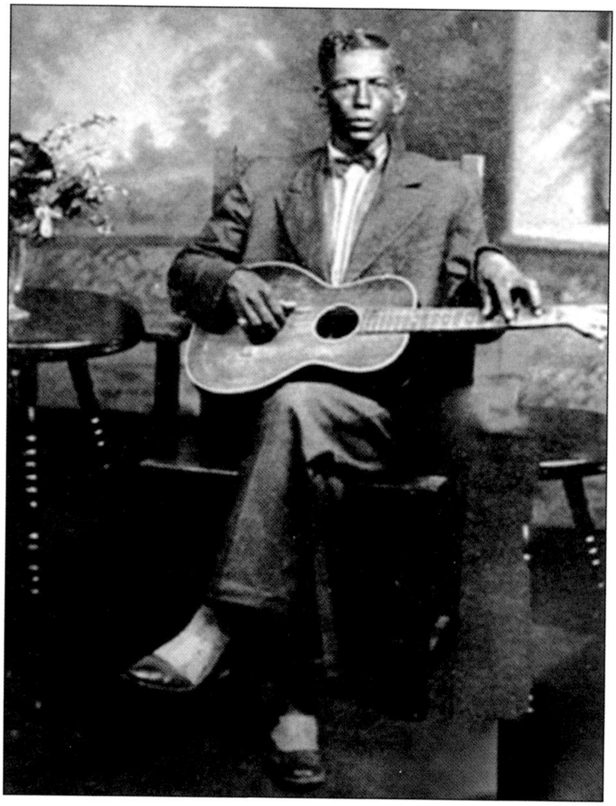

Branch Normal College band members pose in Pine Bluff in 1881 with the school's president, J.C. Corbin (second row, third from the left). The traditions established at UAPB, particularly in jazz and choral music, had a strong impact on the Delta Lowlands. (UAPB University Museum and Cultural Center.)

Charley Patton, the Mississippi-born blues pioneer, lived and performed in Dermott around 1910, according to Millie Torry, his ex-wife. US Census information recently discovered by blues researchers also suggests that Patton possibly lived in Dermott around 1930. Patton is considered by most scholars as the "Father of Delta Blues." His presence in the Lowlands as a resident and as a local artist undoubtedly contributed to the area's music development and, possibly, to his own artistic growth. (Courtesy of KPLU Radio.)

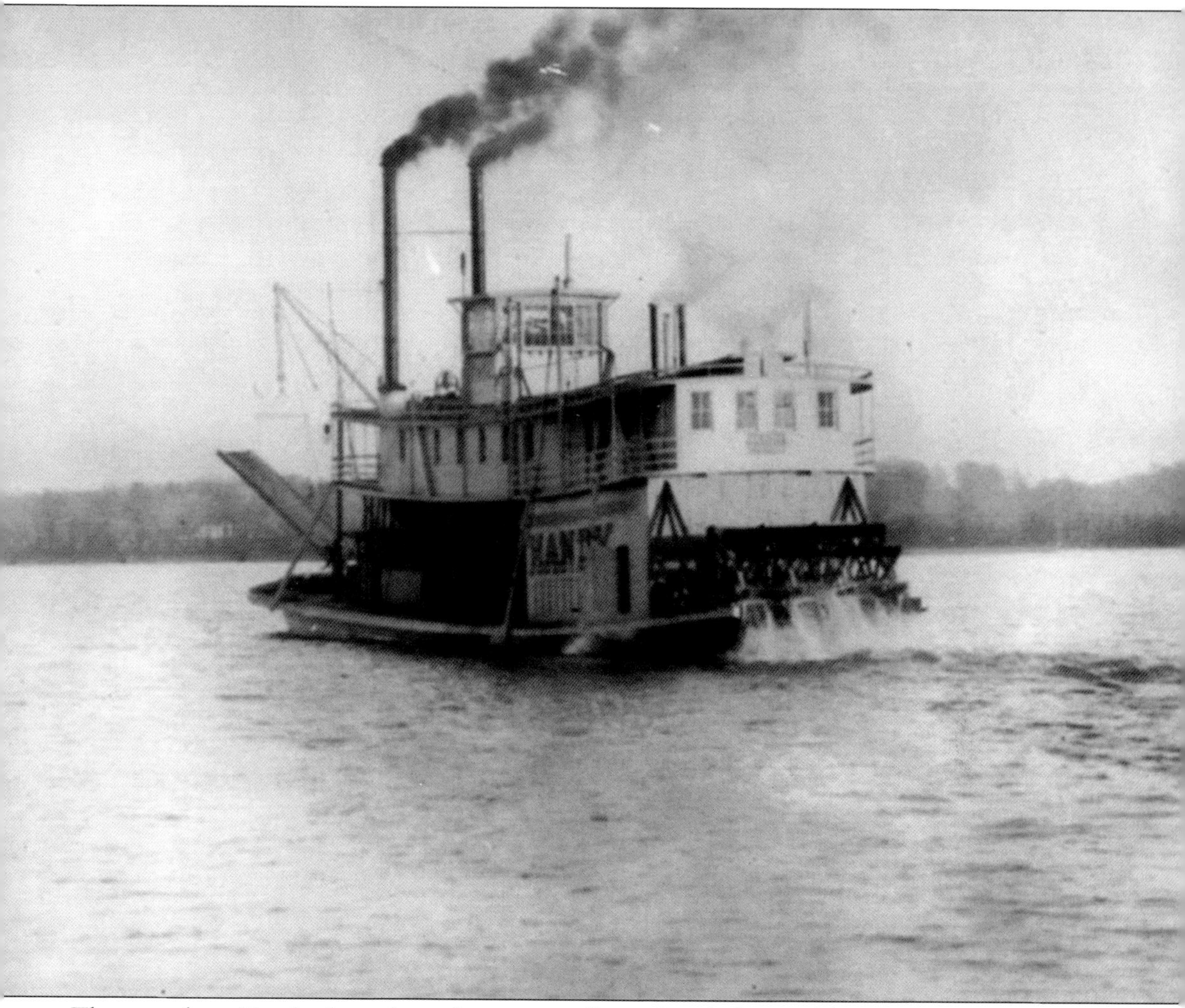

The steamboat *Handy* plows through waters on Bayou Bartholomew (the world's longest bayou) around 1905, probably near Chicot County. Bayou Bartholomew, the Arkansas River, and the Mississippi River supported steamboats, which provided a constant stream of live entertainment to the Delta Lowlands in the late 1800s and early 1900s. One observer wrote in 1911, "I would not give my recollections of the pleasure I enjoyed on a Bartholomew boat crowded with passengers . . . a dance on board every night and flirting with girls . . . for any recollection of my life." (Courtesy of Raul Ransom.)

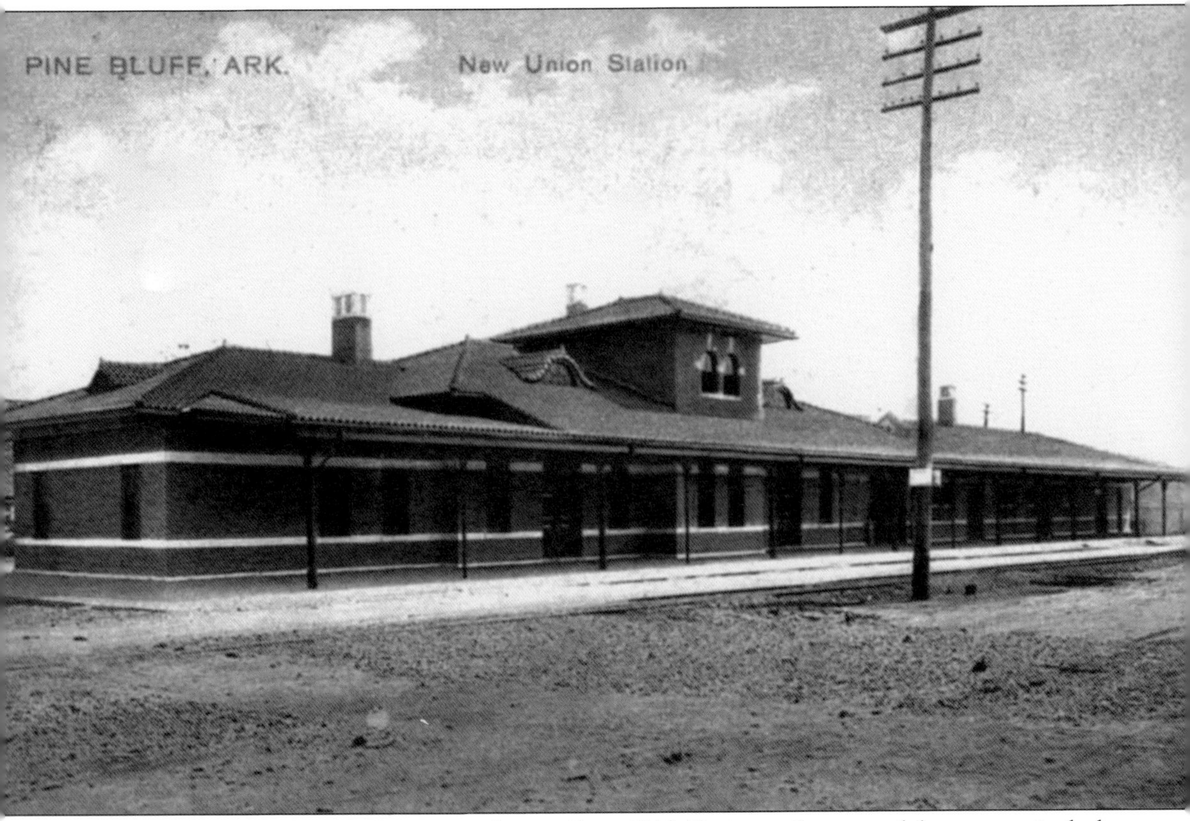

Pine Bluff's Union Station Depot stands proudly in 1910. Trains, railways, and depots, particularly in Jefferson County, have been integral to the Lowlands' music and film story. J. Mayo Williams, member of the Blues Hall of Fame and producer from Pine Bluff, left for Illinois with his family after his father was murdered at a railway station in Jefferson County. Actress Helen Seamon, who played in *The Wizard of Oz*, was sent to Hollywood on the wages of her father, who worked as a ticket agent at the Union Station Depot. According to his biography, Big Bill Broonzy, born in the Altheimer area, was told by a white man at the Union Depot to remove his military uniform upon returning from World War I because "No n*gger is gonna walk around here with Uncle Sam's uniform on up and down the street," prompting Broonzy's move to Chicago, where his music success began. Dr. Julius Lester, one of the most celebrated American children's authors, raised in the summers in Pine Bluff, wrote and recorded a critically acclaimed folk song, "Pine Bluff Freight Train Blues," about his childhood fascination with the area's lumbering trains. Jazz great Miles Davis recalled in his biography his childhood train trips to Pine Bluff from East St. Louis, eating his mother's packed fried chicken on the way to visit his grandfather in the Noble Lake area each summer. Singer Johnny Cash and his family rode the train to Pine Bluff's Union Station in 1937 to stay with relatives in the city, according to his biography, when the family farm was hit by a natural disaster. He later wrote a song about the event. Finally, an early-1900s Cotton Belt branch line, "The Peavine," which ran through Altheimer, shared the name of a popular blues song, "The Peavine Blues," which also characterized a Mississippi branch line. Scholars state that the name "Peavine," referring to the many branches of an actual pea vine, was a metaphor for freedom among Southern blacks. (Courtesy of William Allen.)

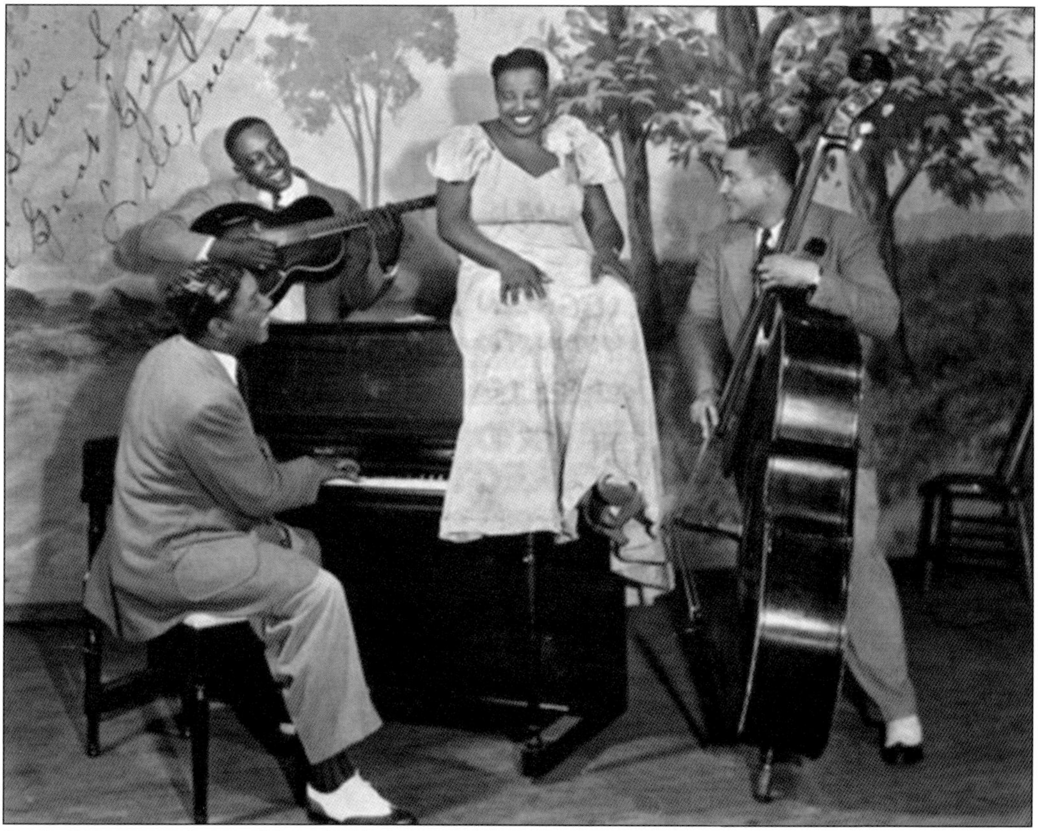

Big Bill Broonzy (second from left), from Jefferson County, accompanies singer Lil Green and her band in 1941. As a teenager in Pine Bluff around 1917, Broonzy played his fiddle, as he recounted in interviews with Studs Terkel and on the *Big Bill Sings Country Blues* album, saying: "I played for big picnics. They called them two way picnics. . . . They cooked big pigs and things like that. A two-way picnic is something where they have a big stage, two stages. . . . The white on the one stage and Negroes on the other stage. . . . There would be one band it would be white dancing on this side and colored on the other side." (Courtesy of Frank Driggs Collection.)

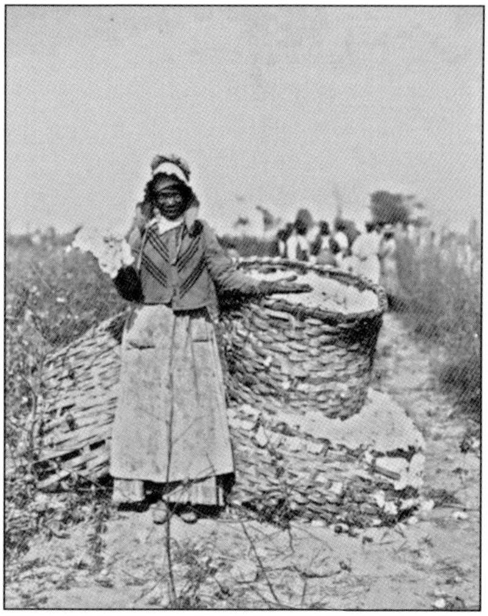

A cotton-picker stands in a Desha County field in the early 1900s. The Delta's extreme discrimination and hardship for blacks helped birth the region's premier contribution to American music, the blues. This genre was no less fed by virulent oppression and hardship in the Delta Lowlands. Lincoln County maintained for decades one of the most notorious US prisons, in which scores of largely black prisoners were systematically tortured. Jefferson County had what is thought to be the largest mass lynching in US history and led the state in total lynchings. Chicot County had the largest number of slaves in Arkansas and a reputation for cruel abuse. Blues was forged in the crucible of these conditions. (Courtesy of Arkansas History Commission.)

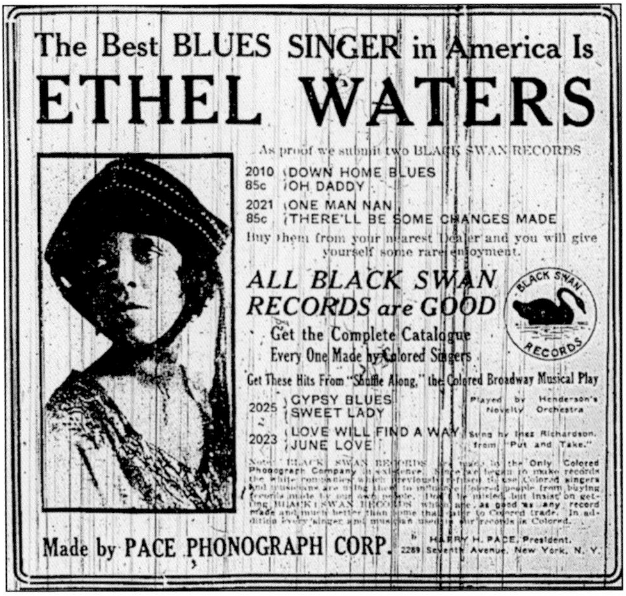

Commercial popular music in the United States started with the surprising success of early-1920s blues. In the 1920s, a small cadre of African American female blues singers, including Ethel Waters, Bessie Smith, Ma Rainey, Mamie Smith, Jefferson County's Sippie Wallace (see page 27), and a few other black women were among the nation's first major record-sellers in any genre. Their unexpected success jump-started the record industry and created the earliest template for recording stardom. When Ethel Waters visited Pine Bluff in 1921 for a two-day performance, she embodied the innovation of all of these black women. (Courtesy of Pace Phonograph Corp.)

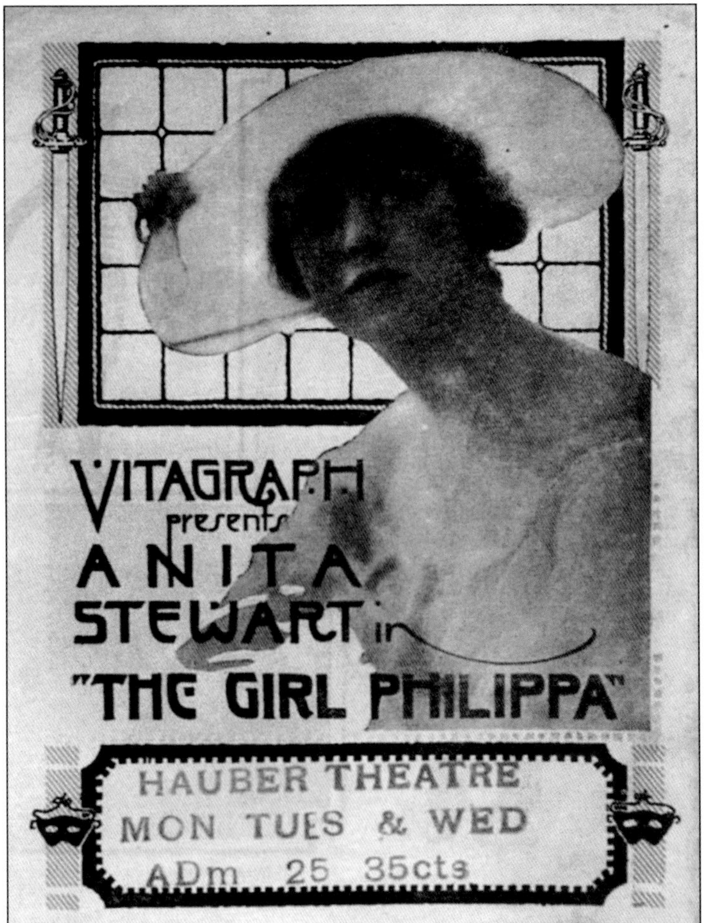

A placard at Pine Bluff's Hauber Theater invites the public to a show. Before movies, crowds attended live shows in the Delta Lowlands at venues like the 1880s opera houses in Pine Bluff, Arkansas City, and Lonoke. A *New York Times* reporter described a converted livery stable in Pine Bluff being used after the opera house burned down in 1899: "The ticket office is a wonder of architectural ingenuity, the entrance being from the top by way of the hayloft. . . . The treasurer sells all reserved seats from memory. And this recently caused a small riot when the treasurer took one too many drinks and sold the first row twice." (Courtesy of Jimmy Cunningham Jr.)

Two

Music Legends of the Delta Lowlands

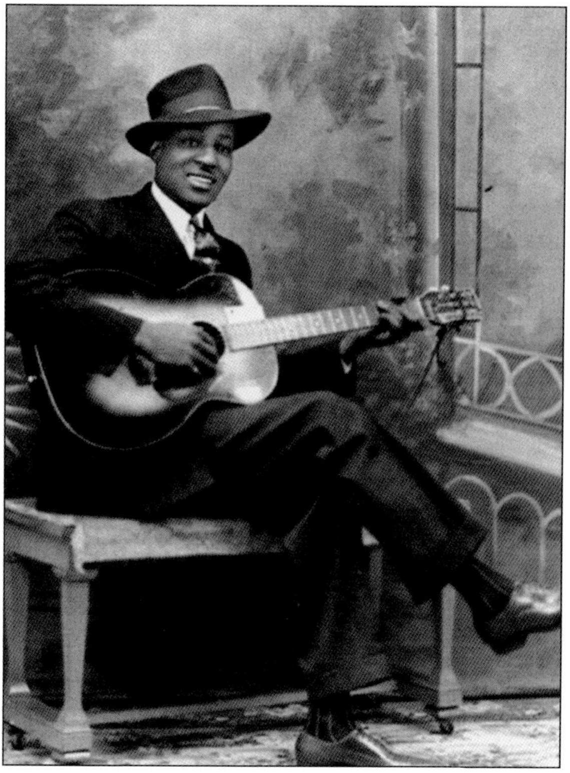

"Big Bill" Broonzy, born near Altheimer and raised in Pine Bluff, according to Broonzy scholar Robert Reisman, was one of the biggest influences in blues history. He reigned in the genre from the late 1920s through the early 1940s. A member of the first class of Blues Hall of Fame inductees, a Grammy nominee, and the first blues artist to have a biography published, Broonzy recorded over 300 songs. He is credited with bringing blues to Europe, as detailed in the 2013 BBC documentary *The Man Who Brought Blues to Britain: Big Bill Broonzy*. Scores of musicians, including the Rolling Stones, the Beatles, Muddy Waters, Eric Clapton, and many others credit him as a seminal influence. His "Glory of Love" has appeared in Steven Spielberg's *The Terminal* (2004), *Intolerable Cruelty* (2003) starring George Clooney, and in other films. *Guitar World Presents the 100 Greatest Guitarists of All Time* included Broonzy among its pantheon of the best guitarists ever. (Courtesy of Frank Driggs Collection.)

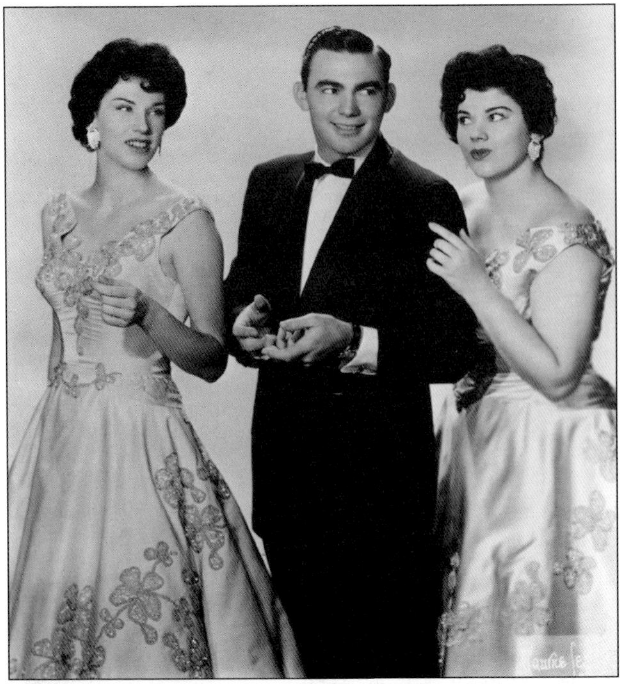

The Browns were a polished, Grammy-nominated country music sibling trio. Maxine (left), Jim Ed (center), and Bonnie were Sparkman, Arkansas, natives who moved to Pine Bluff in grade school. The Browns had 21 chart-topping country music hits between 1954 and 1968, including their number one hit, "The Three Bells." They have appeared on network television numerous times, including *The Ed Sullivan Show*, *The Sopranos*, and others. (Courtesy of Maxine Brown.)

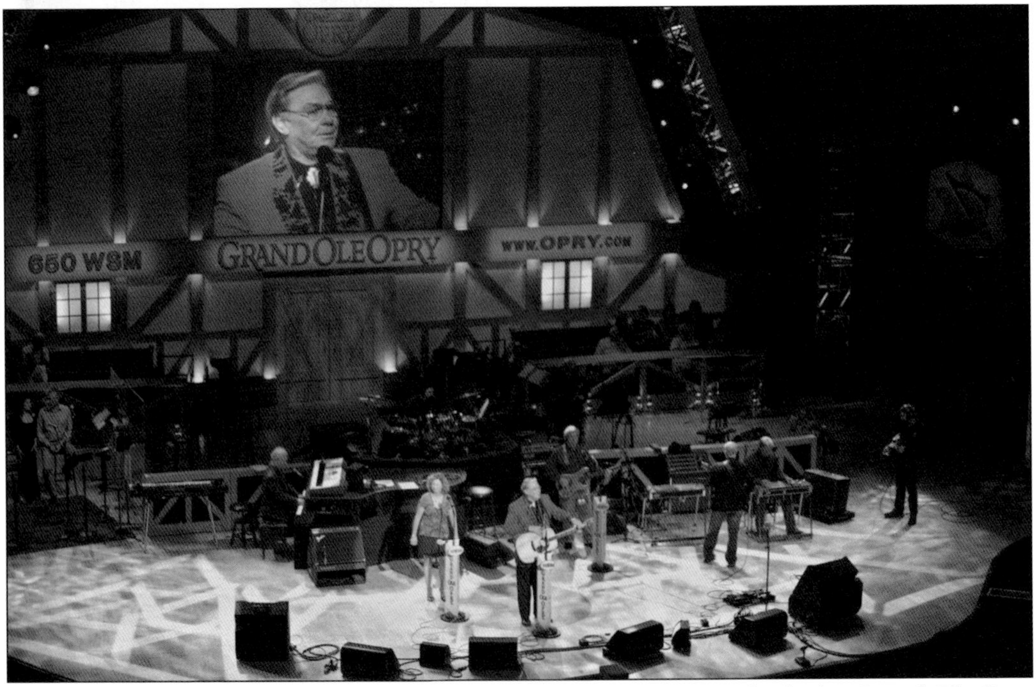

Jim Ed Brown, a country music legend with Pine Bluff roots, hosts both the *Grand Ole Opry* and the *Country Music Greats Radio Show*. After leaving his sibling group, the Browns, in 1965, he began a solo career, racking up almost 40 Billboard chart songs from 1967 to 1981. He was nominated for a Grammy in 1979 for his duet with Helen Cornelius, "If the World Ran Out of Love Tonight." He and Cornelius won three Country Music Association (CMA) awards in 1979. Brown's music appeared in the 2010 movie *Temple Grandin*. (Courtesy of Albert Herring.)

Smokie Norful's 2002 album, *I Need You Now,* helped him earn Grammy, Stellar, Dove, Soul Train Music, and NAACP Image awards. His blend of soul, R&B, and funk fused into gospel has earned him fans worldwide. He grew up largely in Pine Bluff, attended grade schools there, graduated from UAPB, and taught in the local public schools before moving to Illinois to start his professional singing career. Norful's album *Forever Yours* won a Grammy in 2015. (Courtesy of Krisanne Johnson.)

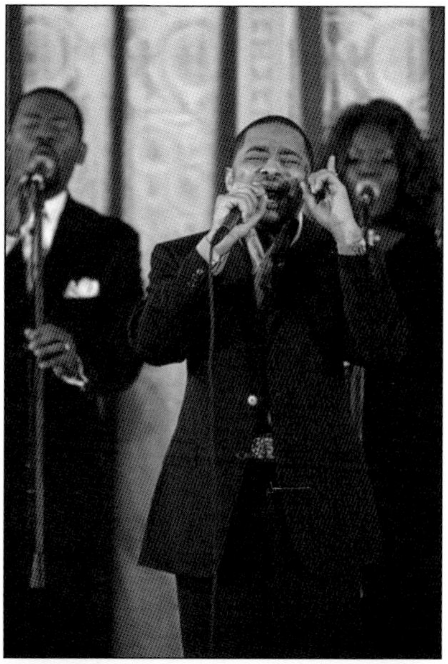

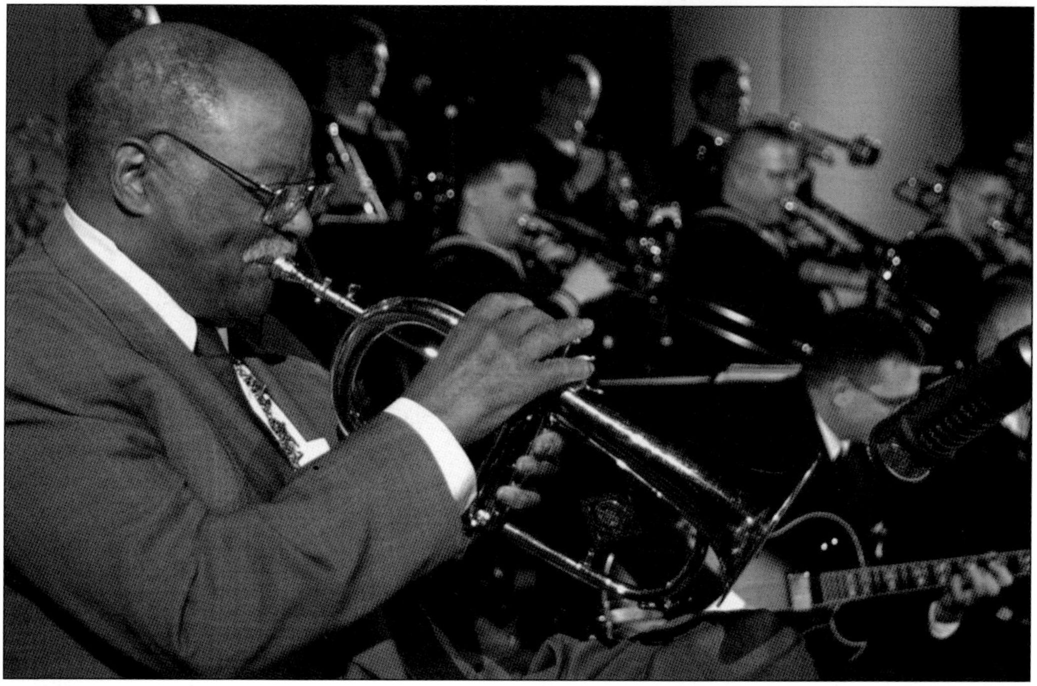

As a Grammy Lifetime Achievement recipient and one of the five most-recorded jazz musicians ever (over 900 recordings), Clark Terry is a legend. The St. Louis–born trumpeter and flugelhornist moved to Pine Bluff in his senior years and has taught jazz at UAPB, inspired local jazz festivals bearing his name, and has mentored musicians from all over the world at his Pine Bluff home. Terry has performed for eight US presidents and has played with Duke Ellington, Sarah Vaughn, Miles Davis, and numerous others. The 2014 documentary *Keep on Keepin On,* about Terry's mentoring of blind music prodigy Justin Kaughlin, was filmed, in part, in Pine Bluff. Terry also cohosted with comedy legend Bill Cosby season three of the online children's show *OBKB*, taped in 2010 before a live audience in Pine Bluff. (Courtesy of US Navy.)

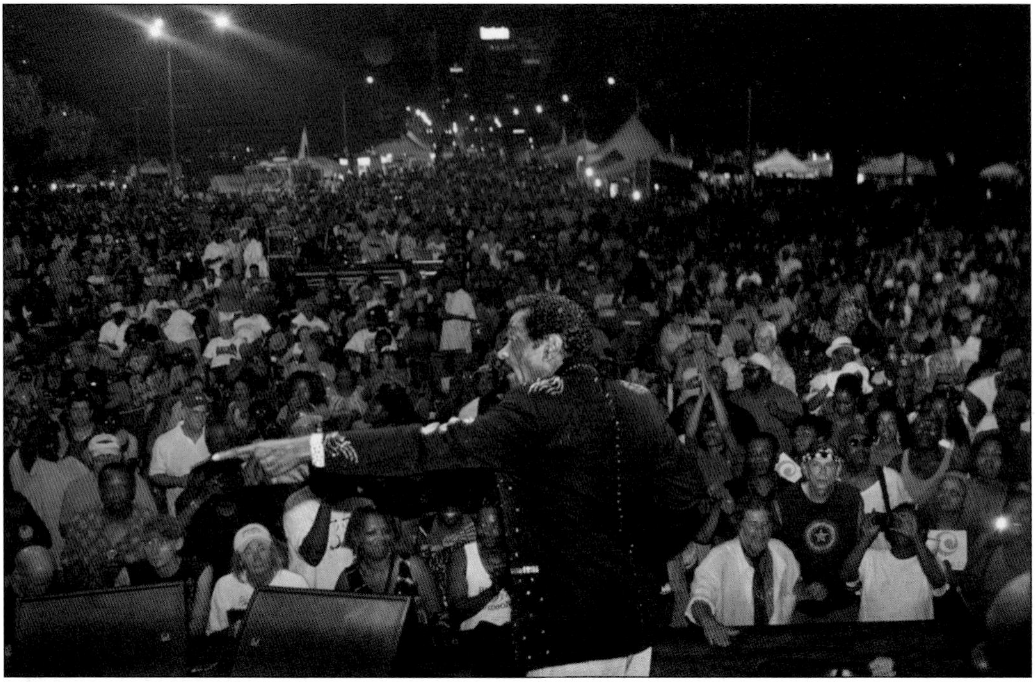

Bobby Rush, a two-time Grammy nominee and member of the Blues Hall of Fame, moved to Sherrill at 11 years old and began playing house parties in Ladd. He first played in a band at a Pine Bluff juke joint, Nappy's, and was first compensated at another Pine Bluff juke joint, Jitterbugs, where he was paid in hamburgers, chitlins, and fried catfish. A guitarist, harmonica player, and vocalist, Rush has played internationally and has won numerous awards. His music has been in movies such as *Black Snake Moan* (2007), starring Samuel L. Jackson, and several documentary films. He appeared on *The Tonight Show with Jimmy Fallon* alongside actor Dan Aykroyd in 2014. (Courtesy of Entice Hal.)

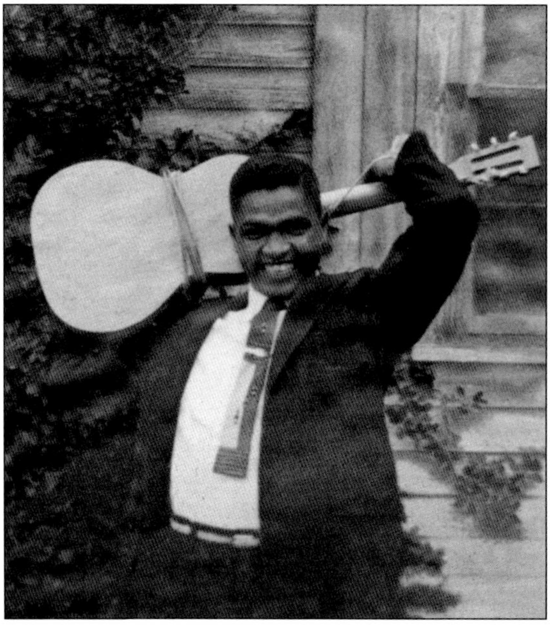

A teenaged Bobby Rush displays his showmanship skills in Altheimer around 1952. In a *Blues Access* magazine interview, he relates his Sunday experiences in Sherrill with his preacher dad: "I'd go to church and the choir would be singing. . . . The ladies would be shouting and everything. . . . My dad would go back and preach [at another church out of town] in the afternoons. I wouldn't go back to church with him. I'd play the guitar outside my house. And the same people that had been shoutin' in church in the morning service, man, they'd be boogie-woogiein' with me, havin' a ball!" (Courtesy of Bobby Rush.)

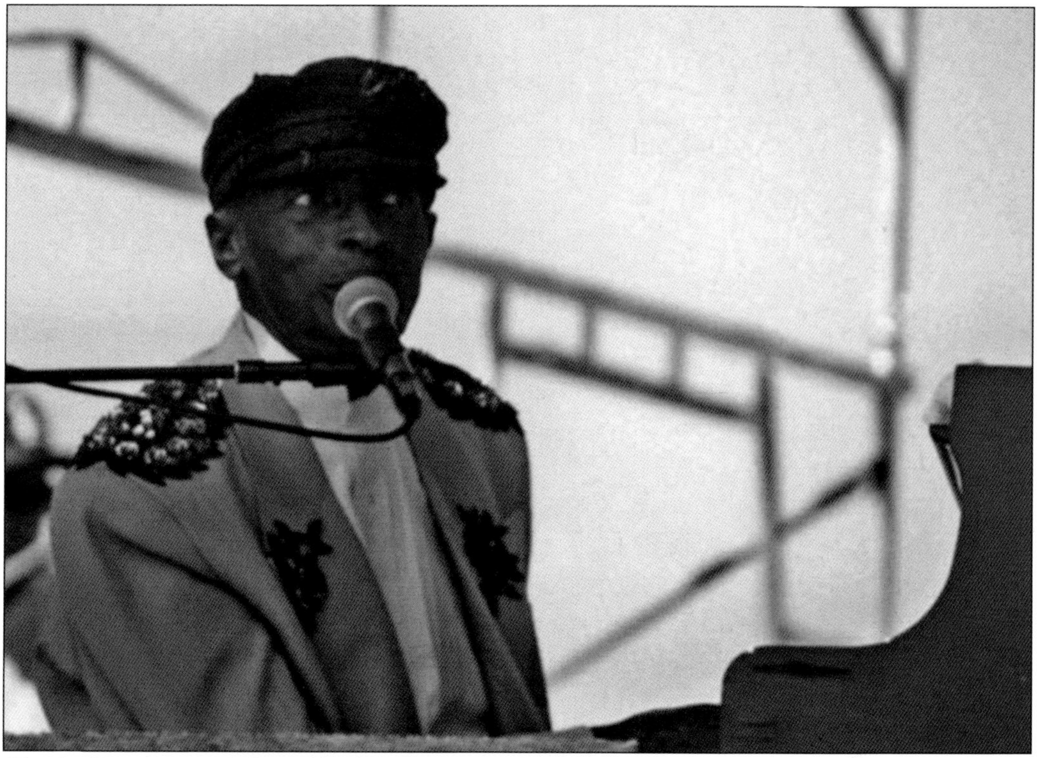

Charles Brown, a member of both the Blues Hall of Fame and the Rock and Roll Hall of Fame, moved to Pine Bluff from Texas City, Texas, in the early 1940s and worked at the Army Arsenal as a chemist. Frustrated with the racism he experienced there, he moved to California, where he churned out 13 top-10 R&B hits from 1946 to 1960. Brown's music appears in the sound tracks for movies like *Friday After Next* (2002), *Cast Away* (2000), *Home Alone* (1990), and many others. (Courtesy of S. Sumori.)

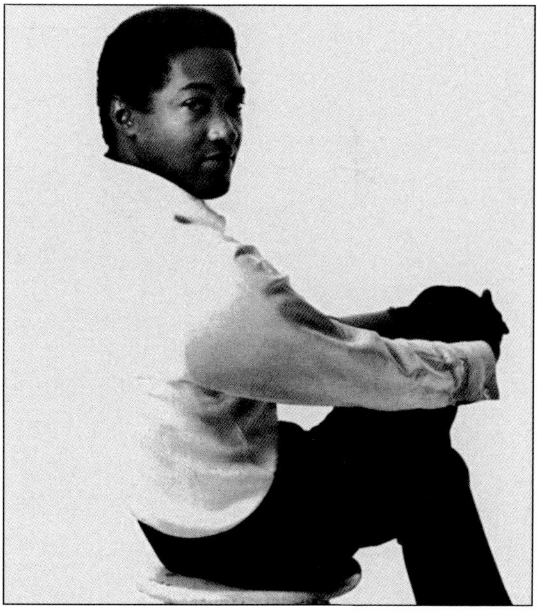

Sam Cooke crooned to millions with a velvety voice. According to *Boogaloo: The Quintessence of American Popular Music*, Cooke's first professional appearance came around 1951 in Pine Bluff after joining the gospel group the Soul Stirrers. Reportedly, he only knew two songs and had a pencil-thin mustache to make him look older. Though he was out-sung by veterans like the Pilgrim Travelers on that day, Cooke was swarmed by Pine Bluff female audience members at the intermission, foreshadowing his later celebrity appeal. (Courtesy of RCA Victor Records.)

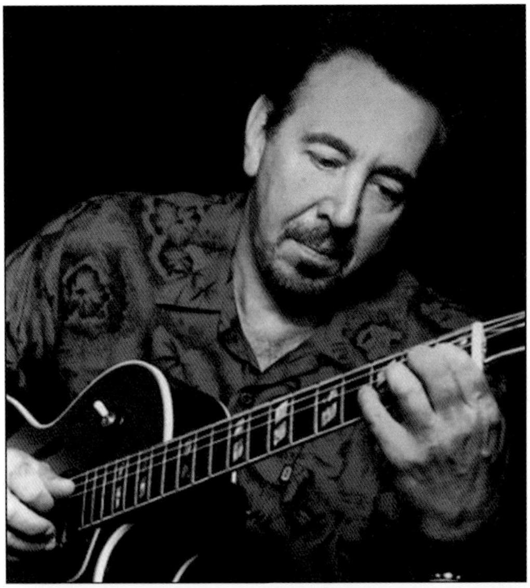

William "Louie" Shelton is one of the most celebrated session guitarists in American music. He is an inductee in the prestigious Musician's Hall of Fame and has been an accompanist and producer for scores of superstars. Born in Little Rock, he moved to Pine Bluff as a teenager and had the life-altering experience of watching Elvis Presley perform at his junior high there. Determined afterward to find music success, Shelton eventually played and produced for such giants as Lionel Richie, Boss Skaggs, Neil Diamond, The Jackson Five, Marvin Gaye, and scores of other greats. As a solo artist, Shelton has recorded five albums. His film work on sound tracks includes *The Life and Times of Judge Roy Bean* (1972), starring Paul Newman, *Klute* (1971), and *J.W. Coop* (1971). (Courtesy of Louie Shelton.)

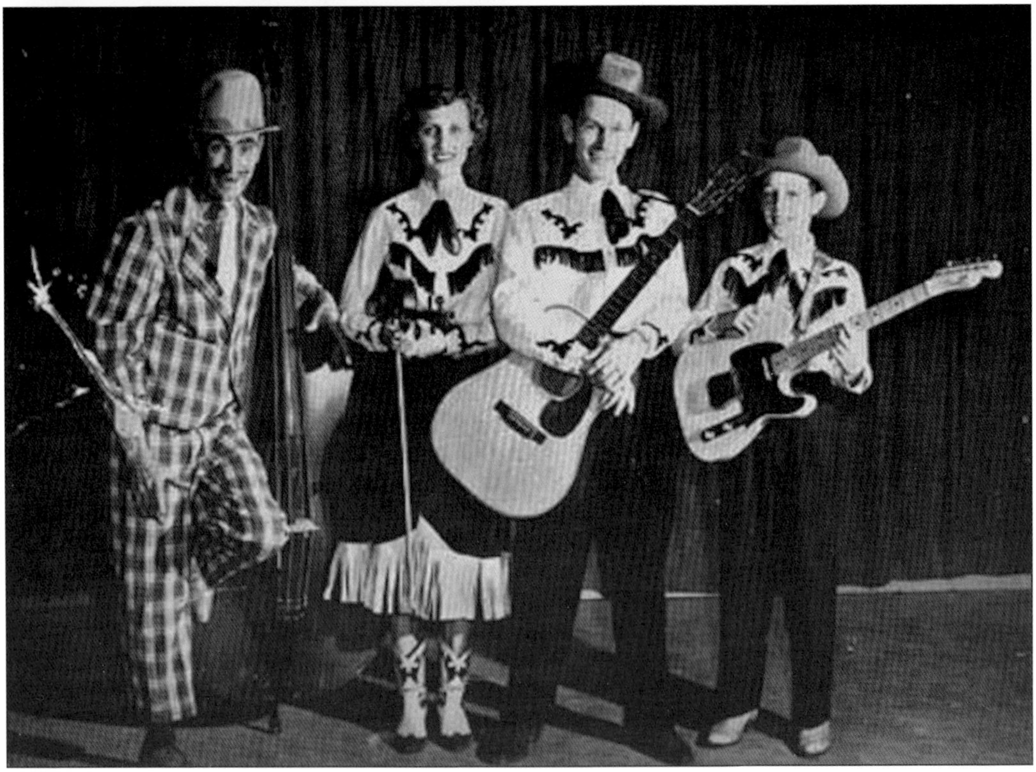

A young Louie Shelton (far right) is pictured with Shelby Cooper and the Dixie Mountaineers in the 1950s. Cooper (second from right) was the Pine Bluff radio station manager for KCLA and was also the lead member of the Dixie Mountaineers, a regional country music group. Sara Jane Cooper (second from left), Shelby's wife, was a vocalist and writer who cowrote Tex Ritter's No. 1 1945 country song "You Will Have To Pay" (which also appeared in the sound track for the 1945 movie *Enemy of the Law*). Shelton lived with the Coopers in Pine Bluff as a teenager and sang with them on radio and television programs. (Courtesy of Louie Shelton.)

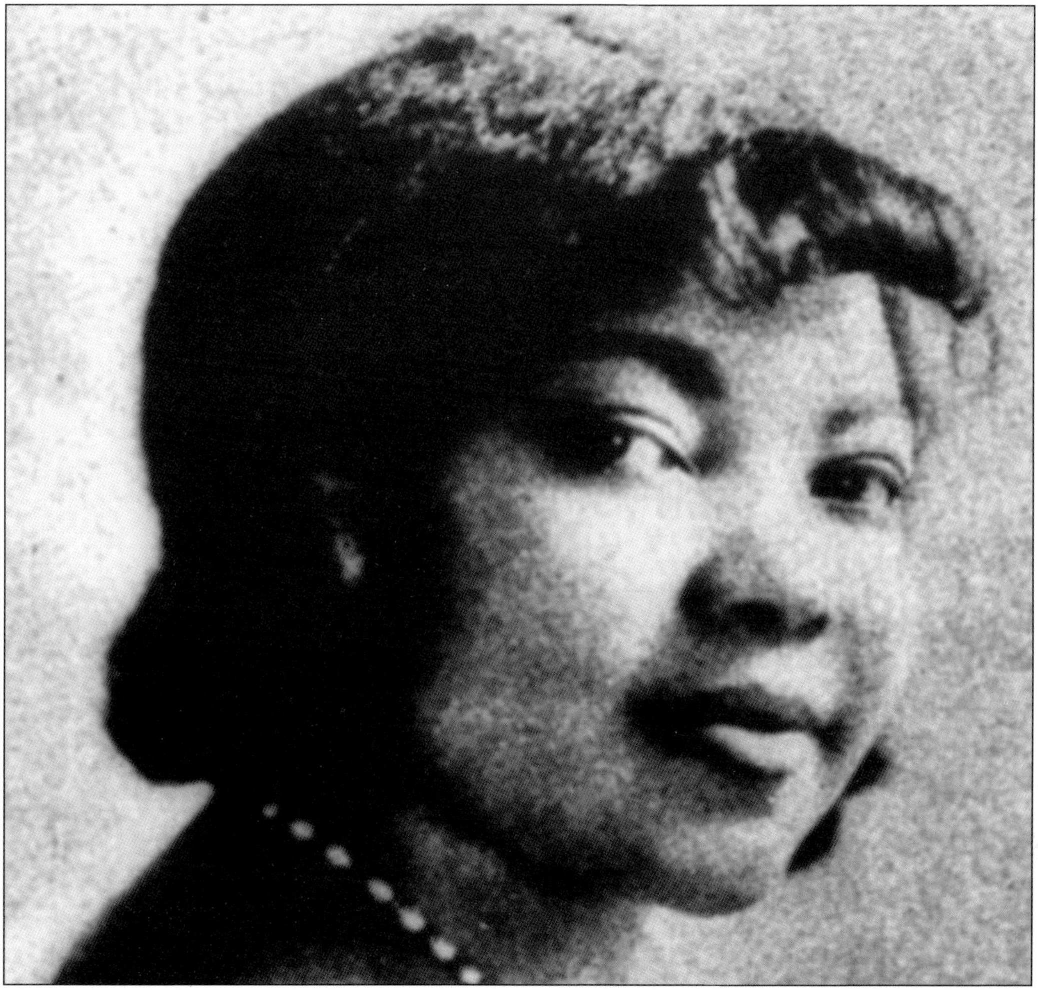

Pioneering blues singer Beaulah "Sippie" Wallace was presumably born in Plum Bayou, Arkansas, and later moved to Houston, Texas, based on the research of historians Bob Eagle and Eric LeBlanc in *Blues: A Regional Experience*. She was the daughter of former slaves from Pine Bluff whose mother was reportedly born in an area contraband camp during the Civil War in 1865. One of the first commercially successful blues stars, Wallace's record sales from 1923 to 1929 were second only to Bessie Smith's, according to *Living Blues* magazine. She and a small group of black female blues singers in the 1920s literally transformed popular music and the recording industry when they became the first large-selling recording artists in the United States. Their success sent record companies in other genres scrambling to duplicate their accomplishments and set in motion America's fascination with recorded popular music. Wallace also collaborated with her talented brothers, George and Hersal. A member of the Blues Hall of Fame, she performed with such greats as Louis Armstrong, King Oliver, and Bonnie Raitt. In 1982, she was nominated for a Grammy. Wallace's music is on the sound track for the movie *The Reaping* (2007). (Courtesy of Lindsey Marks.)

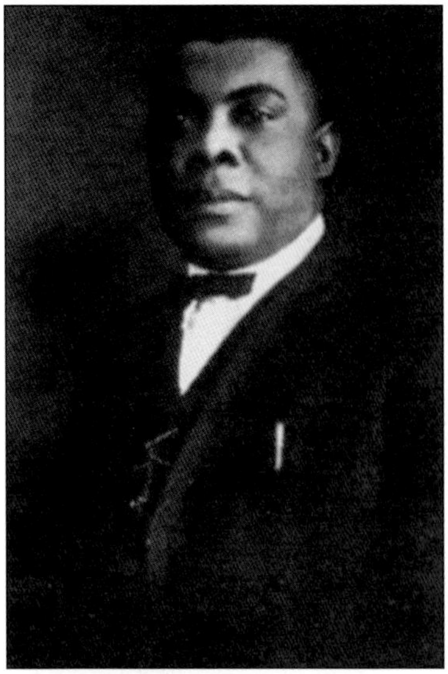

George Washington Thomas, a legendary pianist, songwriter, and publisher, was the older brother of Sippie Wallace. He was born in Plum Bayou, Arkansas, according to researchers, and moved to Houston by age 13. Historians credit Thomas with writing the first song with a boogie-woogie bass line, 1911's "New Orleans Hop Scop Blues," and with recording the first boogie-woogie song, "The Rocks," in 1923 (under the pseudonym Clay Custer). His pioneering work helped spawn revolutionary changes in popular music for decades, as boogie-woogie became integral to several music genres. Thomas composed an estimated 100 blues songs and had several hits. He also collaborated with his sister, Sippie, and younger brother, Hersal. His music can be heard on the sound track for the television miniseries *Baseball: A National Heirloom* (1994). (Courtesy of Lindsey Marks.)

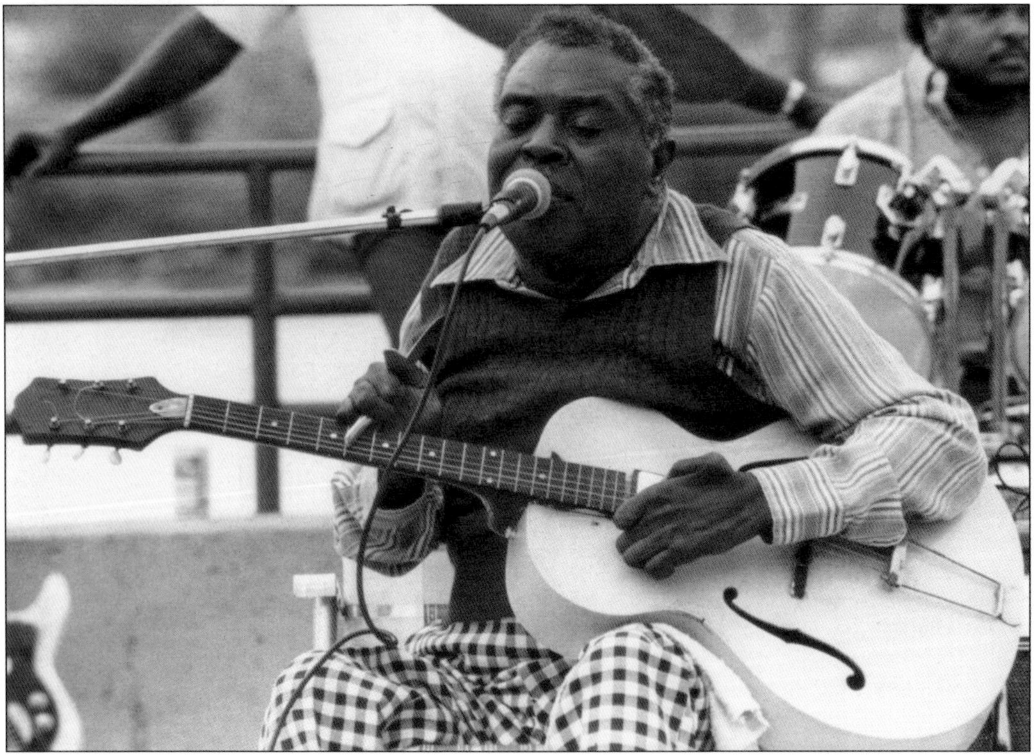

Cedell Davis, called "the last original Delta bluesman," is a National Endowment for the Arts National Heritage Fellowship nominee whose albums have been cited in nearly every published blues encyclopedia. The *New York Times* said of Davis, "[He] plays with a special verve and style . . . and stumps with a furious rock beat." Davis has been featured in two documentaries and has been the subject of his own documentary about his life and his music. Davis lived in Pine Bluff for over 45 years, playing at the Jungle Hut juke joint while traveling worldwide. At 89 years old, he is currently making preparations for another album. His movie sound track credits include *Santa's Slay* (2005) and *Tempted* (2001), staring Burt Reynolds. (Courtesy of Paul Barrows.)

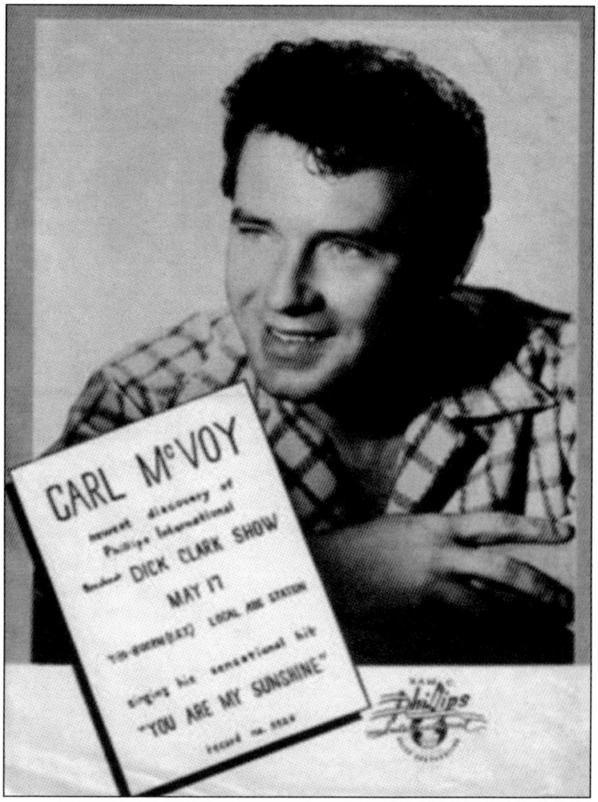

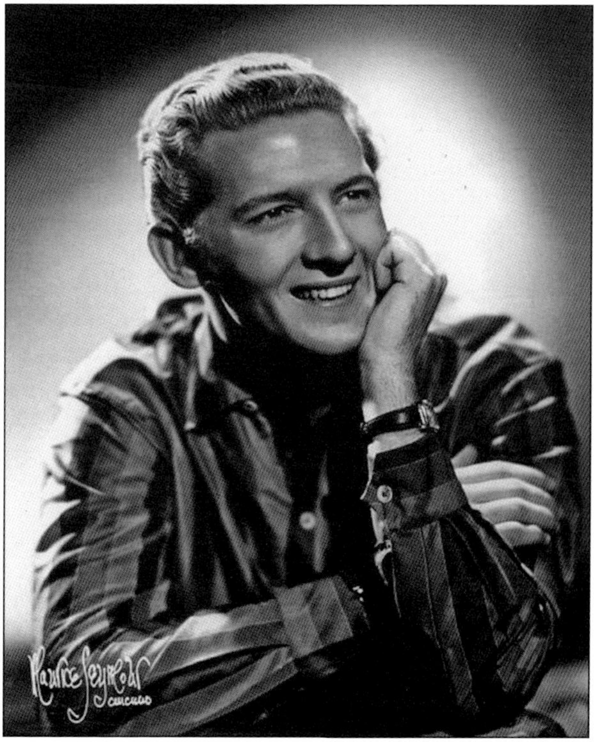

Carl McVoy (above) moved to Pine Bluff as a teenager from Epps, Louisiana, and later found success with his 1958 hit "You Are My Sunshine." According to *Good Rockin' Tonight: Sun Records and the Birth of Rock 'n' Roll*, McVoy's cousin, Jerry Lee Lewis (below), stayed with him in the summer of 1945 in Pine Bluff. McVoy, who recently learned to play boogie-woogie piano, had begun to master it. While in Pine Bluff that summer, McVoy taught Lewis how to play boogie-woogie music on piano. Rev. Jimmy Swaggart, a cousin of both McVoy and Lewis, says in *Swaggart: The Unauthorized Biography of an American Evangelist*: "Shortly after that, he [Lewis] was sent to Pine Bluff. He came back in six weeks with more piano skills than the stodgy teacher could have drilled in him in a lifetime. His cousin, Carl, had taught him the honky-tonk style that was irreverently called Holy Ghost Boogie." Lewis later became a rock 'n' roll star known for his rollicking piano playing, using the boogie-woogie elements he learned in Pine Bluff. (Above, courtesy of Hillbilly Country Collection; below, courtesy of Maurice Seymour.)

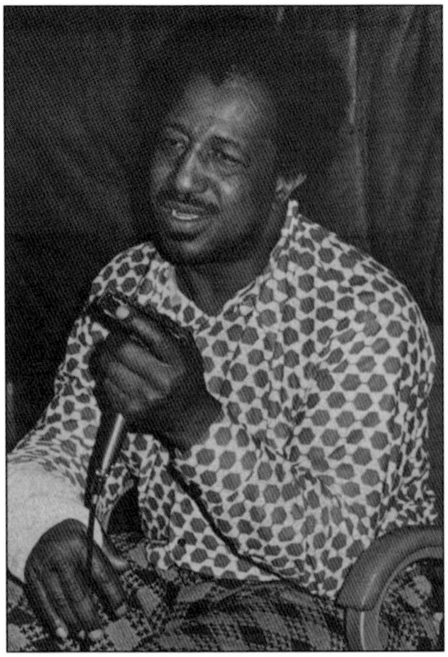

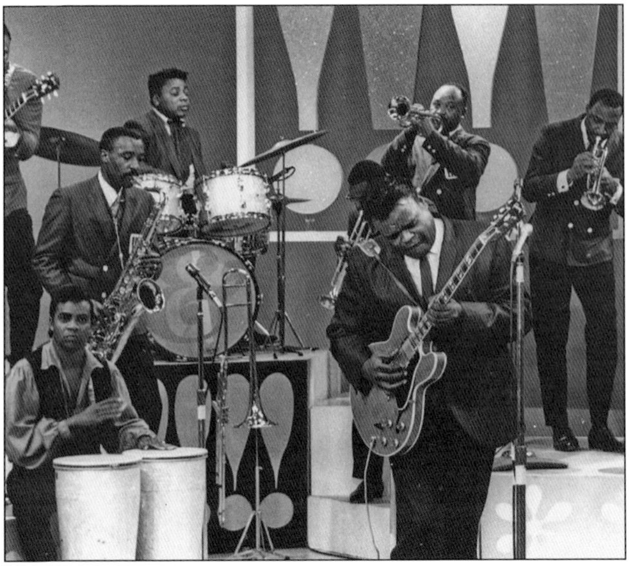

Earlee Payton (left) of Pine Bluff was a Chicago blues harmonica player during the 1940s and 1950s who helped launch the career of Rock and Roll Hall of Fame member and blues great Freddie King (right, with guitar). When King arrived in Chicago as a teenager, he first played professionally with Payton and his Blues Cats. Payton mentored King and introduced him to the Chicago club scene. King cut his first record, "Country Boy," with Payton and Robert Lockwood in 1956, according to *The Blues Encyclopedia*. (Both, courtesy of Jim O'Neal and the Beat.)

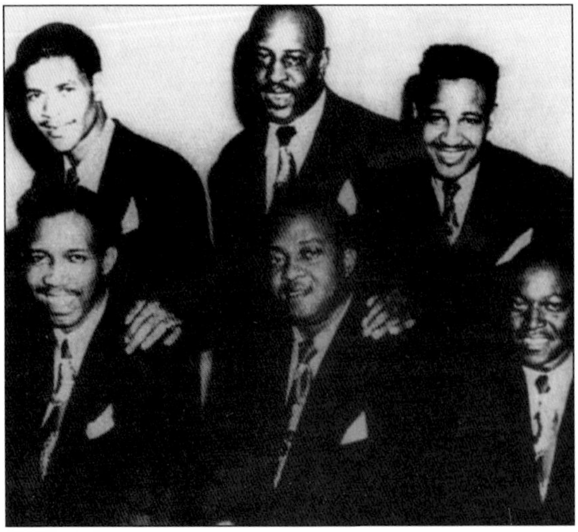

Gospel quartet pioneer Roscoe Robinson (top row, left), of Dermott, poses with the Southern Sons around 1963. He began singing gospel music in 1951 with groups like the Highway Q.C.s, the Fairfield Four, and the Five Blind Boys of Mississippi. However, by the mid-1960s, he became a successful soul-music singer with a string of *Billboard* hits, including his million-seller "That's Enough." He went back to gospel in the 1970s as a member of the Grammy-winning Blind Boys of Alabama. Robinson has been twice inducted into the Gospel Quartet Hall of Fame and has sung with Aretha Franklin, Patti Labelle, B.B. King, and many others. (Courtesy of Opal Nations.)

Before legendary African American music producers like Quincy Jones, Berry Gordy, and Dr. Dre, the godfather of black music producers was Pine Bluff–born J. Mayo "Ink" Williams. The first African American producer for a major record company, he became the most successful producer of black music, largely blues, from the 1920s to the 1940s. Williams, a member of the Blues Hall of Fame, discovered, produced, and/or wrote for legends like Ma Rainey, Jelly Roll Morton, Muddy Waters, Mahalia Jackson, and Louis Jordan, among others. Songs he wrote or cowrote, like Little Richard's "Keep a-Knockin'," have been covered by many music giants. Williams's songs have also appeared in movies, like *Ray* (2004) starring Jamie Fox, *Life* (1999) starring Eddie Murphy and Martin Lawrence, and *The Buddy Holly Story* (1978). Many scholars also credit Williams with helping to create the subgenre of jump blues, arguably the progenitor of rock 'n' roll. (Courtesy of Chicago Reader.)

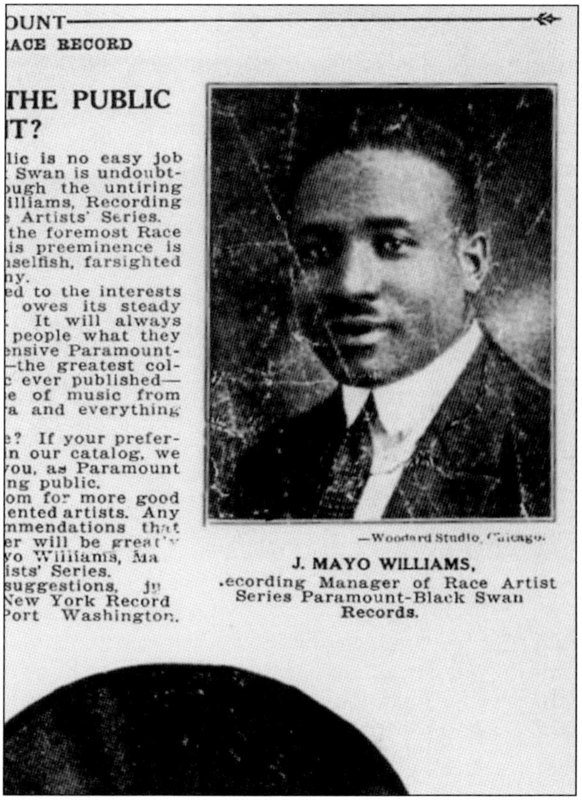
OUNT
ACE RECORD

THE PUBLIC
T?

lic is no easy job
Swan is undoubt-
ugh the untiring
illiams, Recording
Artists' Series.
the foremost Race
is preeminence is
iselfish, farsighted
ny.
ed to the interests
owes its steady
It will always
people what they
nsive Paramount-
—the greatest col-
ever published—
e of music from
a and everything

? If your prefer-
n our catalog, we
ou, as Paramount
ng public.
om for more good
ented artists. Any
mmendations th:t
er will be great'
o Williams, Ma
ists' Series.
suggestions, jı
New York Record
Port Washington.

—Woodard Studio,

J. MAYO WILLIAMS,
Recording Manager of Race Artist Series Paramount-Black Swan Records.

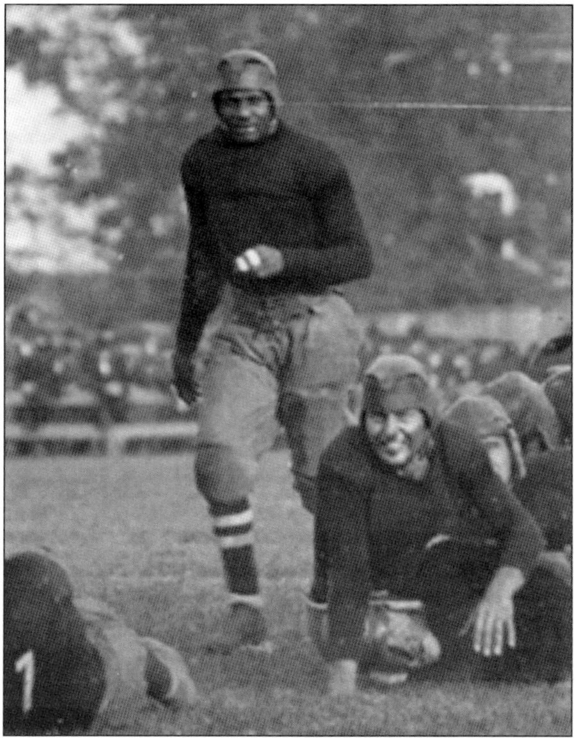

The legendary Pine Bluff producer J. Mayo Williams (seen here around 1922) was one of the first three African American players in the National Football League, playing alongside activist Paul Robeson. However, Williams never disclosed to music officials that he was concurrently a professional football player. Additional information about his life is referenced in *The Encyclopedia of Arkansas Music*. (Courtesy of Alpha Gamma, Inc.)

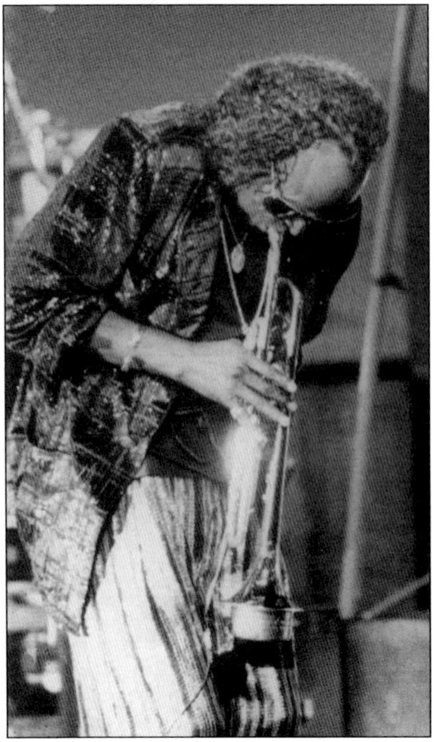

Jazz legend Miles Davis, nine-time Grammy winner and a member of the Rock and Roll Hall of Fame, spent his childhood summers in Jefferson County. Davis's father was born and raised in the Noble Lake area. His grandfather was a longtime Noble Lake resident and one of the earliest fish farmers in Arkansas. In the 1920s, the Davis family lived not far down Highway 65 from the Jones family, Varner natives, who later migrated to Michigan and gave birth to another jazz legend, Betty Carter, in 1929. (Courtesy of Rui Britto.)

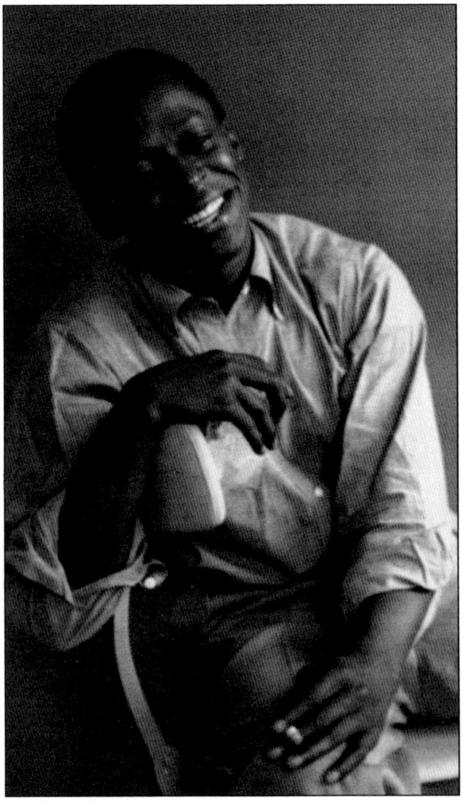

Miles Davis's earliest music roots extend to 1930s Jefferson County, where his parents would send him from East St. Louis each summer to spend time with his grandfather in the Noble Lake area. Davis says of his Jefferson County music experiences in *Miles: The Autobiography*: "I also remember how the music used to sound down there in Arkansas . . . especially at the Saturday night church. Man, that [expletive] was a [expletive]. I guess I was about six or seven. We'd be walking on these dark country roads at night and all of a sudden this music would seem to come out of nowhere, out of them spooky-looking trees. . . . I remember somebody would be playing a guitar the way B.B. King plays. And I remember a man and a woman singing and talking about getting *down*! . . . That music was something, especially that woman singing. But I think that kind of stuff stayed with me. . . . That *kind* of sound in music, that blues, church, back-road funk kind of thing, that southern . . . rural sound and rhythm. I think it started getting into my blood on them spook-filled Arkansas back-roads after dark when the owls came out hoot-ing. . . . It's hard to pinpoint where it [music] all began for me. But I think some of it had to have started on that Arkansas Road." (Courtesy of Tom Palumbo.)

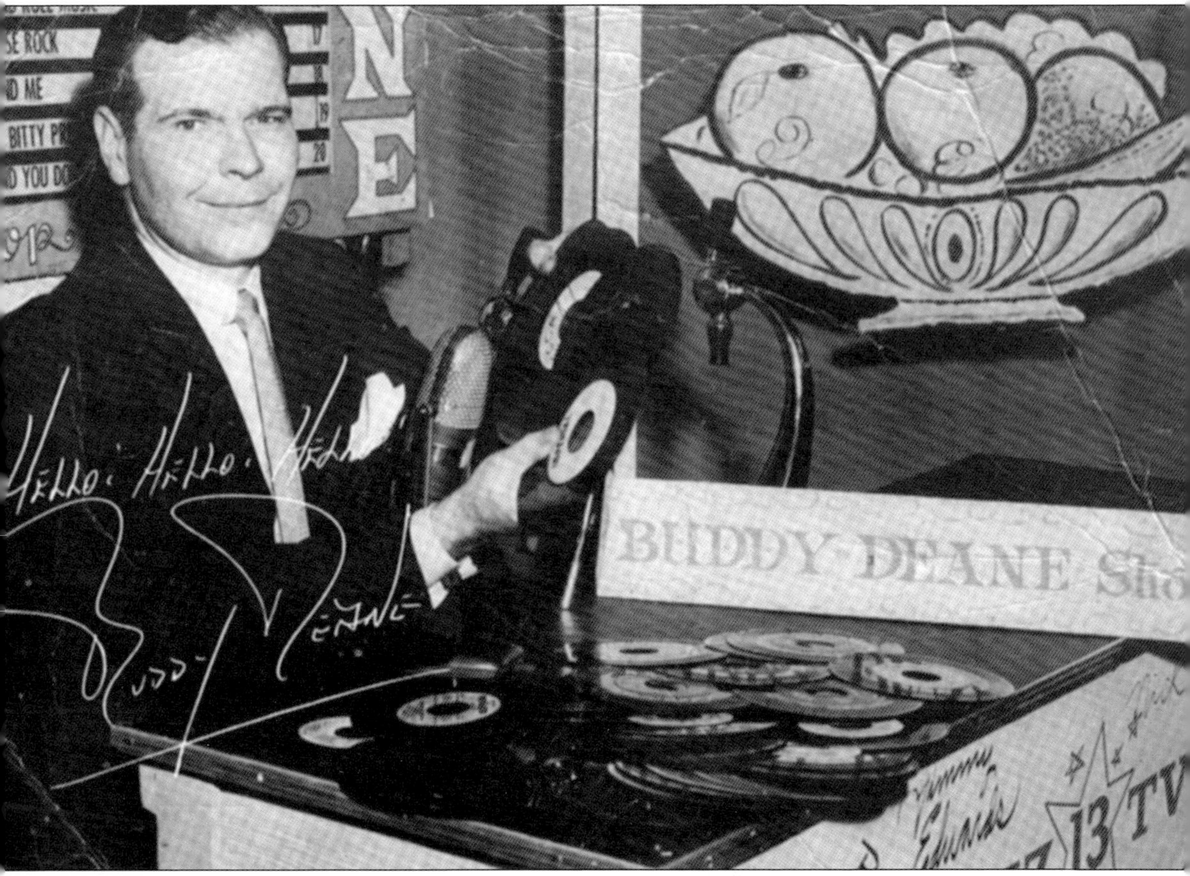

Buddy Deane, known as "the Morning Mayor," was a popular deejay in Pine Bluff and the owner of KOTN radio station for almost 40 years. His shows featured news, music, and informative interviews. While in Baltimore in the 1950s, he was one of the earliest radio deejays in the country to play rock 'n' roll music daily. In 1962, working at WITH radio, he was voted the number-one disc jockey in the nation by *Billboard* magazine. (Courtesy of Arlene Kozak/*Buddy Deane Show*.)

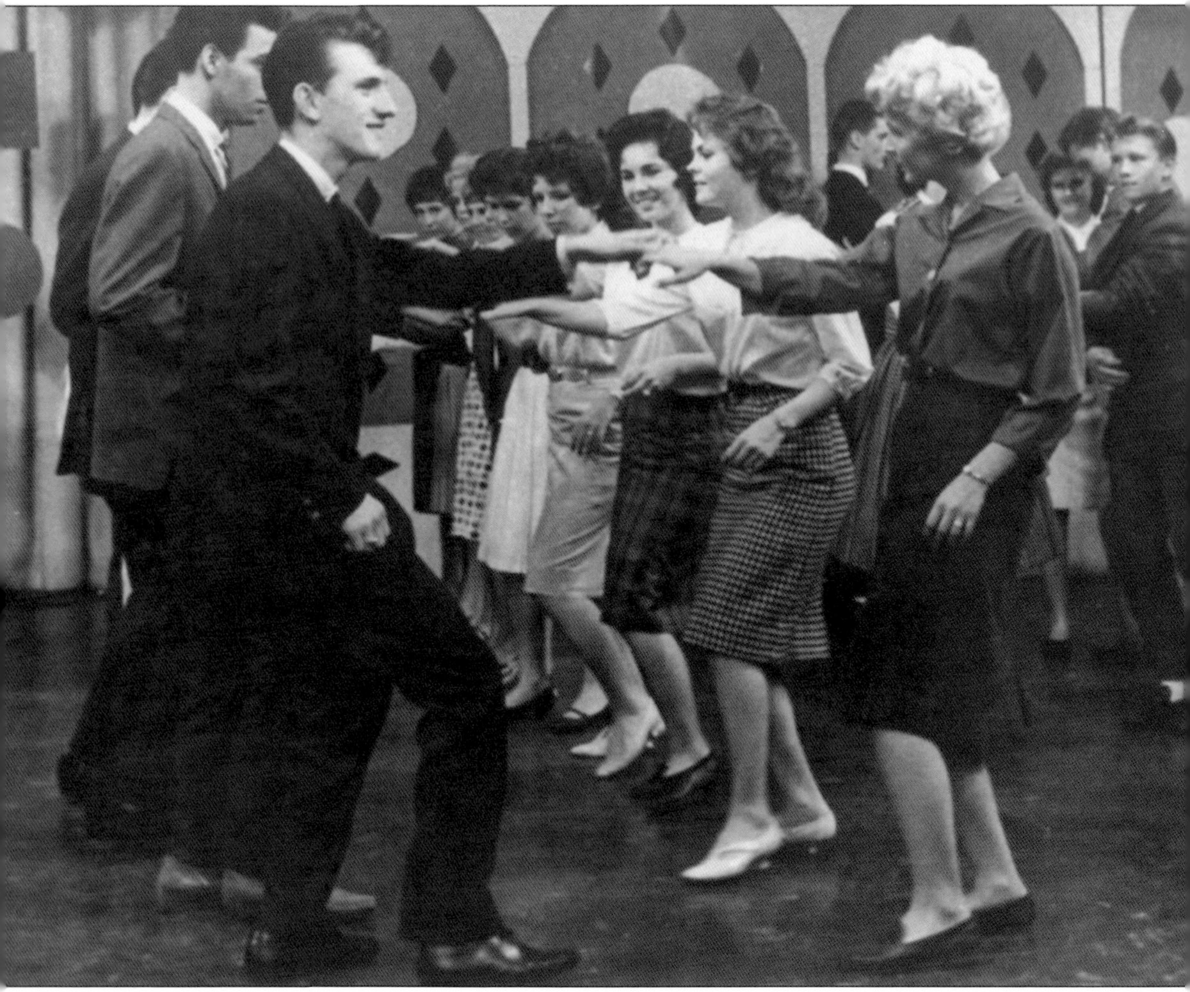

The Buddy Deane Show was a groundbreaking teen dance program that aired on Baltimore television from 1957 to 1964. It was one of the first television programs in the country to highlight teens dancing to rock 'n' roll. Bill Haley and the Comets first performed "Rock Around the Clock" on his show. In 1964, it was cancelled by WJZ-TV's management because of pressure to integrate its cast. The 1988 movie *Hairspray* was loosely based on the longtime Pine Bluff resident's dance show. (Courtesy of Arlene Kozak/*Buddy Deane Show*.)

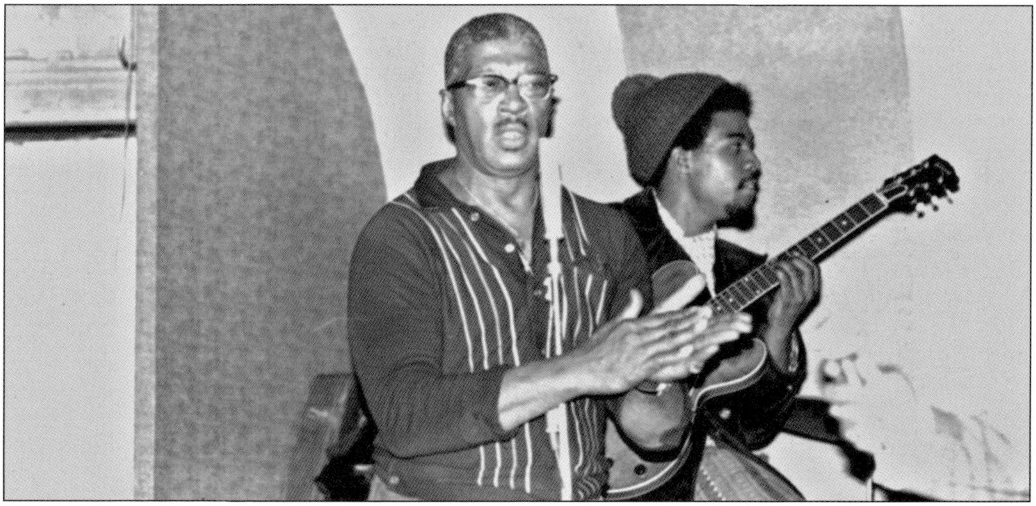

William "Big Bill" Hill, a native of England, Arkansas, moved to Chicago in the 1950s when blues was transforming rock 'n' roll. He became a well-known disc jockey, playing blues and R&B for newly emerging audiences. In 1963, he joined famed producer Leonard Chess's WVON (Voice of the Negro) and became a radio giant in Chicago. Hill later helped influence the development of the popular television program *Soul Train* and often served as a guest host in its early years. (Courtesy of Special Collections Department of the University of Mississippi.)

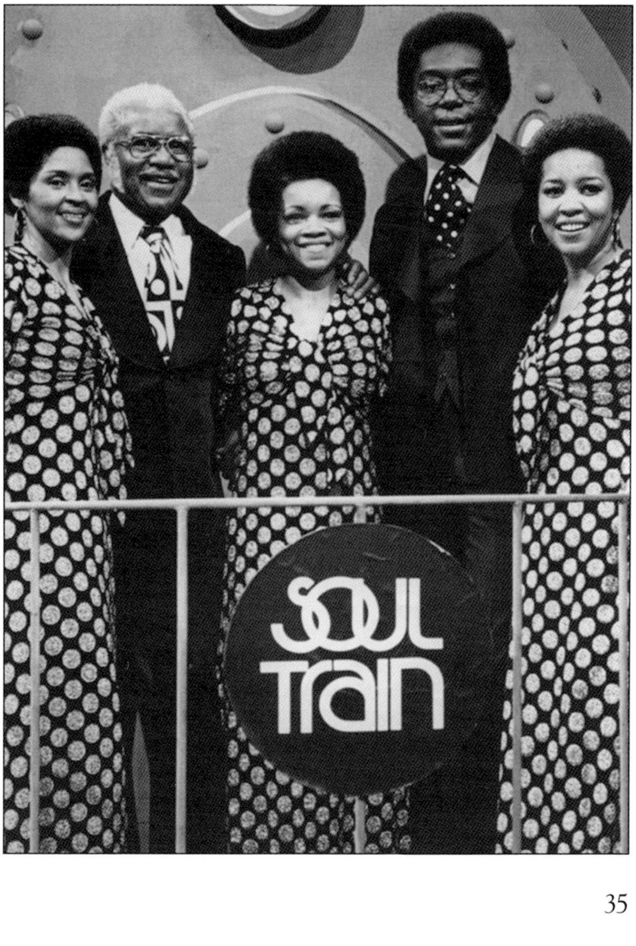

When Chicago radio disc jockey and England, Arkansas, native "Big Bill" Hill started hosting a preteen dance show, *Red Hot & Blues*, in 1967 for WCIU-TV, a young executive, Don Cornelius (second from right), had just joined the news staff. Cornelius closely followed the dance show, noting its strengths and weaknesses, as he began considering an improved format. In 1970, Cornelius developed his own teen dance show, *Soul Train*. According to the show's first producer, Drew Leach, Cornelius was highly influenced by Hill's show and even borrowed stylistic elements from it for his new dance program. Cornelius is seen here with the Staple Singers. (Courtesy of L.P. Drew.)

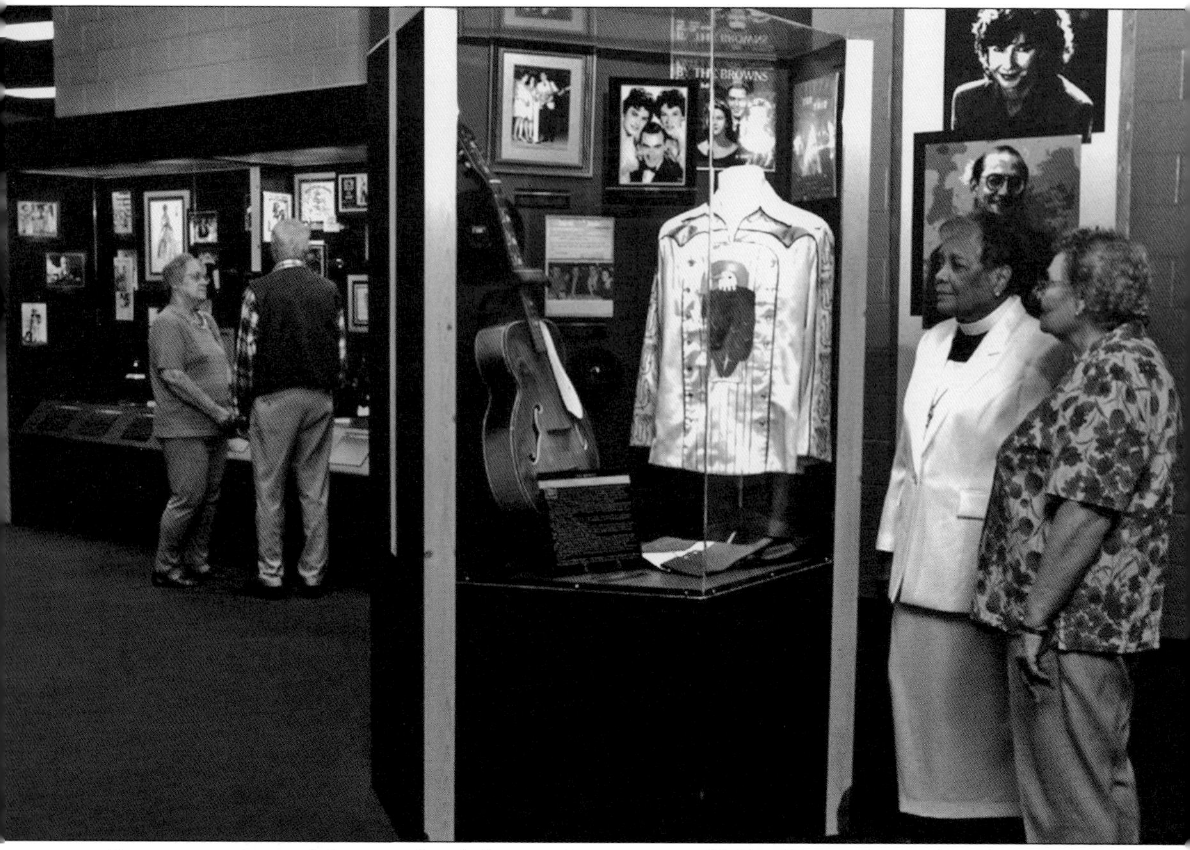

Spectators view exhibits at the Arkansas Entertainers Hall of Fame, housed at the Pine Bluff Convention Center. Showcasing legends from the state of Arkansas in music, film, television, and radio, the hall of fame has been operational since 1996. While a few inductees from the Delta Lowlands have been highlighted there, many others have not. The hope is that far more hall of fame inductees from the region will be recognized in the future even as additional mediums like festivals, academic institutes, museums, conferences, outdoor art galleries, murals, film screenings, and others are developed to illustrate and interpret the powerful Delta Lowlands music and film story. (Courtesy of Arkansas Department of Parks and Tourism.)

Three

Songs Connected to the Delta Lowlands

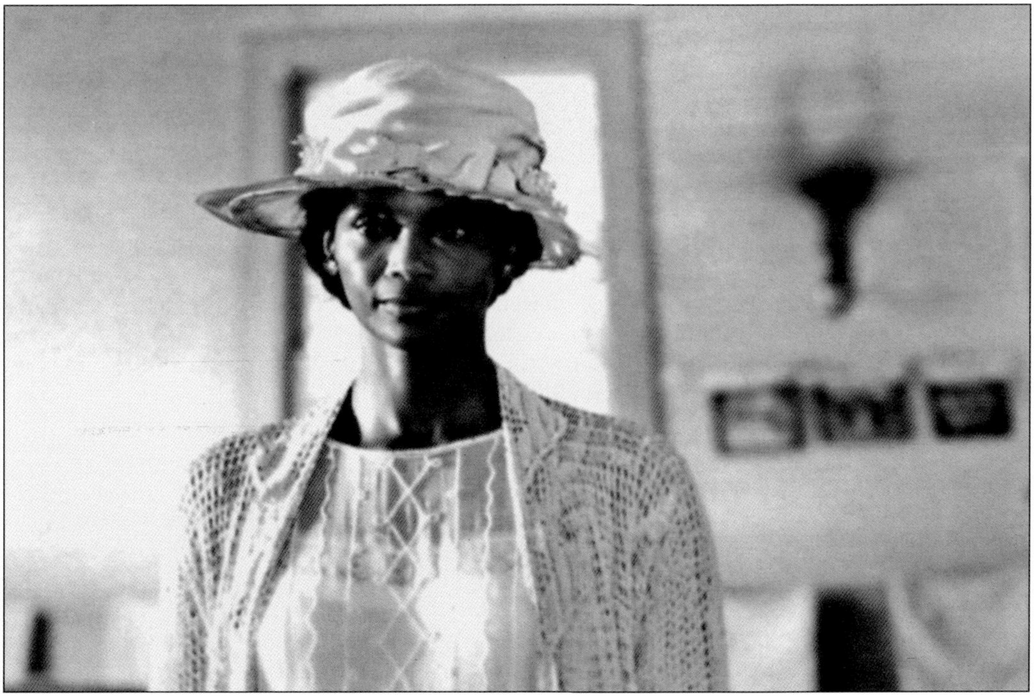

The 1985 movie *The Color Purple* featured Margaret Avery, shown here as the character Shug Avery. Earlier in the movie, Shug wails a raucous blues song called "The Dirty Dozens" in a juke joint scene with Hollywood greats Danny Glover, Laurence Fishburne, and Whoopi Goldberg. The cowriter of this 1920s hit song was Blues Hall of Fame member and Pine Bluff native J. Mayo "Ink" Williams. The song was part of the movie's Oscar-nominated sound track, produced by Quincy Jones. (Courtesy of Warner Bros. Productions.)

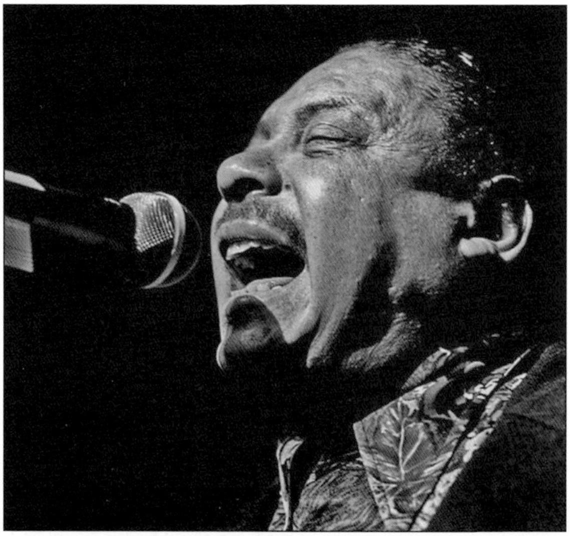

"Piney Brown Blues," by legendary bluesman "Big" Joe Turner, became a 1940 hit and was later recorded by Count Basie, Muddy Waters, Frank Sinatra, and many others. The song references one of two brothers, Walter "Little Piney" Brown or Jefferson "Big Piney" Brown, nicknamed because of their Pine Bluff roots according to the *Kansas City Star*. While it is not clear which brother the song refers to, the brothers both managed popular jazz clubs in Kansas City's famed Eighteenth and Vine District in the 1920s and 1930s. They had storied reputations for helping artists in need and became figures in local lore, according to music historians. (Courtesy of Studio Films.)

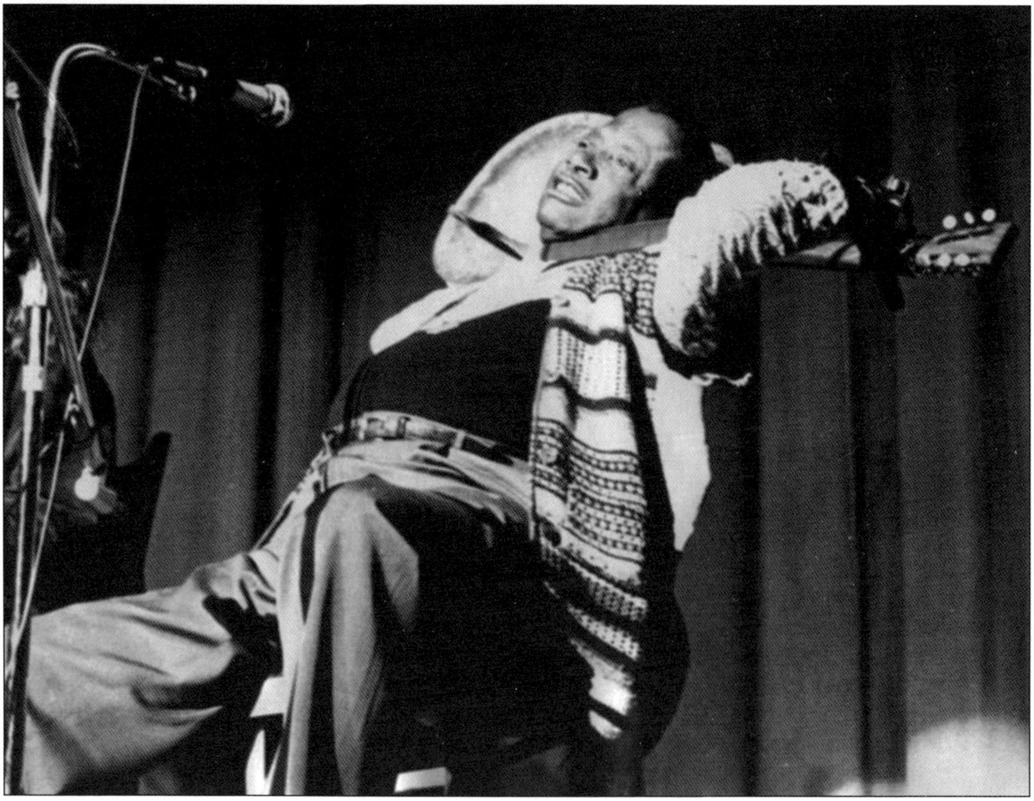

"Pinebluff Arkansas," recorded by Mississippi-born Blues Hall of Fame member Bukka White in 1937, was a song about White's girlfriend. She lived in Pine Bluff, a place where he often performed. White had just been sentenced to two years in Mississippi's Parchman Farm Prison but had secured a special release to record two singles before beginning his sentence. He thought that "Pinebluff Arkansas" would be the big seller. Instead, the B side, "Shake 'Em on Down," became the smash hit and a popular blues standard. Still, critics consider "Pinebluff Arkansas" one of White's best early recordings. (Courtesy of Jim O'Neal.)

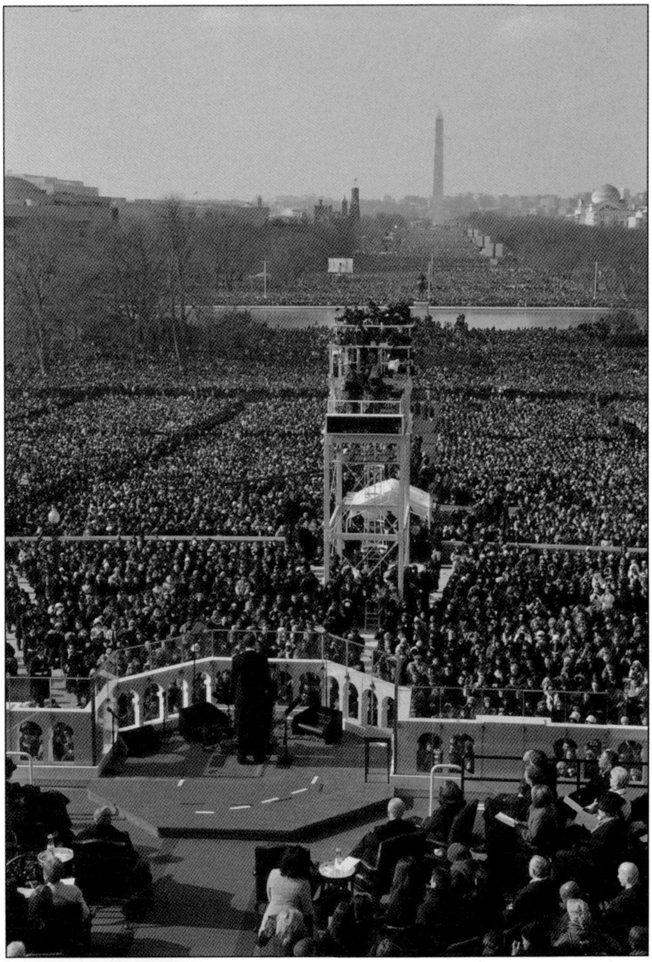

The 2009 inauguration of Pres. Barack Obama at the US Capitol was the occasion on which pioneering civil rights activist Rev. Joseph Lowery, an inaugural speaker, quoted lyrics from Jefferson County blues legend Big Bill Broonzy's 1940s protest song "Black, Brown and White." The song, with its blunt critique of America's racist social and political order, says, "If you're white, you're alright. If you're brown, stick around. But if you're black, oh brother, get back." (Courtesy of Sgt. Thomas Meneguin.)

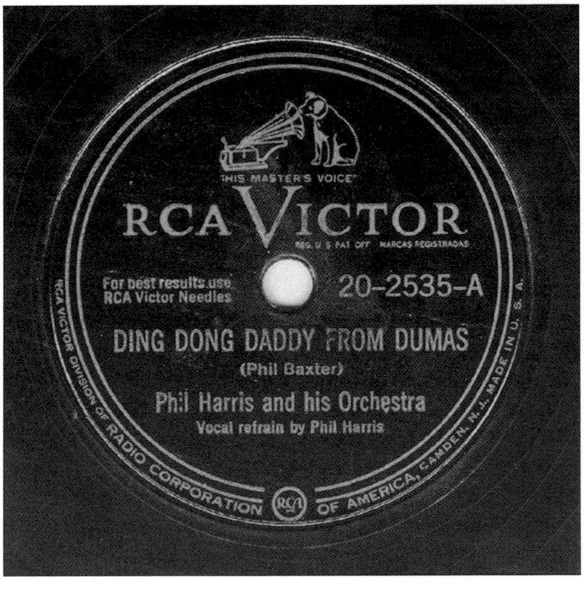

"Ding Dong Daddy from Dumas," written by Phil Harris in 1928, was made popular by Phil Baxter. Both Dumas, Arkansas, and Dumas, Texas, claim that the jazz song was about their towns, a result of separate visits by Harris. The song gained additional popularity with recordings by Louis Armstrong, Arthur Godfrey, and others. The city of Dumas, Arkansas, hosts an annual Ding Dong Days Festival. In other popular culture expressions, the character Ding Dong Daddy from the 2005 cartoon *Teen Titans* was spun from the song title, along with the cartoons "Ding Dog Daddy" (1942) and "Ding Dong Doggie" (1937). (Courtesy of City of Dumas.)

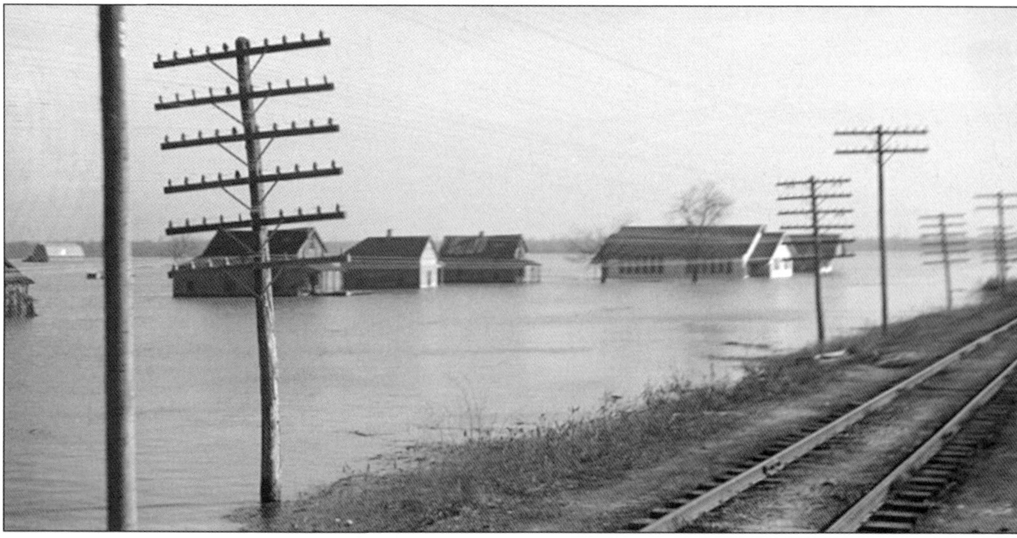

Mississippi River floodwaters engulf Delta land in 1937. Johnny Cash's hit song "Five Feet High and Rising" was written about his childhood experience in that flood. The family lived in the northeast Arkansas Delta town of Dyess when the levy broke. His song says, "We gotta head for higher ground. / We can't come back till the water comes down." In fact, Cash is referencing his family taking refuge in Pine Bluff at his grandfather's house for a month as they waited for the waters to recede, according to *Johnny Cash: The Biography*. The song reached No. 14 on the Billboard Hot Country and Western charts in 1959. (Courtesy of Library of Congress.)

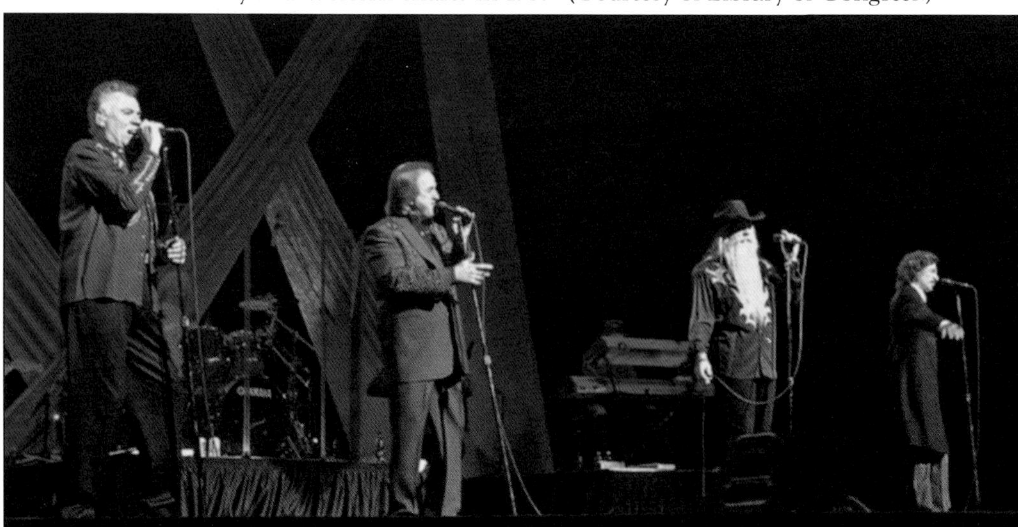

"Thank God for Kids" is a beloved country music Christmas song by the Oak Ridge Boys. According to *More Stories Behind the Best-Loved Songs of Christmas*, by Ace Collins, when the group performed the song for the public in Pine Bluff during a 1982 HBO television special, they were amazed that the crowd, many crying and cheering, gave it a rousing ovation of several minutes. The song had been unsuccessfully released in the 1970s by the group and had been largely forgotten. The overwhelming Pine Bluff response prompted its rerecording and subsequent commercial success. More important, this moment in Pine Bluff, according to lead singer Duane Allen, helped renew the group's focus and maintained their cohesion as they were considering breaking up. (Courtesy of C.D. Divan.)

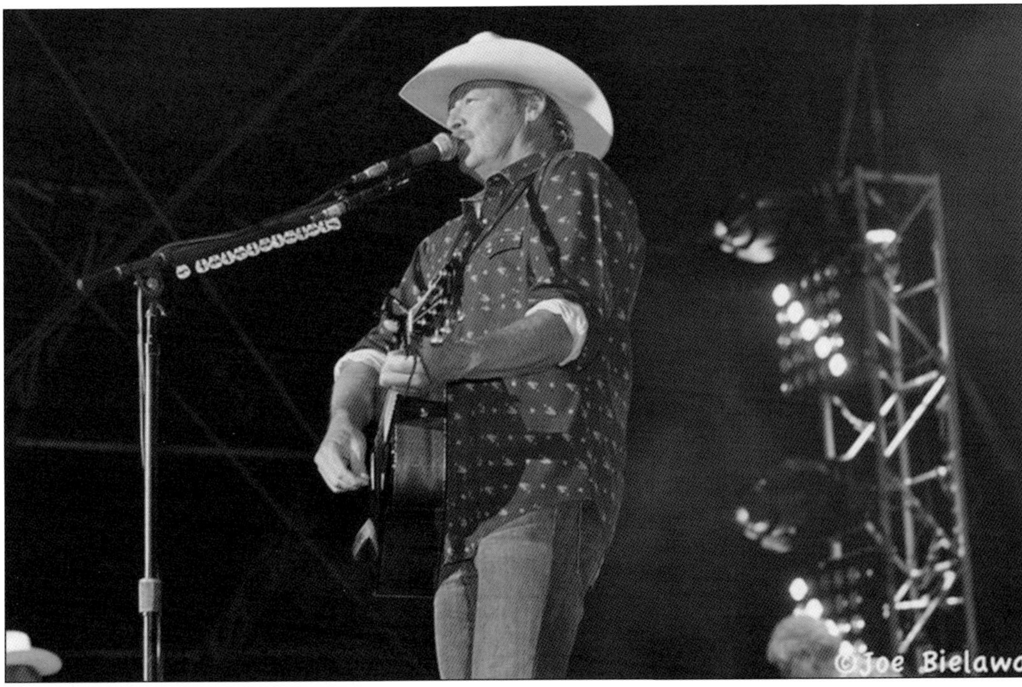

"I'd Love You All Over Again," by country superstar Alan Jackson, was the singer's first number-one hit on the *Billboard* Hot Country chart. The 1991 song was written by Jackson in a Pine Bluff hotel room during a concert tour, according to the *Chicago Tribune*. It was in tribute to his wife on their 10th wedding anniversary. (Courtesy of Joe Bielawa.)

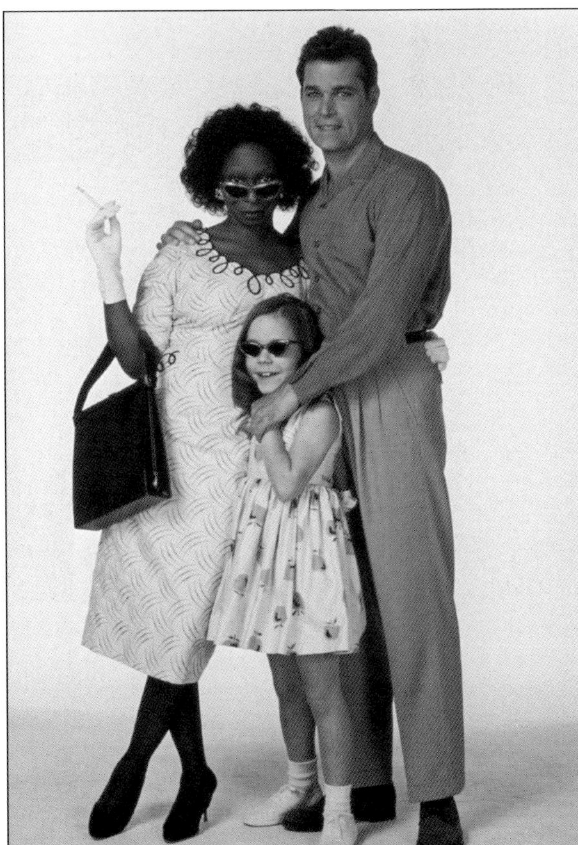

Corrina, Corrina, a 1994 movie starring Whoopi Goldberg (left), Ray Liotta (right), and Tina Majorino (center), was about a relationship that revolved around the main character's love of jazz and blues. The movie's name and anthem were taken from a 1932 hit cowritten by Blues Hall of Fame member and Pine Bluff native J. Mayo Williams. The song has been covered by such greats as Bob Dylan, Willie Nelson, Wynton Marsalis, Jerry Lee Lewis, Rod Stewart, Muddy Waters, and Dean Martin. (Courtesy of New Line Cinema.)

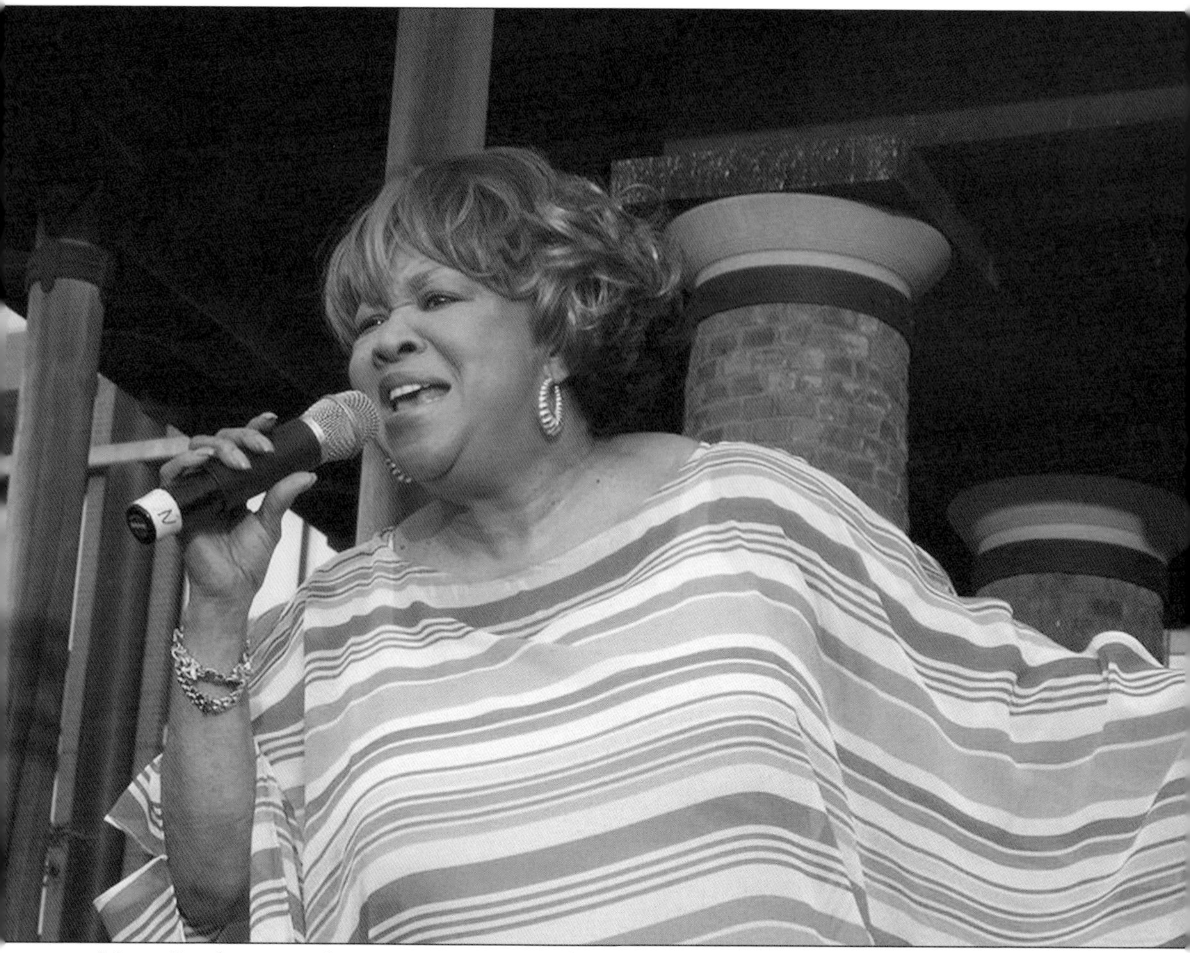

Mavis Staples is seen here singing to a crowd in 2007. When "On My Way To Heaven" was sung by Staples during a 1958 Pine Bluff concert featuring the Staple Singers, Rev. Cleo Franklin, and Aretha Franklin, a young deejay, Al Bell, was moved to tears by her voice, according to *I'll Take You There: Mavis Staples, the Staple Singers, and the March up Freedom's Highway*. It was the first time he had heard Mavis sing a solo. After the concert, he spoke with her and said, "Something happened between the two of us that night, a bond occurred . . . that I don't have words to describe." The bond that formed in Pine Bluff resulted, by 1968, in Al Bell, now the head of Stax Records, signing the Staple Singers. When Bell was producing their song "I'll Take You There" in 1971, he was going through Mavis's vocal tracks, trying to find the perfect sound for the final version. When he finally found it, he exclaimed that what he had captured in this version was reminiscent of the raw emotion he had first heard 10 years before in Pine Bluff. Bell said, "It was Mavis, Mavis, Mavis—*that* Mavis I saw in Pine Bluff in the '50s singing. . . . Whatever was in there emotionally and spiritually came out." The song went on to become one of the group's biggest hits. (Courtesy of Jalylah Burrell.)

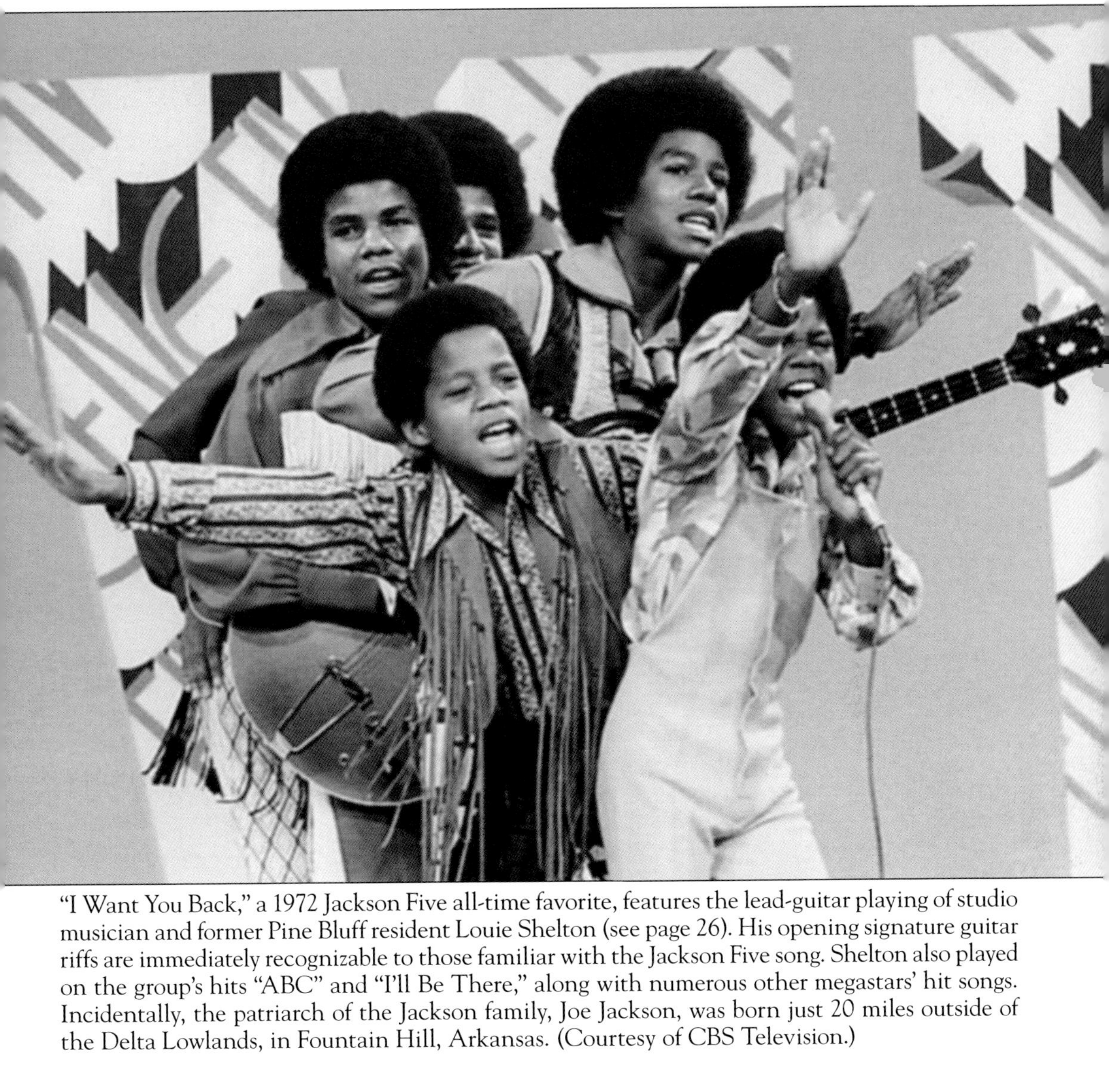

"I Want You Back," a 1972 Jackson Five all-time favorite, features the lead-guitar playing of studio musician and former Pine Bluff resident Louie Shelton (see page 26). His opening signature guitar riffs are immediately recognizable to those familiar with the Jackson Five song. Shelton also played on the group's hits "ABC" and "I'll Be There," along with numerous other megastars' hit songs. Incidentally, the patriarch of the Jackson family, Joe Jackson, was born just 20 miles outside of the Delta Lowlands, in Fountain Hill, Arkansas. (Courtesy of CBS Television.)

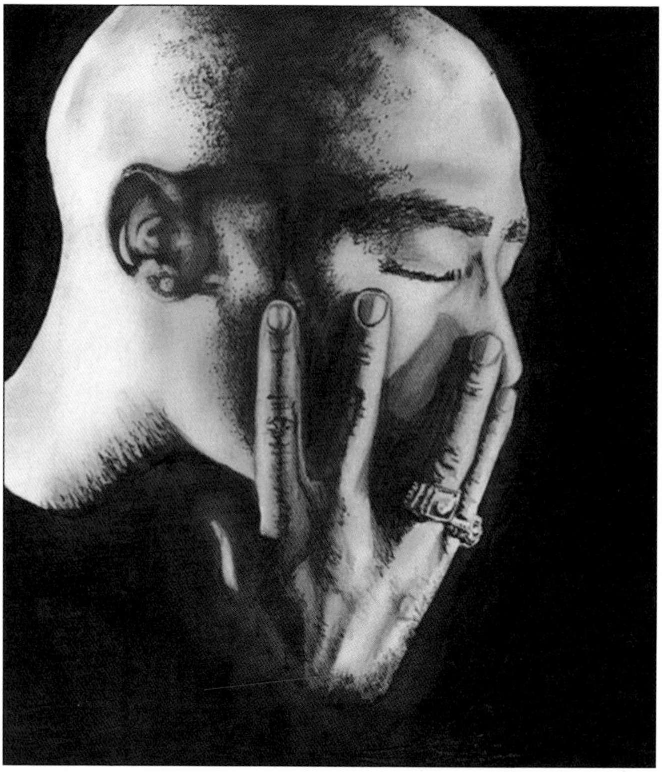

"Ghetto Gospel" by rapper Tupac Shakur became a hit following the rap icon's 1996 murder. The song references former Pine Bluff native and Black Panther Party icon Bobby Hutton, who, in 1968, was the first Panther gunned down by police in the country. Hutton's name became synonymous with police brutality following accounts of his execution-style murder while in custody. His name has been invoked in other rap songs, like Smif-N-Wessun's "Still Fighting," The Coup and Dead Prez's "Get Up," and Paris's "Panther Power." Incidentally, a shooting at Tupac's 1993 Pine Bluff concert infamously led to the largest monetary judgment ($16 million) against him in his career. (Courtesy of Makaveli75.)

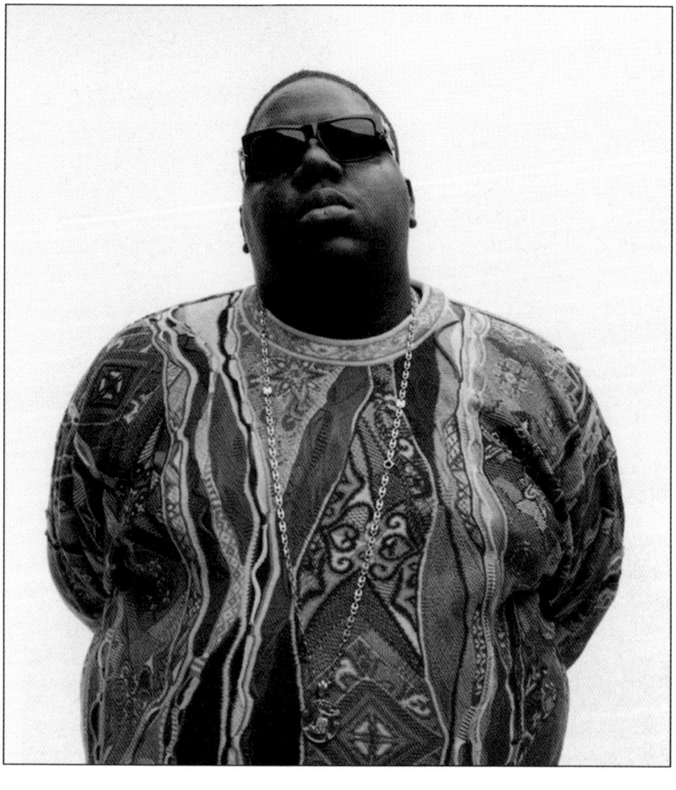

Notorious B.I.G. (pictured), in his 1994 hit song "Juicy," asks, "Remember 'Rappin Duke'? Da ha, da ha. You never thought hip hop would take it this far." This is a reference to the novelty rap song "Rappin' Duke," a 1984 hit by Shawn Brown. He was a UAPB graduate who resided in Pine Bluff, working as a disc jockey at KCAT. His song, which was also immortalized in a Beastie Boys release, made *Billboard*'s rap charts. (Courtesy of Bad Boy Records.)

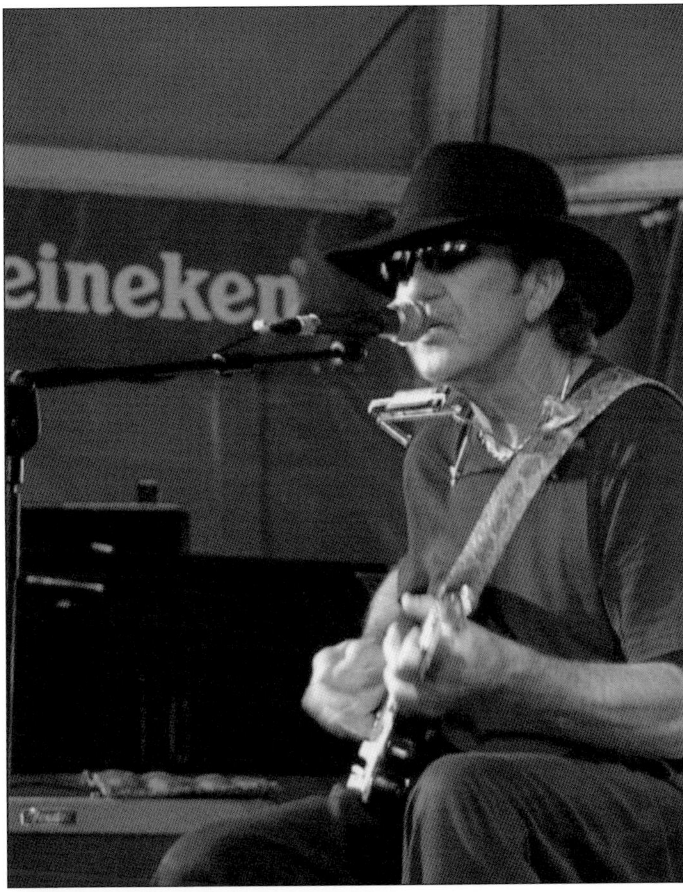

"They Caught the Devil and Put Him in Jail in Eudora" was by Tony Joe White, a blues-rock recording star and *Billboard* charting artist. The 1971 song was a fanciful story about the capture of a supernatural prisoner in Eudora, Arkansas. (Courtesy of Raul Mesa.)

Main Street in Pine Bluff bustles with traffic in the 1960s. "Draggin' Main Street" was written in 1955 by the Grammy-nominated country music group the Browns. The inspiration for the song was the group's 1950s weekend experiences cruising Pine Bluff streets as teens on thoroughfares like Cherry Street, Main Street, and others. Some Pine Bluff locals took offense to the song, culminating in a stinging editorial by a local newspaper highly critical of the lyrics. (Courtesy of Paul Perdue.)

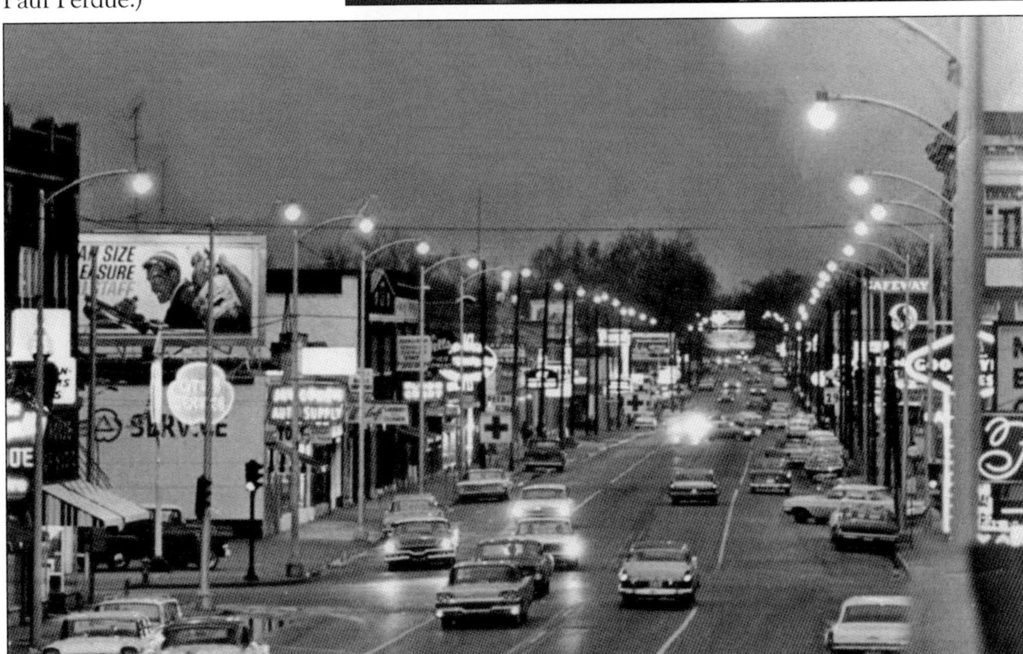

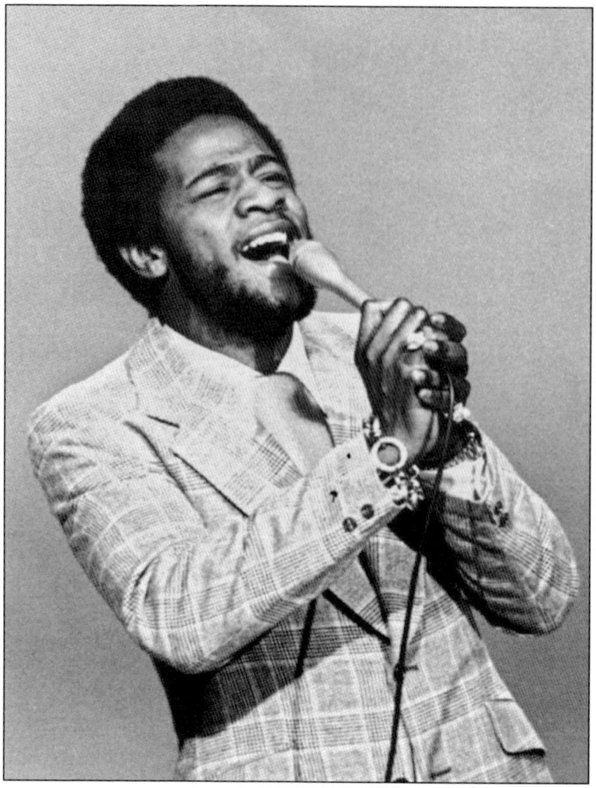

The 1971 blockbuster hit "Let's Stay Together," by soul legend Al Green, was cowritten by Green, record executive "Papa" Willie Mitchell, and former UAPB student and drummer for Booker T. & the M.G.s Al Jackson Jr. The trio created the song in a Memphis studio, laid the music track, then gathered locals who were drinking outside to listen to Green lay the vocals, according to an interview with Mitchell. The song gained recent attention in 2012 at Harlem's Apollo Theater when President Obama famously crooned a portion of it to the audience before a speech. (Courtesy of *The Mike Douglas Show.*)

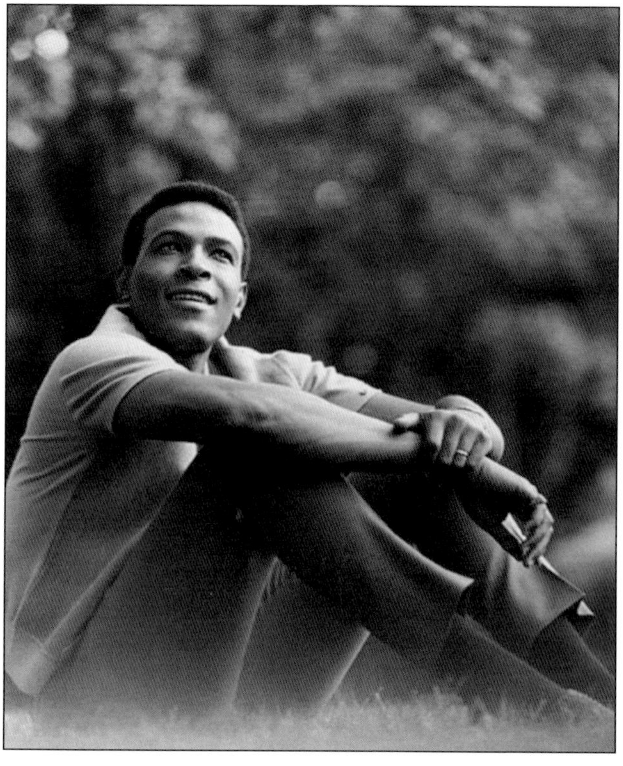

One of the most famous recorded love songs, "Let's Get It On," was cowritten in 1973 by the R&B great Marvin Gaye and former UAPB graduate and Pine Bluff resident Ed Townsend. Townsend teamed up with Gaye and originally wrote the song with a religious theme following Townsend's release from an alcohol rehab facility. However, after several iterations, including a political version, the two decided to tweak the composition into a love song which ultimately became one of Gaye's biggest smash hits. (Courtesy of J. Edward Bailey.)

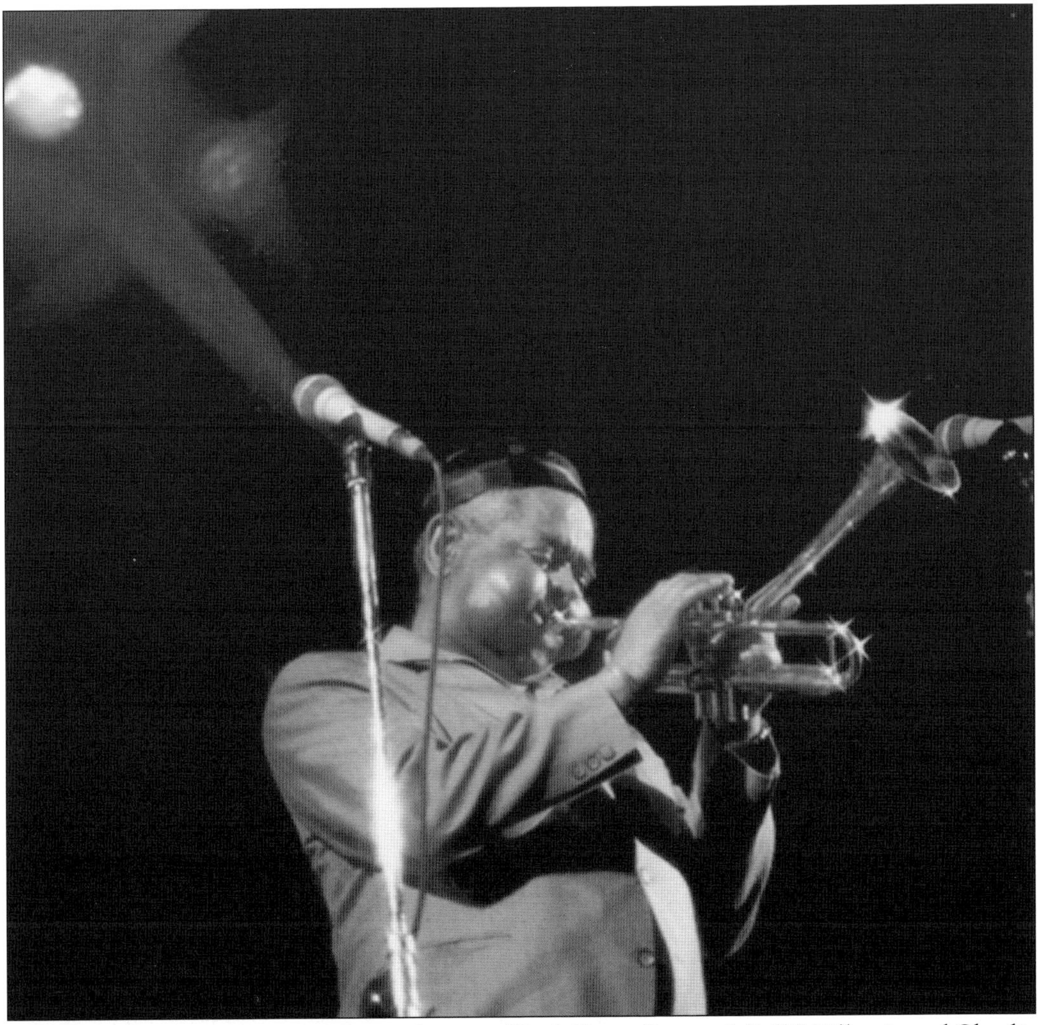

Jazz great Dizzy Gillespie never forgot the song "Dark Town Strutter's Ball." Gillespie and Charlie "Bird" Parker were playing on tour with Earl Hines's band in Pine Bluff at a military camp in the 1940s. A white farmer tossed a quarter at Gillespie, insisting, "Boy, play me some of that 'Darktown Strutter's Ball'," according to his account in *DownBeat: The Great Jazz Interviews*. However, Gillespie ignored him. The farmer angrily left, but waited until Gillespie went to the bathroom. He then took a bottle and crashed it against Gillespie's head. Gillespie, bloodied and dazed, started to lunge for the man, but Parker, realizing the trouble that could follow fighting a white man in the Jim Crow South, pushed Gillespie away. An ambulance transported Gillespie to the local black Pine Bluff hospital to treat his bleeding head wounds. The incident underscored the dangers of black artists playing for white audiences in the segregated South. (Courtesy of Pino Alpino.)

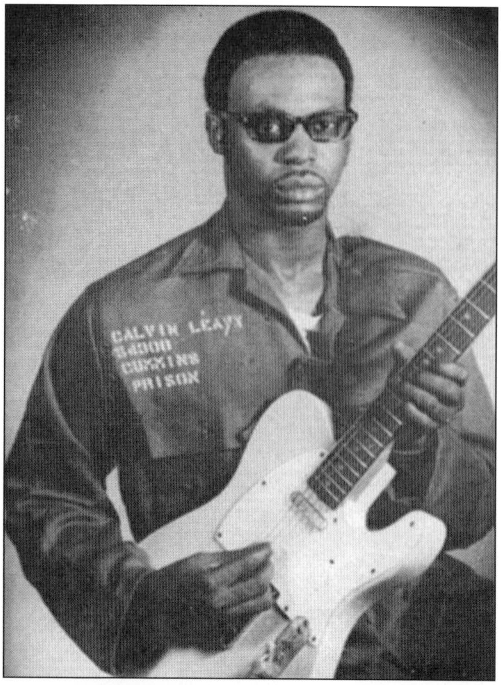

"Cummins Prison Farm" skyrocketed up the *Billboard* charts in 1970, becoming a hit. The blues song, by guitarist and singer Calvin Leavy, a native of Scott, Arkansas, described the hard life of incarceration at the state's maximum-security penal facility, Cummins Prison. Its success spawned multiple covers by bluesmen Magic Slim, Tommy Bankhead, and others. Ironically, Leavy, an exceptional vocalist with other recorded singles, was sentenced to prison in 1991 at Cummins and died as a prisoner at Pine Bluff's Jefferson Regional Medical Center in 2004. (Courtesy of the Lenox Store.)

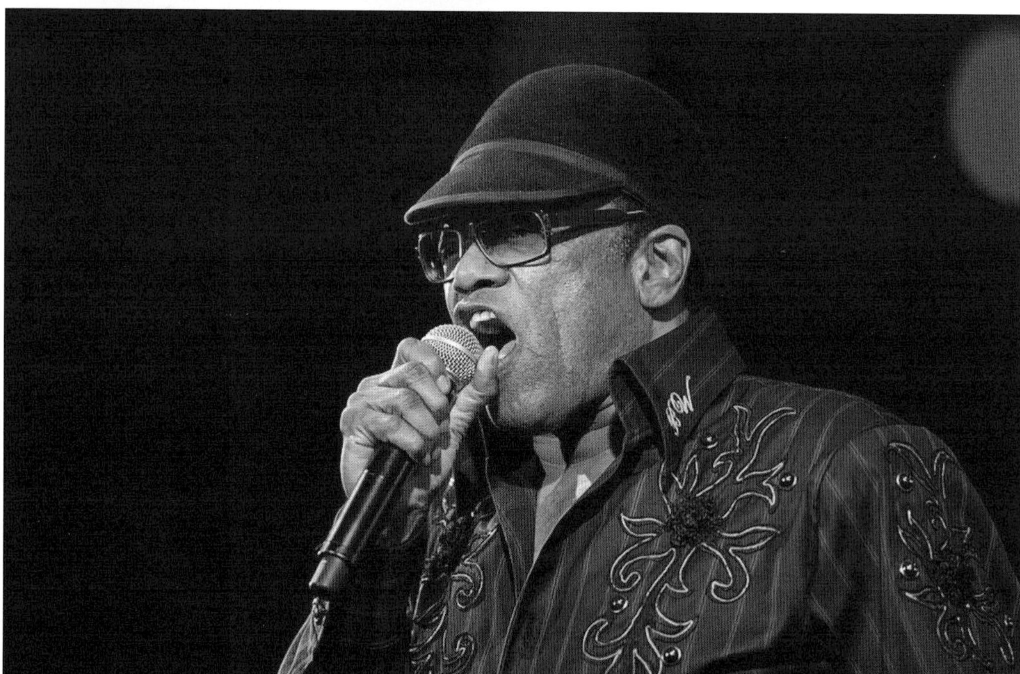

"Arkansas State Prison," by soul powerhouse Bobby Womack, envisioned a fabled escape from an Arkansas prison. His 1970 lyrical portrait of the bleakness of prison life and the inhumane conditions in an Arkansas prison is chilling. When he sings, "No one knows how many they list as missing," this is clearly a veiled reference to the 1960s rumors about the secret mass graves at Cummins Prison. The prison was later characterized in the 1980 movie *Brubaker*. (Courtesy of Bill Ebbesen.)

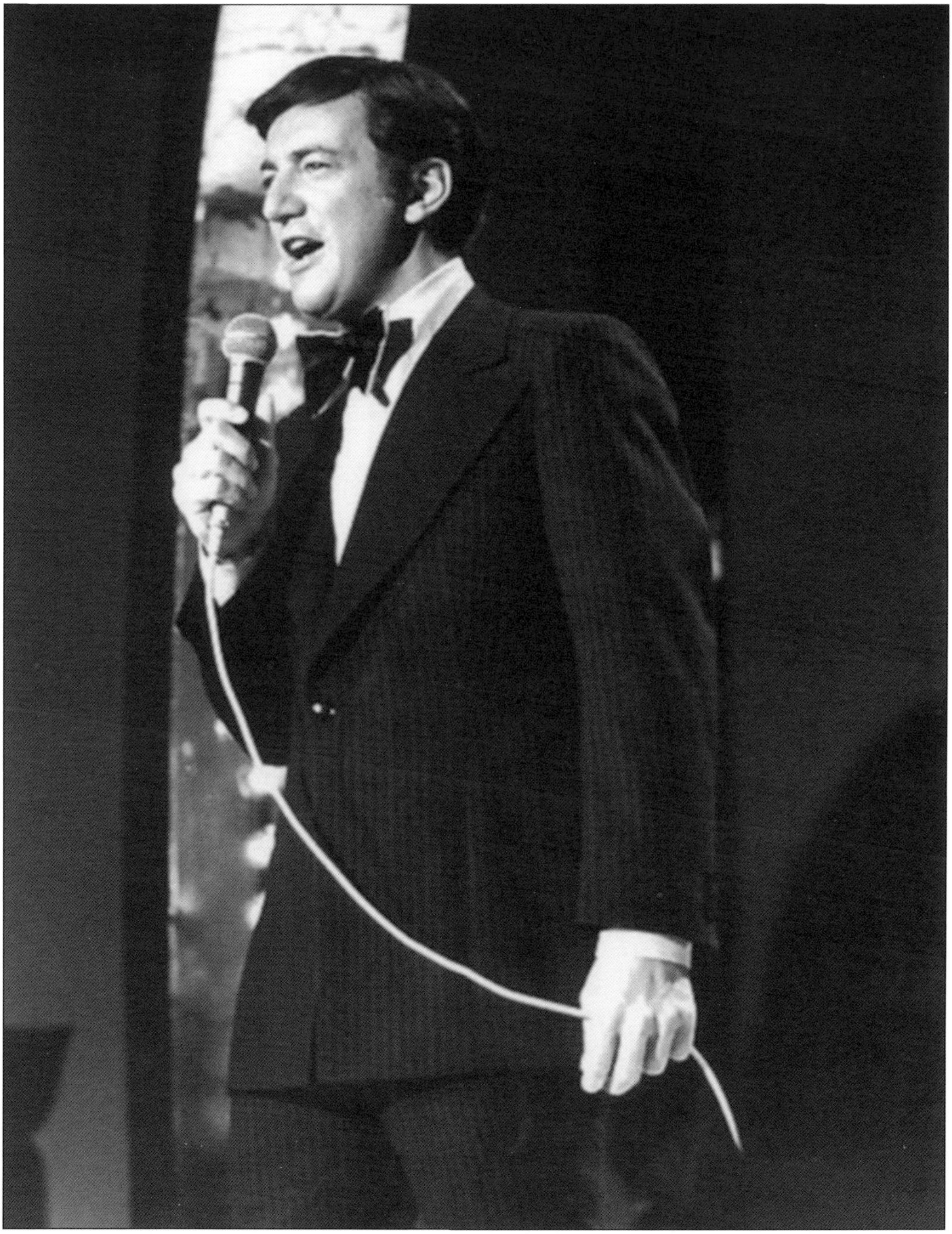

"Long Line Rider," a 1968 protest song by Grammy Award–winning singer and Oscar-nominated actor Bobby Darin, highlighted the cruel conditions to which Arkansas inmates were subjected. It also referenced unmarked graves filled with bodies that had suffered abuse and torture at Cummins Prison. In 1969, Darin walked off the set of *The Jackie Gleason Show* because he was not allowed to sing the song. (Courtesy of NBC Television.)

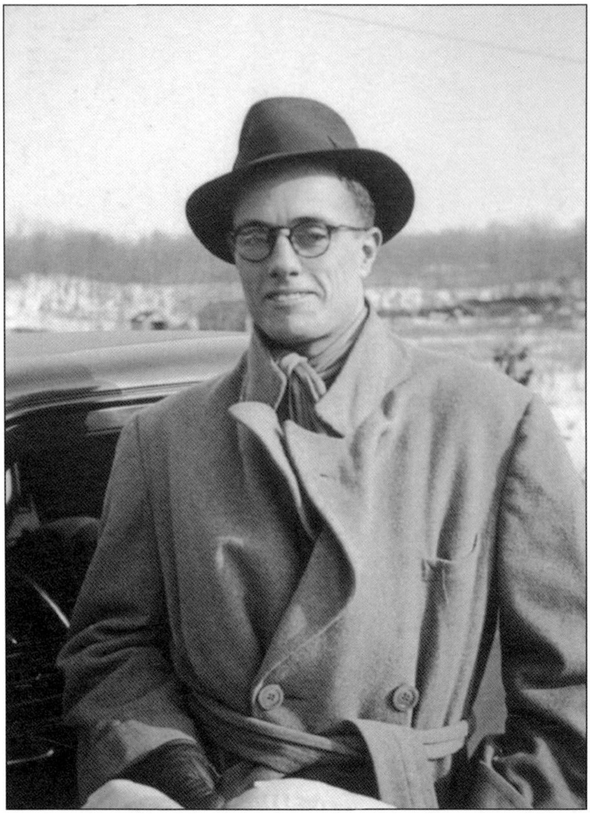

"Rock Island Line" became popular when folklorists/ethnomusicologists John (left) and Alan Lomax, along with legendary blues/folk artist Huddie "Lead Belly" Ledbetter, visited Tucker and Cummins Prisons in 1934. They recorded numerous songs in Southern prisons and local communities in a federally funded journey focusing on rare African American folk songs, many dating back to slavery. When they heard Kelly Pace singing "Rock Island Line" at Cummins with other convicts, they recorded him leading the song. A host of musical greats later covered the song, including Lead Belly, Johnny Cash, Odetta, Harry Belafonte, John Lennon, Paul Simon, Paul McCartney, and Little Richard. Also of note, Lomax later interviewed and recorded Jefferson County legend Big Bill Broonzy and Desha County blind gospel songwriter Charles Haffer Jr., revealing important dynamics in early blues, gospel, and folk music. (Both, courtesy of Library of Congress.)

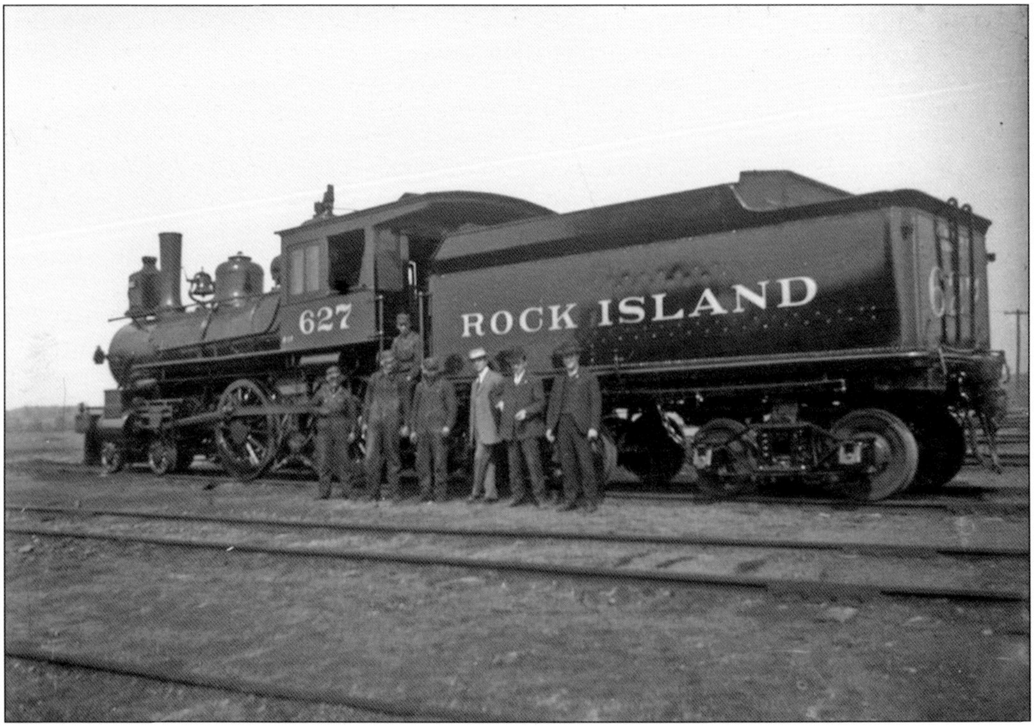

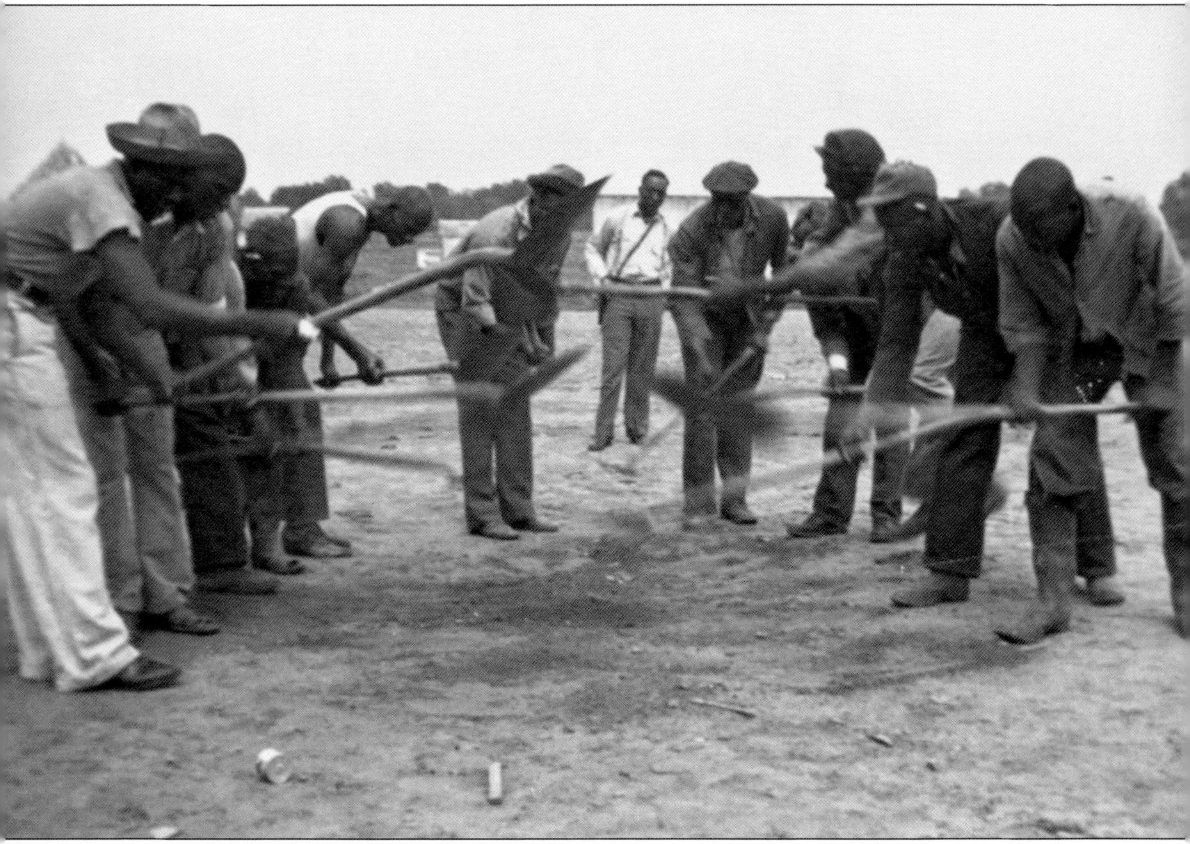

Here, Cummins prisoners sing as researcher Alan Lomax photographs them in 1934. The first full-length recording of the now-popular African American spiritual "Children Go Where I Send Thee" was made at Cummins Prison in 1939. According to the *Encyclopedia of Great Popular Song Recordings, Vol. 2*, John and Alan Lomax and Huddie Ledbetter recorded prisoner Kelly Pace, who led the song. Lomax recorded Pace leading 37 other rare songs during his 20-plus-year stint at Cummins. The song has been recorded by music greats as diverse as Tennessee Ernie Ford, Nina Simone, Mahalia Jackson, Ricky Scaggs, and many others. It was also a part of the movie sound track for *Christmas Lilies of the Field* (1979), starring Billy Dee Williams. Numerous other folk and blues songs with origins dating back to slavery were captured in the legendary Lomax recordings featuring additional inmates at facilities in Tucker, Pine Bluff, and Grady between 1934 and 1939. (Courtesy of Library of Congress.)

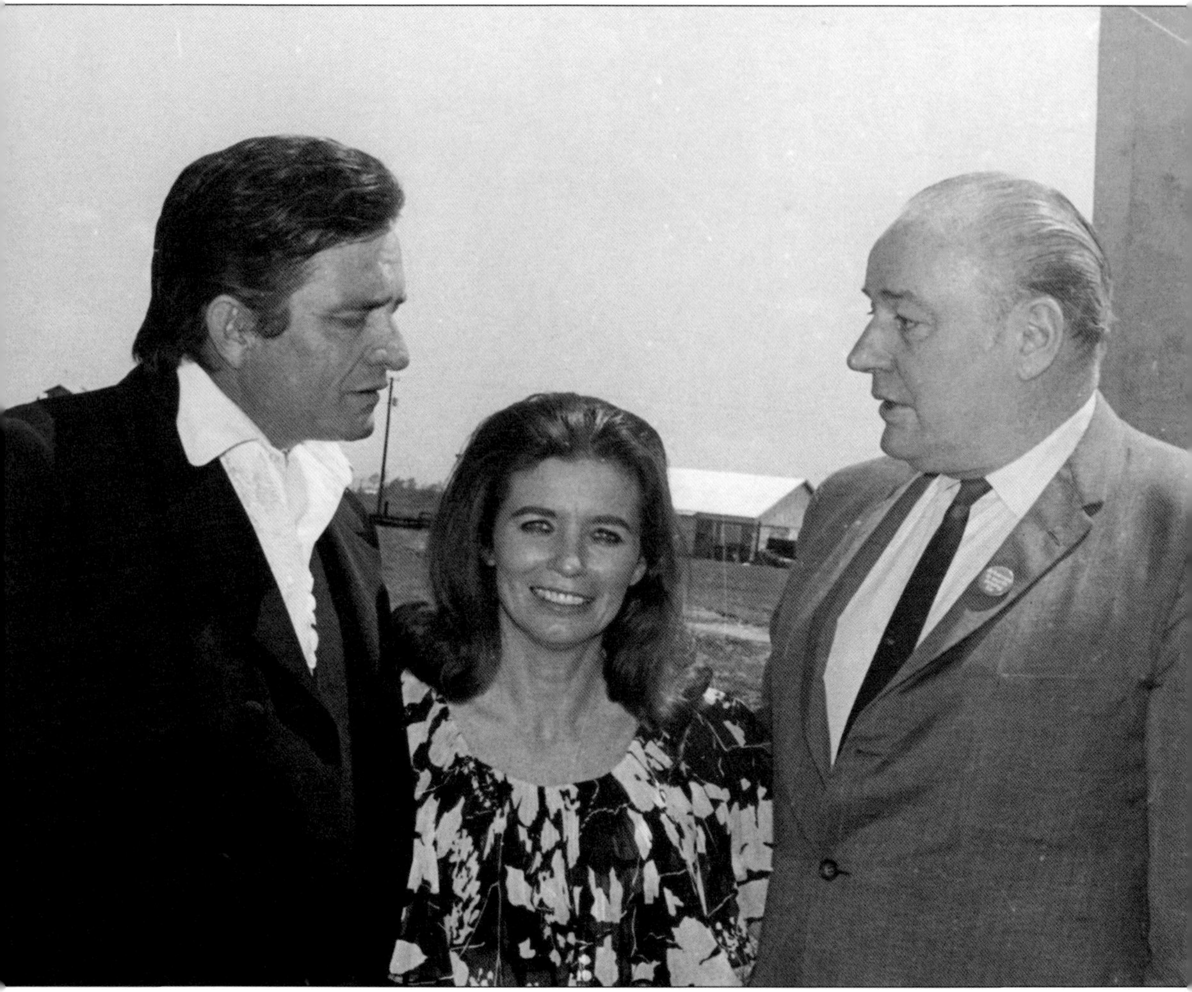

Country music legends Johnny (left) and June Carter Cash (center) talk with Arkansas governor Winthrop Rockefeller in 1969 before a Cummins Prison concert. Johnny Cash sang "When I Get Out of Cummins" at the concert, drawing attention to the deplorable prison system in Arkansas. They system was ruled unconstitutional by the US Supreme Court in 1970. With charges of mass graves of prisoners and documented use of torture (such as the "Tucker Telephone," which ran electrical current through inmates' genitalia), Cash felt obligated as a prison-reform advocate and as a fellow Arkansan to visit the troubled institution. He also sang "Rock Island Line" there, which Cummins inmate Kelley Pace sang 30 years prior, during the Lomax/Lead Belly recordings. Some historians suggest that Cash's Cummins Prison visit marked the official beginning of prison reform in Arkansas. Just three weeks after his concert, the legislature began dismantling the prison's self-supporting system. In 2012, the BBC produced a radio documentary on Cash's Cummins visit called *Johnny Cash and the Forgotten Prison Blues*. (Courtesy of University of Arkansas at Little Rock Center for Arkansas History and Culture.)

Four

The UAPB/Delta Lowlands Music Connection

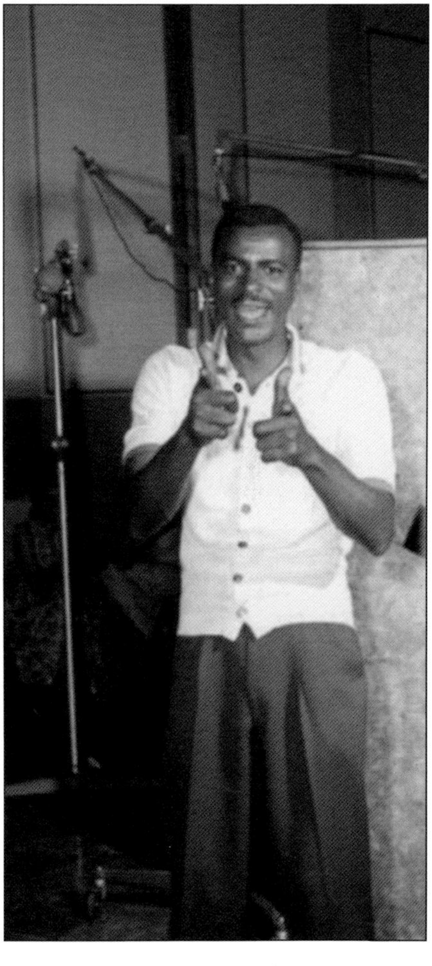

When Ed Townsend, UAPB graduate and Pine Bluff resident, recorded "For Your Love" in 1958, Dick Clark signed him to perform in the first month of his new dance show, *American Bandstand*. The song shot to number 13 on the *Billboard* charts. Following this, Townsend had a brief recording career, but he focused his efforts on songwriting. He wrote and produced other chart-topping songs for major artists, none more famous than "Let's Get It On," cowritten with Marvin Gaye. Townsend also scored music for the movies *Black Fist* (1974) and *The Ultimate Thrill* (1974). (Courtesy of Corbin Photos.)

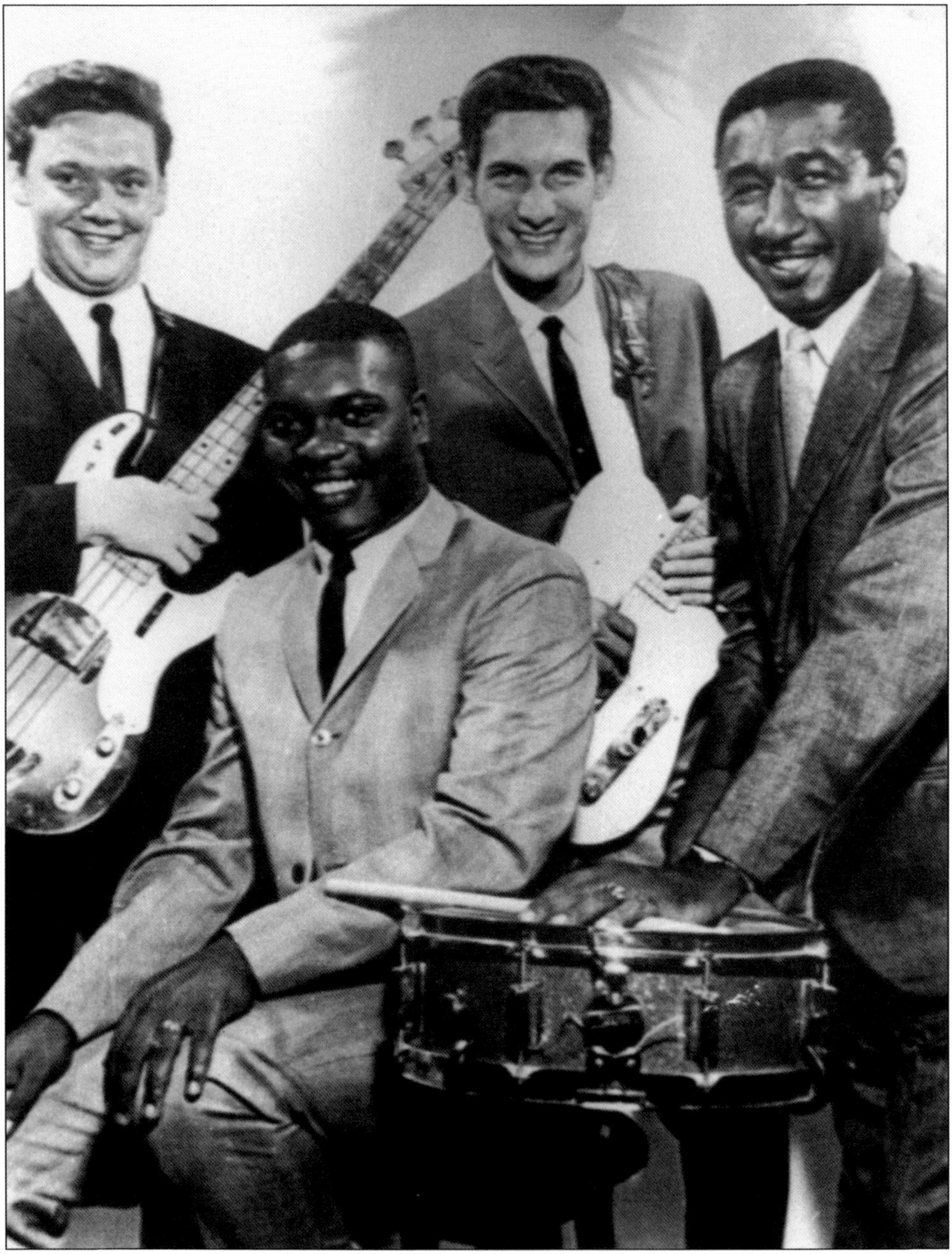

Memphis-born Al Jackson Jr. (right) was a Grammy winner, former UAPB student, songwriter, producer, and drummer. As a member of the legendary Stax Records house band in the early 1960s, he played on hits by Otis Redding, Sam & Dave, Eddie Floyd, Rufus Thomas, Albert King, Isaac Hayes, Wilson Pickett, and others. Because of his keen songwriting abilities, artists also used Jackson to help write and produce many of the defining songs of the Memphis sound of the 1960s and 1970s. The Stax house band, Booker T. & the M.G.s (pictured), had its own incredible success, eventually taking it to the Rock and Roll Hall of Fame. Jackson also individually worked on other projects, including cowriting Al Green hits such as "Let's Stay Together," "I'm Still in Love with You," and "I'm So Tired of Being Alone." He has over 90 credits in movies and television programs. Musicradar.com ranks Jackson in its 100 most influential drummers of all time. (Courtesy of *Billboard* magazine.)

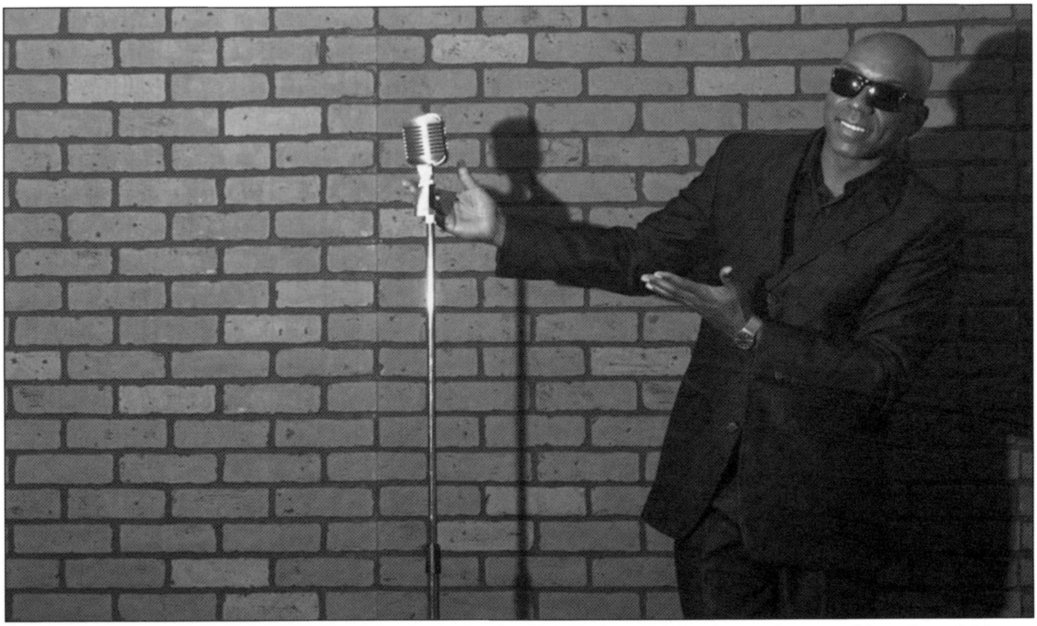

Chicago-born Larry Braggs, a UAPB graduate, lead vocalist for the legendary soul/jazz band Tower of Power for 13 years, and currently an independent recording artist, has wowed audiences all over the world with a three-octave vocal range. His vocals helped propel Tower of Power to eight *Billboard* chart-topping jazz albums in his tenure. Braggs has also appeared in movies such as *Player 5150* (2008), *Wildcats* (1986), and *A Soldier's Story* (1984). (Courtesy of Larry Braggs.)

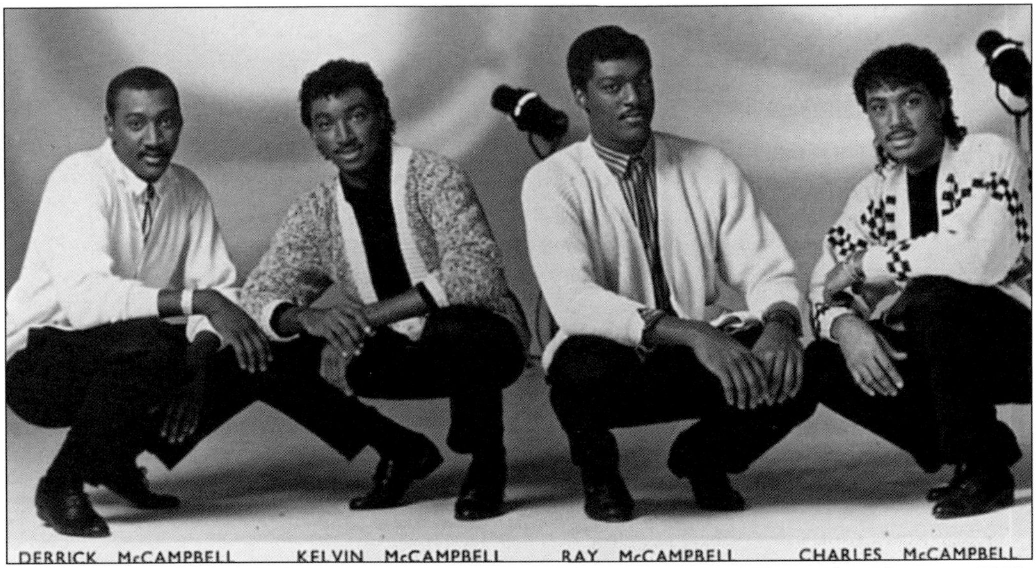

The Mac Band had a No. 1 hit, "Roses are Red," on the Billboard Black Singles Charts in 1988. The group featured the talented voices of the McCampbell brothers from Flint, Michigan, including Derrick "D-Mack" McCampbell (first person from the left), a UAPB graduate. The success of their first album included productions by Babyface and Atlantic Star yielding national tours and television exposure like their 1990 *Soul Train* appearance with the rap group Salt-N-Peppa. From 1988 to 1992, the band produced three albums and placed other songs on the R&B charts both in the United States and the United Kingdom. (Courtesy of Miller Rand.)

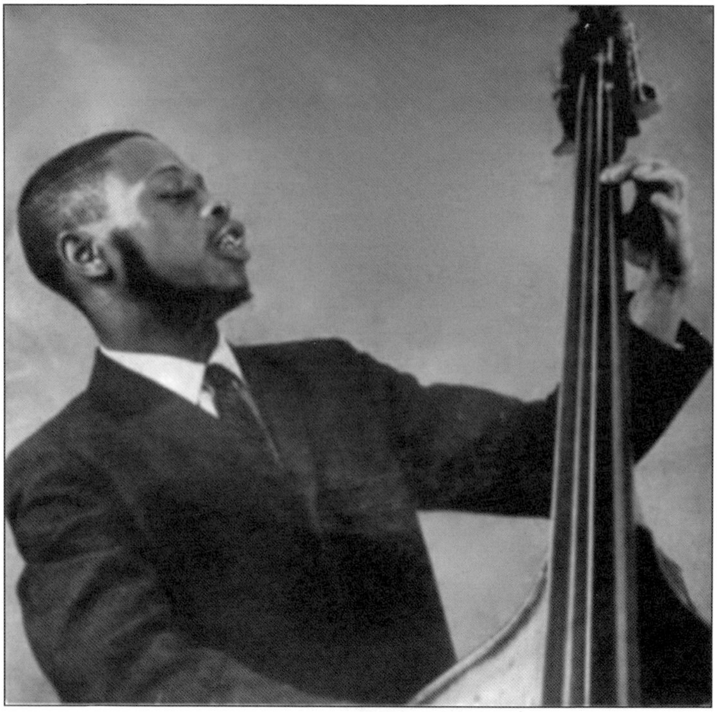

Jamil Nassar (George Joyner), a UAPB graduate born in Memphis, was a talented jazz bassist who also played tuba. He accompanied many greats, including B.B. King, John Coltrane, Sonny Rollins, Ahmad Jamal, and Red Garland. His extensive body of music can be found in almost 40 albums from 1958 to 1998. The *All Music Guide to Jazz* cites his work. He also appeared in the 1996 movie *The Preacher's Wife*, starring Denzel Washington and Whitney Houston. (Courtesy of Laura Rainey.)

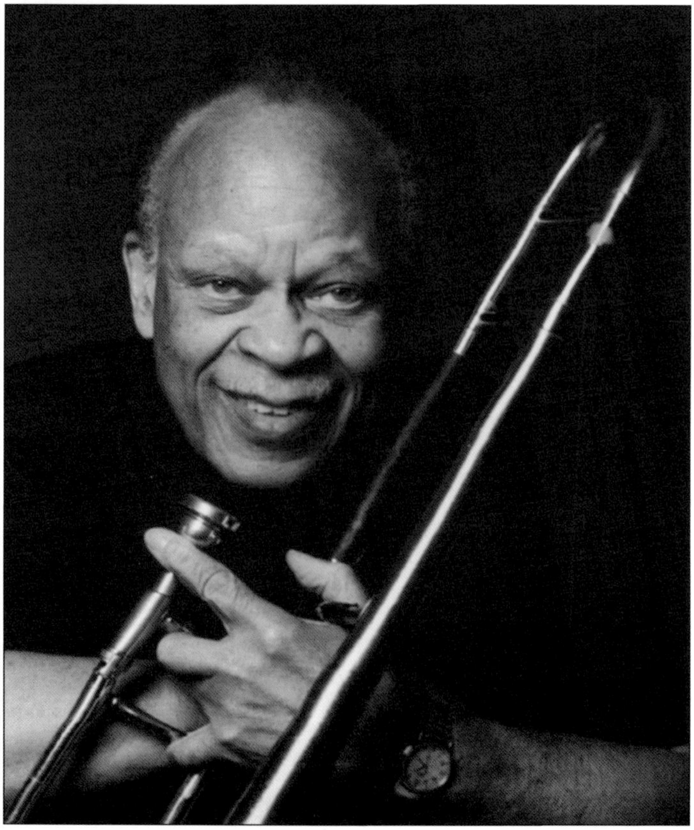

Memphis's Garnett Brown, a graduate of UAPB, is a celebrated trombonist. He has worked with Lionel Hampton; Quincy Jones; Herbie Hancock; Bobby Bland; B.B. King; Prince; Captain and Tenille; Earth, Wind & Fire; and others. He appears on over 40 albums as a sideman. Brown orchestrated, arranged, and conducted the music for the 1989 movie *Harlem Nights* (see page 114). His work is referenced in *The Biographical Encyclopedia of Jazz.* (Courtesy of Garnett Brown.)

Morris Hayes, an inductee to the Arkansas Black Hall of Fame and a native of Jefferson, Arkansas, is a producer, keyboardist, and bandleader for the New Power Generation, the backup band for Prince. Hayes graduated from UAPB, then worked his way to Minneapolis, where Prince eventually brought him into his band. Hayes has played with other stars, including Kanye West, Elton John, Whitney Houston, and others. He has written music for shows like Flavor Flav's *Under One Roof*, Martin Lawrence's *You So Crazy*, and HBO's *Laurel Avenue*. Hayes also appeared in the movie *Graffiti Bridge* (1990), directed by Prince. (Courtesy of Morris Hayes.)

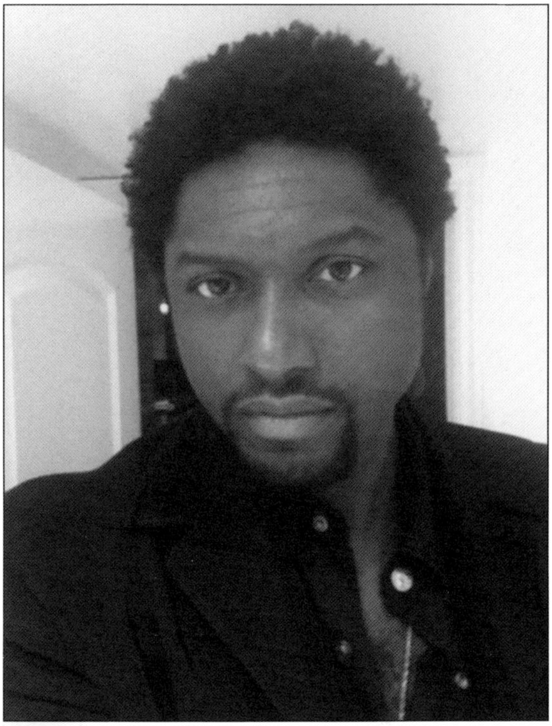

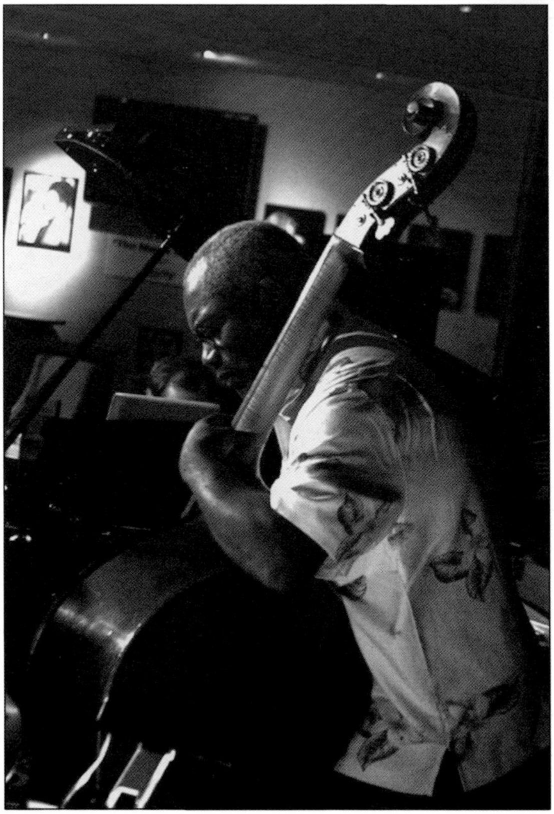

James Leary is a two-time Grammy-winning bassist from Little Rock and a graduate of UAPB. A student of the late Art Porter Sr., he has performed with Nancy Wilson, Frank Sinatra, Sammy Davis Jr., Liza Minnelli, Thelonious Monk, Dizzy Gillespie, the Count Basie Orchestra, and his own group, the James Leary Orchestra. In 1996, he was inducted into the Arkansas Jazz Hall of Fame. He has recorded three albums and has appeared on countless others. Leary's music was on the sound track for movies like *Smouldering Cigarette* (2001) and *Guinevere* (1999), and he has appeared in other movies, like *That Thing You Do!* (1996). (Courtesy of James Leary.)

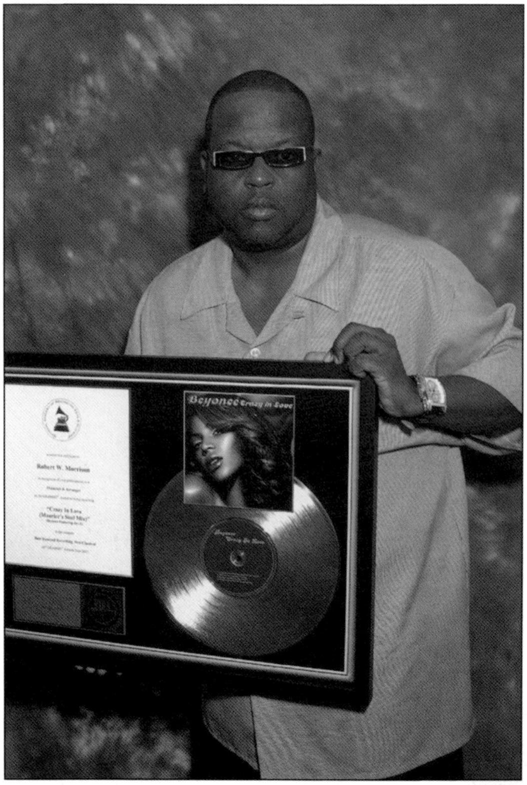

Rob "Diggy" Morrison, a Chicago native, UAPB graduate, keyboardist, writer, and producer is a Grammy Certified award winner for his work with megastar Beyonce. He is gold certified for work with Janet Jackson, Omarion, and Shakira. Morrison has also scored music in movies like *Miami Uncovered* (2015), *The Swan Princess Christmas* (2012), *The Witch of Portobella* (2009), *Tactical* (2008), and others. (Courtesy of Rob Morrison.)

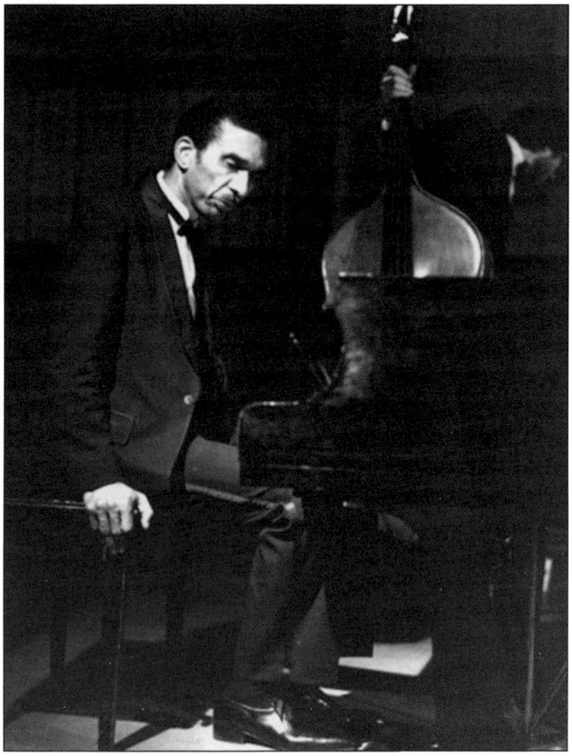

Art Porter Sr., jazz pianist, composer, music teacher, UAPB graduate, and Little Rock native, was celebrated as one of the finest traditional jazz musicians in Arkansas from the 1960s to the 1990s. His Art Porter Trio awed audiences, particularly with his groundbreaking public television show, *The Minor Key*. He produced several albums and was later inducted into the Arkansas Jazz Hall of Fame. He was the father of the late Art Porter Jr., a contemporary jazz artist. (Courtesy of Butler Center for Arkansas Studies.)

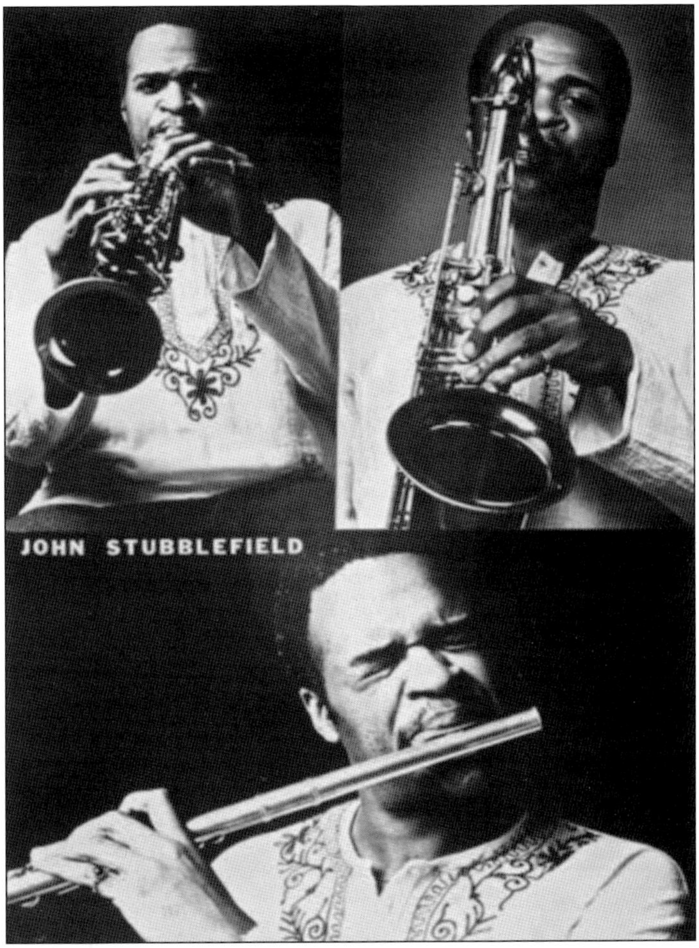

John Stubblefield was one of the most innovative soloists of the post-Coltrane era, according to Allmusic.com. A jazz/blues flutist, saxophonist, and oboist from Little Rock and a UAPB graduate, he collaborated with Charles Mingus, Miles Davis, Nat Adderly, and others. In addition to his work as a sideman, he recorded seven solo albums from 1976 to 1993. *The Biographical Encyclopedia of Jazz* cites his contributions. The video documentary *Dreaming in America* (2005) includes his artistic contributions. (Courtesy of Arkansas History Commission.)

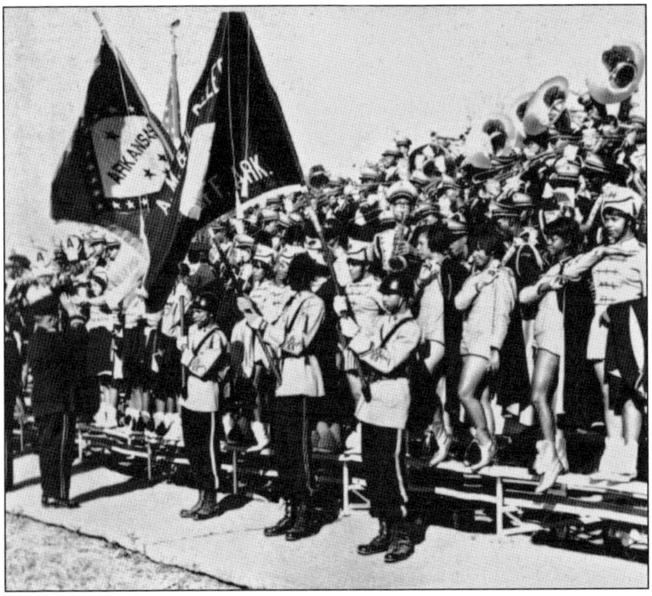

The Arkansas AM&N (UAPB) Marching Band performs here in the 1960s under the direction of Harold Strong (standing on the lower level in front of the flags). Band members were nurtured by directors like Strong, Alma Brown, Odie Burris Jr., Dr. Joseph Miller, Kelvin Washington, and John Graham. Many band members, though not from Jefferson County or the Delta Lowlands, significantly contributed to area music, serving as student teachers in local schools, mentors in community programs, and musicians at churches and clubs/juke joints. (Courtesy of UAPB Archives.)

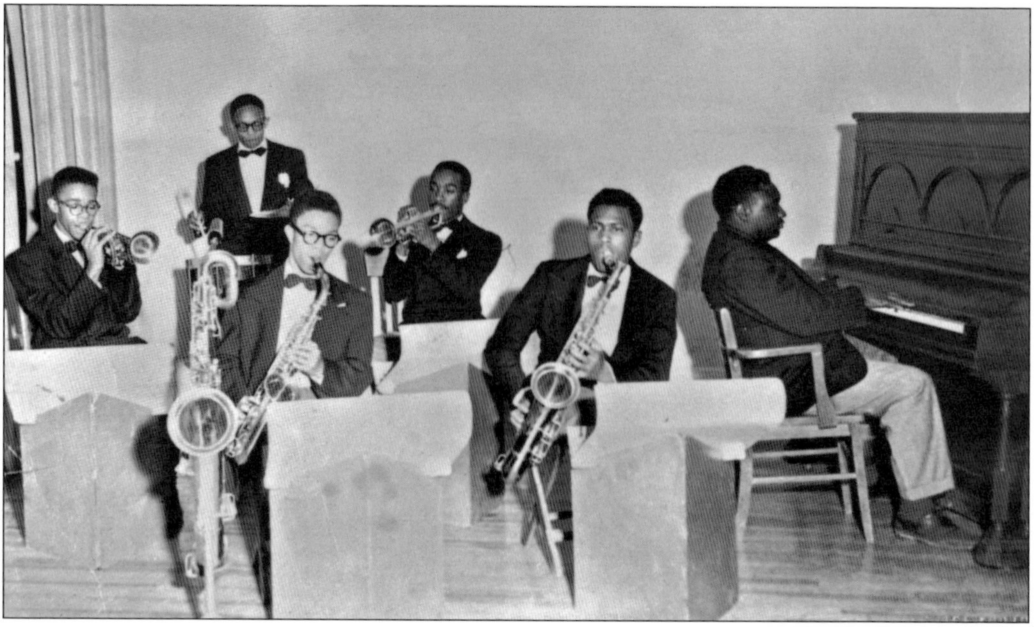

Trenton Cooper (far right) plays with an Arkansas AM&N combo in 1948. Also identified here is Ulysses Dalton III (rear center). Cooper was born in Hope, Arkansas, graduated from Arkansas AM&N, and later became a UAPB administrator. He played with the Drops of Joy, led by popular 1950s R&B artist Jimmy Liggins. Cooper later recorded his own jazz/blues album and other singles while playing clubs throughout Arkansas. His contributions are highlighted in *Our Own Sweet Sounds.* (Courtesy of Arkansas History Commission.)

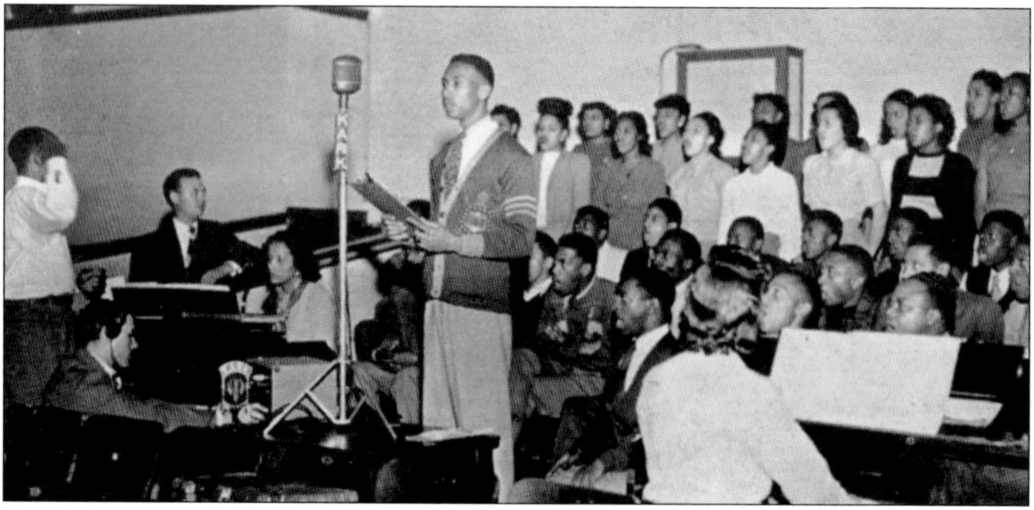

The Arkansas AM&N (UAPB) Vesper Choir performs in a live broadcast on KARK radio around 1948. Vesper Choir directors like Dr. Ariel Lovelace (also former music department chair), Shelton McGhee, and Dr. Michael Bates (current interim music department chair) have molded numerous collegiate singers. Devoted music department chairs like Dr. Grace Wiley, Dr. Josephine Bell, and other distinguished staff like composer Zenobia Powell Perry, W. H. Zachary (also a former Merrill High School instructor), acclaimed contralto soloist Rosa Louise Burge, jazz guitarist Milton Jackson, and many others have made the university's music a powerful force. (Courtesy of UAPB Archives.)

Five

Jefferson County Juke Joints, Honky-Tonks, and Nickelodeons

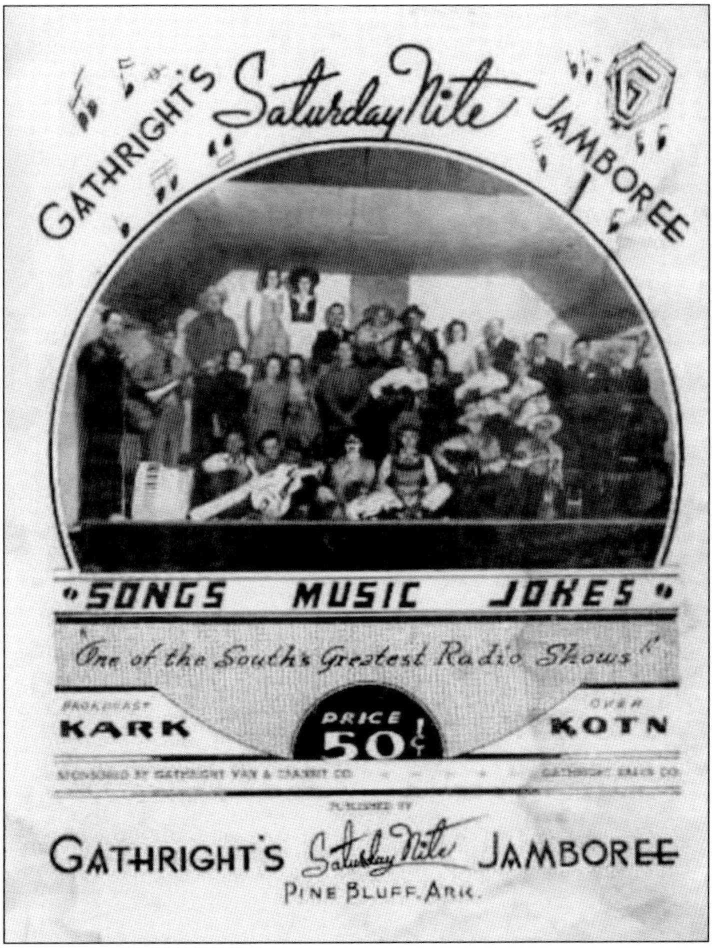

Gathright's Saturday Night Jamboree was Pine Bluff's equivalent of the *Grand Ole Opry*. It was a weekly KARK and KOTN radio broadcast of the best area country music artists. Starting around 1942, country music performers in Pine Bluff began holding jam sessions after hours at Gathright's Van & Storage Co. By 1943, the sessions were so popular and attracted so many fans (who watched from a barn loft) that radio stations began broadcasting live shows. Local talent included Fiddlin' Rufus, the Troubadors, Ruby Heird, the Original Tune Peddlers, Fanny Evans, and others. (Courtesy of Bill Shannon.)

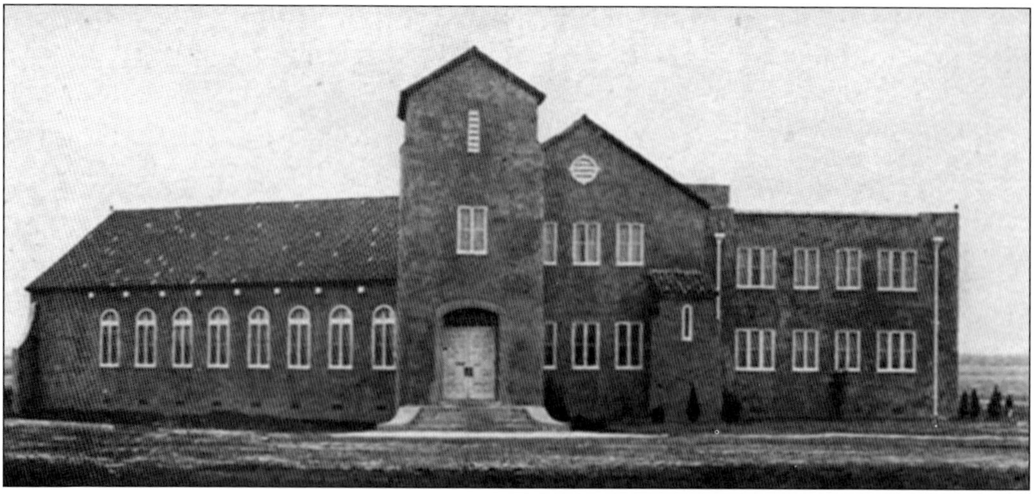

Built in 1929 as a terminal for Pine Bluff's first airfield, Toney Field Airport, this building was later sold to the Elks Lodge for use as a club in the early 1960s. The Elks Lodge hosted performers like B.B. King, Bobby "Blue" Bland, Little Milton, Albert King, and others. The club sold dinners upstairs, including fried chicken, chitlins, and pigs' feet, though patrons had to bring their own liquor. The building burned down, but it was replaced with a new structure in the same general area on US Highway 79 in the early 1970s. (Courtesy of Paul Perdue.)

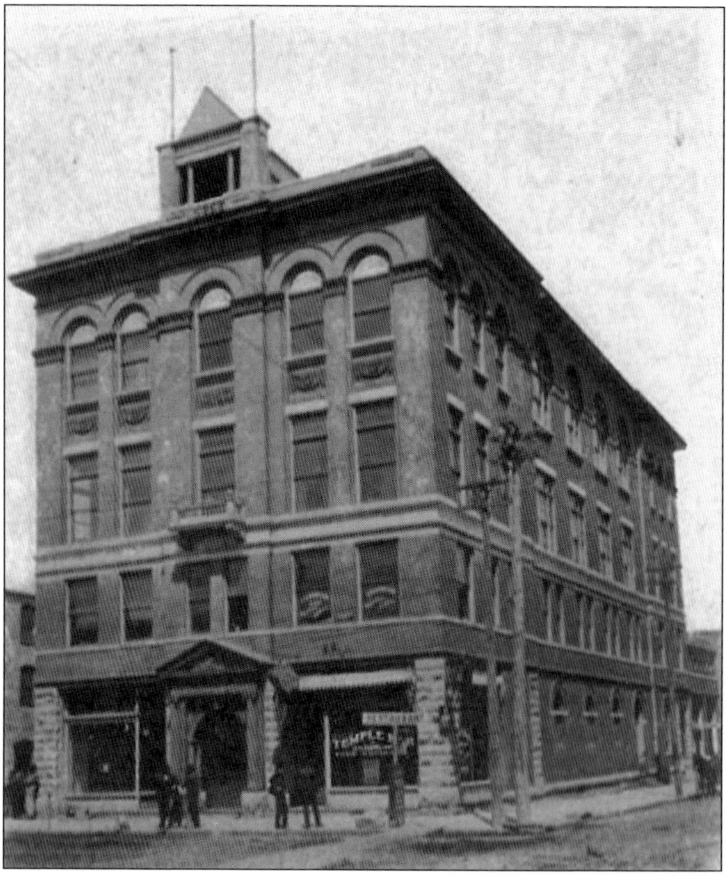

The Masonic Building, erected in 1903 by African Americans for meetings and office space, included a floor that was used for dances and concerts at least through the 1950s. Everyone in jazz and blues performed there (and in the neighboring Old Howard Building on Fourth Avenue and Main Street). Greats like Duke Ellington, Cab Calloway, Count Basie, Earl Himes, Earl Hooker, Sonny Boy Williamson I, John Lee Hooker, and many others came, according to locals. (Courtesy of Arkansas History Commission.)

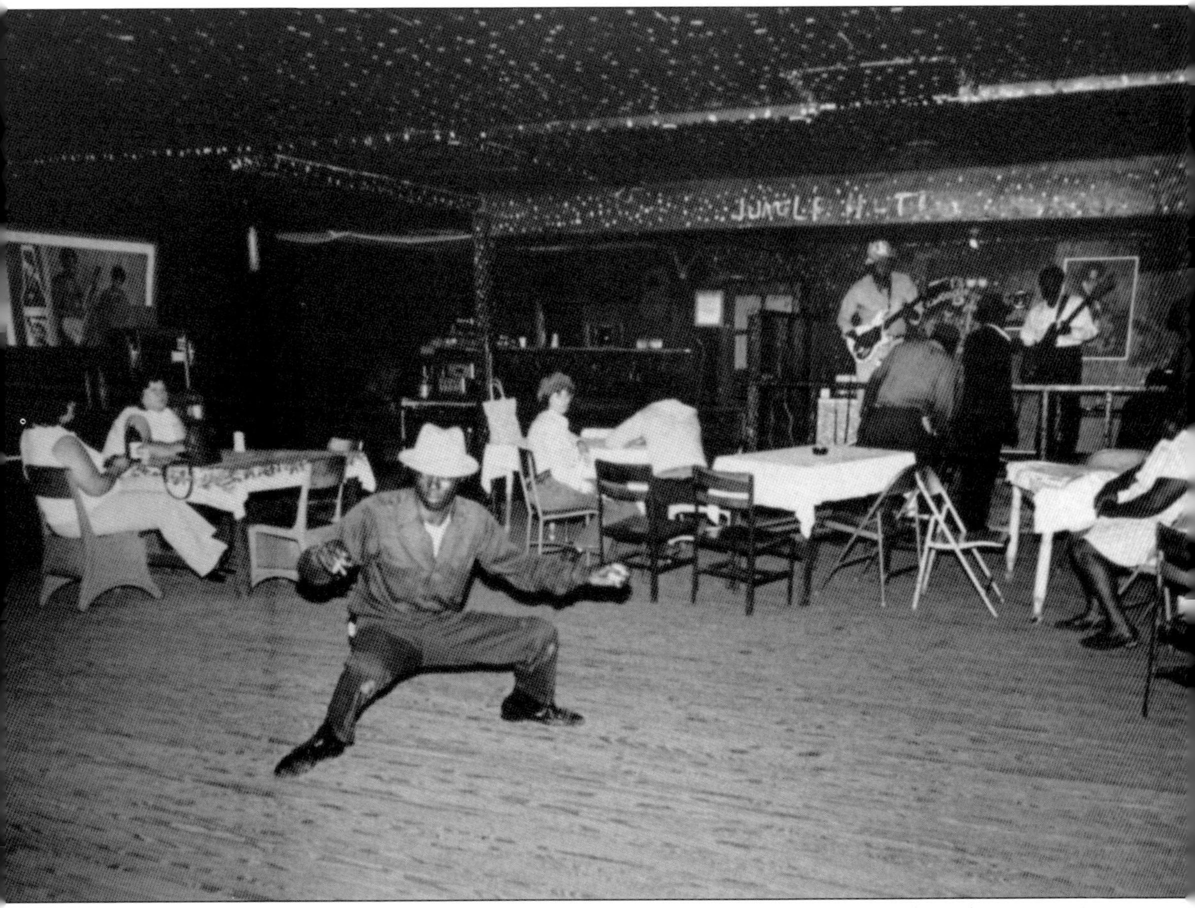

A patron finds his groove at Pine Bluff's Jungle Hut (previously the Jack Rabbit) in the 1970s. A virtual who's who of blues artists brought their best skills to demanding crowds in this legendary juke joint. Blues veteran James "Tail Dragger" Jones remembered sneaking in the club as a child to hear legends Sonny Boy Williamson II and Howlin' Wolf. Blues great Bobby Rush remembered when he and slide guitar legend Elmore James were playing the club in the 1950s and a jealous husband turned over a stove, almost burning down the facility. Local bluesman "Goosey" Willie Moore recorded live there in 1976 for the acclaimed Arkansas blues compilation album "Keep It to Your Self." Other blues artists who often played there included legends like Houston Stackhouse, Robert Nighthawk, James Peck Curtis, Cedell Davis, Johnny "Big Moose" Walker, David "Honeyboy" Edwards, and others. Boyd Gilmore, a 10-year-plus Pine Bluff resident and a cousin to Rock and Roll Hall of Fame member Elmore James also performed at the Jungle Hut frequently. Boyd often boasted that he taught James his legendary slide guitar style. Incidentally, *Blue Suede News* magazine reported that Elmore James moved to Pine Bluff for a period in the 1950s at Gilmore's invitation. (Courtesy of Arkansas History Commission.)

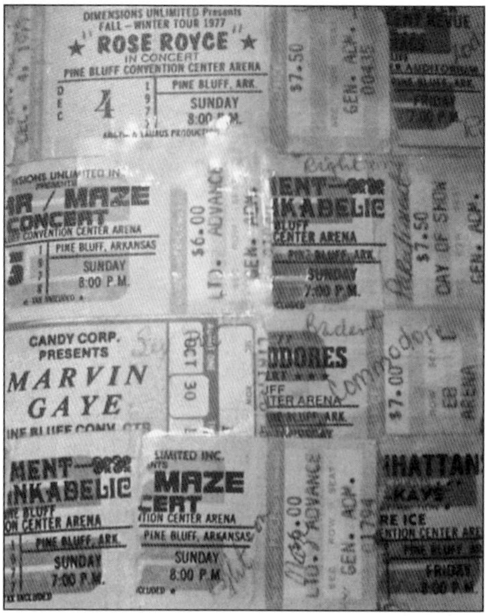

Mary Greenlee Jones-Woods's memory book displays tickets from 1970s and 1980s R&B concerts she attended at the Pine Bluff Convention Center. However, artists of all genres performed there, especially in its early years. Among visiting acts were Willie Nelson, Dionne Warwick, KISS, Waylon Jennings, Barbara Mandrell, Natalie Cole, Prince, AC/DC, Bob Hope, Teddy Pendergrass, the Emotions, REO Speedwagon, and a host of others. (Courtesy of Mary Greenlee Jones-Woods.)

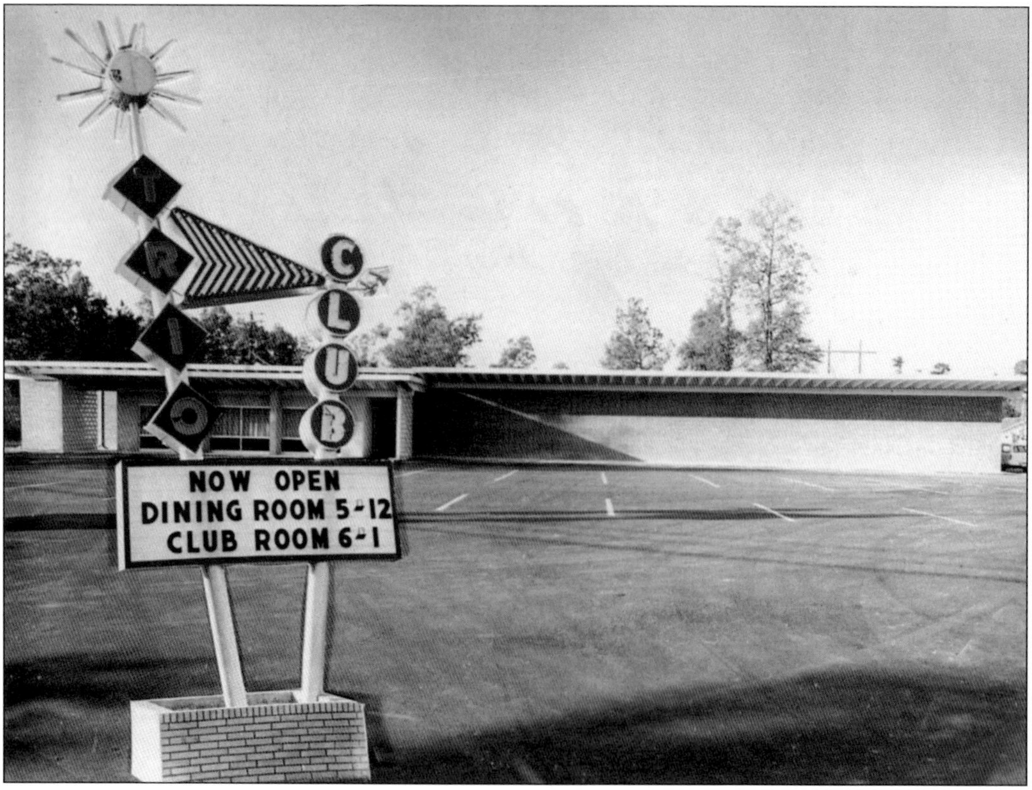

The Trio Club was owned by Floyd and Birdie Brown, the parents of Jim Ed, Maxine, and Bonnie—the country music group the Browns. The popular club served dinners and provided live entertainment in Pine Bluff in the 1950s. It was easily Pine Bluff's most modern club of the day, estimated to cost about $100,000 to construct. Many future stars performed there, including Elvis Presley (Bonnie Brown's former boyfriend), Conway Twitty, Ray Price, and Porter Wagoner. (Courtesy of Maxine Brown.)

Legend Elvis Presley (third from left) poses with members of the popular country music group the Browns (from left to right, Jim Ed, Maxine, and Bonnie) at Pine Bluff's Trio Club in 1956. This was one of numerous trips he made to visit the Browns in Pine Bluff, as he was close with the entire family and spent many weekends there in between performance stops. The Browns toured with Presley before he became a national sensation. In fact, they made the crucial recommendation to Horace Logan of the *Louisiana Hayride* to allow Elvis to perform on the national radio show before he was ever known. This was the first national exposure for him, effectively kicking off his live performance career, according to *Looking Back to See*. (Courtesy of Maxine Brown.)

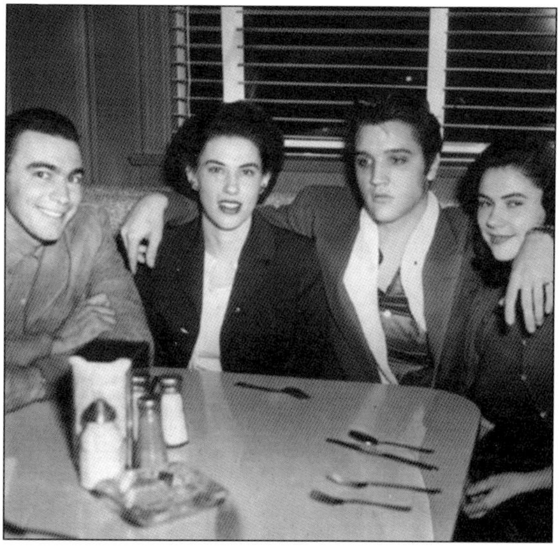

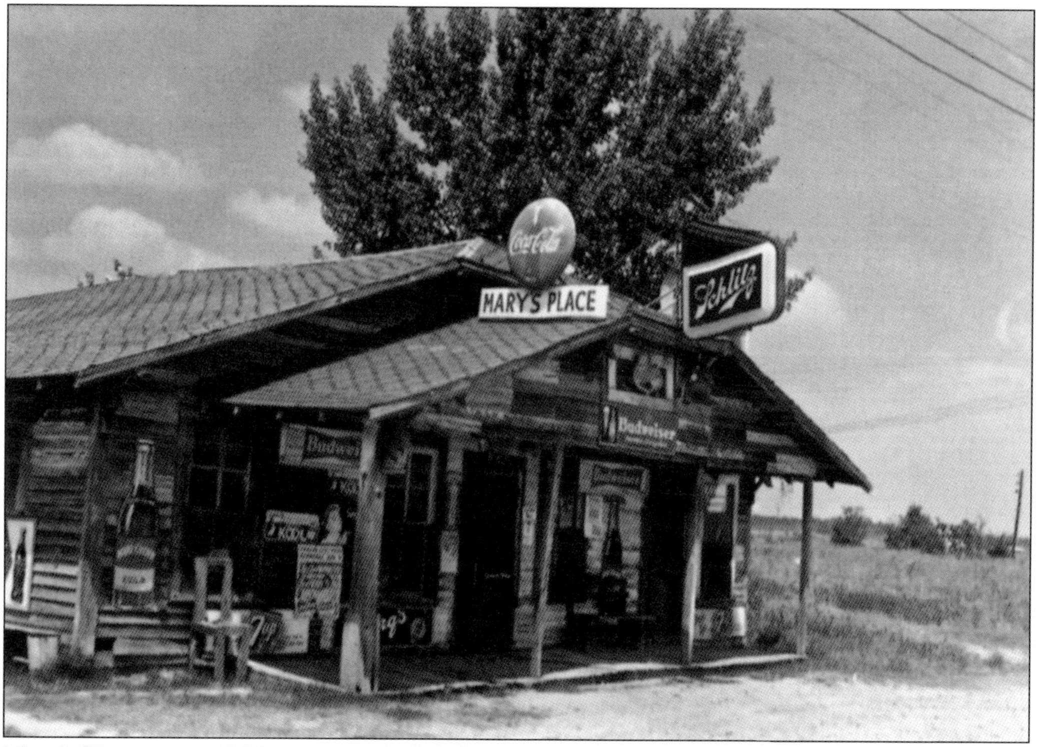

Mary's Place was a 1950s watering hole/juke joint in Humphrey. Other similar juke joint/clubs featuring blues and soul music in Jefferson County included Drums, Jitterbug's, Sturdiks, Nappy's, the Jungle Hut/Jack Rabbit, the Casino, the Gayla Room, the Yellow Front, Fat's Place, the Black Cat, Nita's Penthouse, Collegiate Plaza (now P.J.'s Club), the Georgia Street Ballroom, Rockin' Annie's, and the Swingland Grille, to name a few. While celebrated blues artists visited these places, local blues artists also flourished there like "Pine Bluff Pete," "Little Cooper," "Detroit" Johnnie, "Goosey" Willie Moore, Cedell Davis, Naomi Wimbley, Jackie Wimbley, Ernest Brooks, Marshall Darrough, Duke Bradley, J.C. Haynie, Johnny Turner, Leonard Smith, Trenton Cooper, and others. (Courtesy of Special Collections Department, University of Arkansas Libraries.)

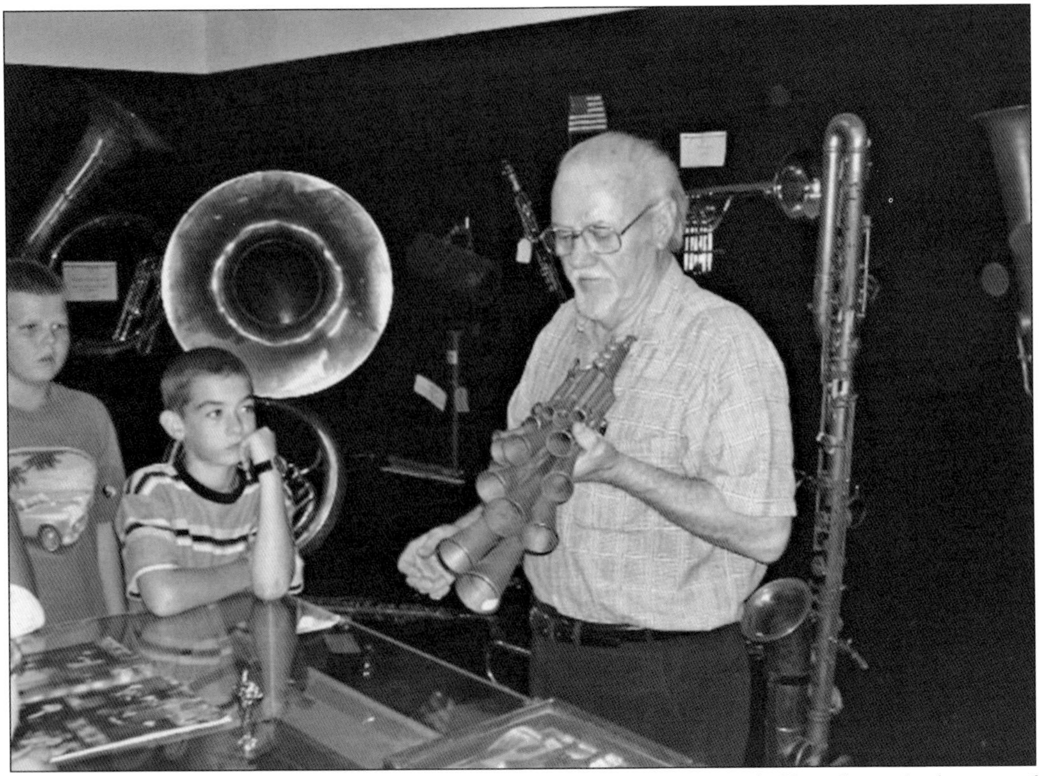

Jerry Horne, former curator and founder of the Band Museum in Pine Bluff, explains the history of a rare instrument. Horne's downtown museum was the 1990s home for the Pine Bluff Community Concert Band and also held public jam sessions. The Band Museum was the only institution in the United States dedicated to the history of band instruments and band music before it closed in 2010. It highlighted Horne's collection of over 1,500 antique instruments dating from the 1700s to the 1950s. (Courtesy of the Online Band Museum.)

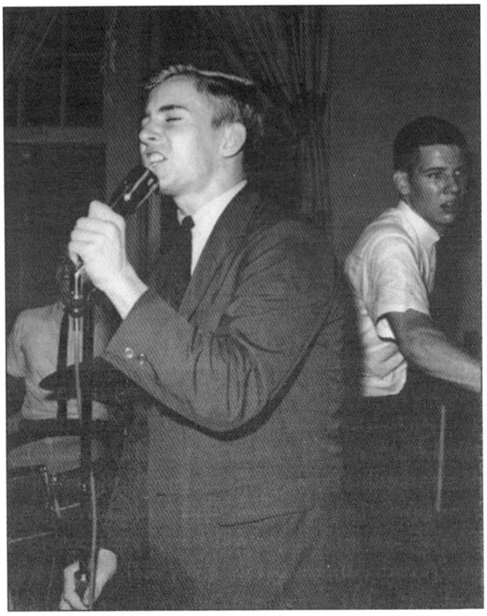

A member of the Playboys sings at Oakland Tavern in Pine Bluff in the early 1960s. Oakland Tavern hosted dances and other functions beginning in the 1930s. Teens enjoyed music and dancing there for as little as 40¢ admission in the 1960s. The Playboys, the Chaps, the Magnificent Seven, the Yardleys, and other local pop/rock garage bands, along with R&B groups like Motha's Funk, Brass Funk, the Zodiacs, Polo, and Willard Harris and the Czars of Rhythm were always draws at area venues. Interestingly, the Playboys claimed a world record for playing the longest continuous tune, "Shout," for 1 hour and 16 minutes. (Courtesy of Paul Perdue.)

Hazzard Gymnasium at Arkansas AM&N College (UAPB) often held concerts, like this 1960s performance by James Brown. The campus also hosted performers at the Hathaway/Howard Fine Arts building, including Duke Ellington in the 1960s. The popular funk group Cameo played at Pumphrey Stadium in the 1970s, and the HYPER Complex was the homecoming concert site for 1980s acts like Roger Troutman and the Zap Band, hip-hop's Run-DMC, and R&B's Mint Condition in the 1990s. (Courtesy of Special Collections Department, University of Arkansas Libraries.)

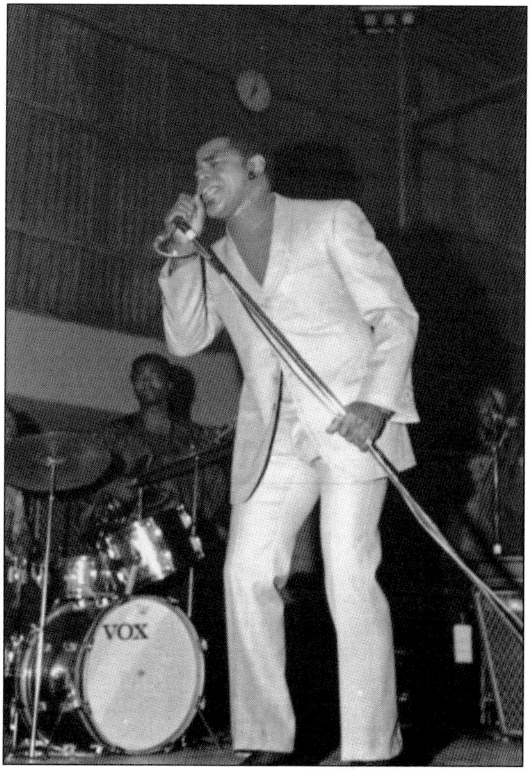

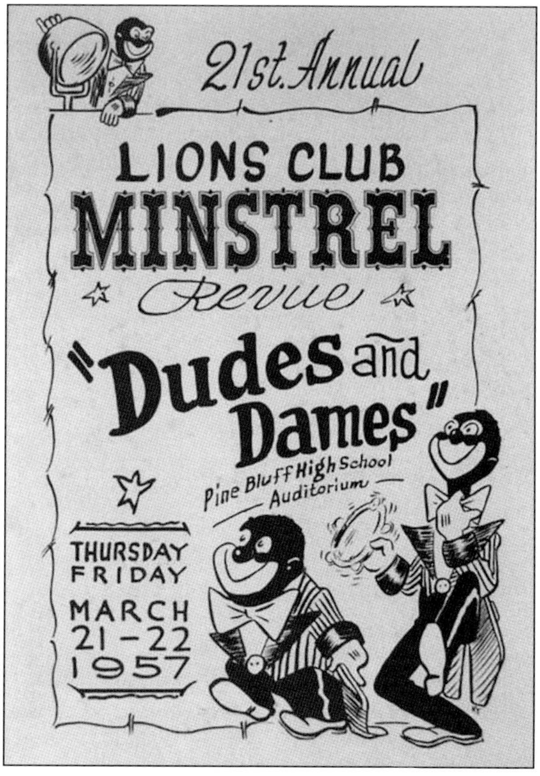

A 1957 flier for a minstrel revue at Pine Bluff High School uses racist imagery, standard for the era. Area high schools like Merrill, Watson Chapel, St. Peter Catholic, Pine Bluff High, Townsend Park, and Coleman often held concerts featuring local groups and major acts. (Courtesy of Jimmy Cunningham Jr.)

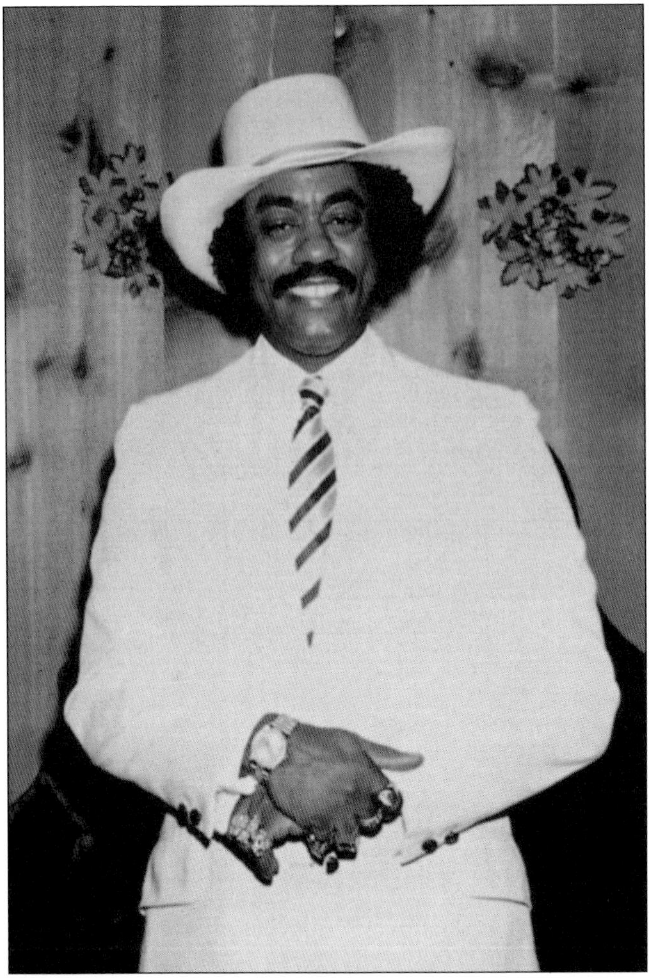

Soul/blues artist Johnny Taylor poses at Pine Bluff's PJ's Club after a 1980s concert. In addition to being one of Arkansas's most well-known dance clubs, it has also been a concert site for many music acts over the years. (Courtesy of Special Collections Department, University of Arkansas Libraries.)

Local country clubs, exclusive in both race and class, provided Pine Bluff's white elite families with a venue for social events, like this 1948 dance at Eden Park Country Club. (Courtesy of Paul Perdue.)

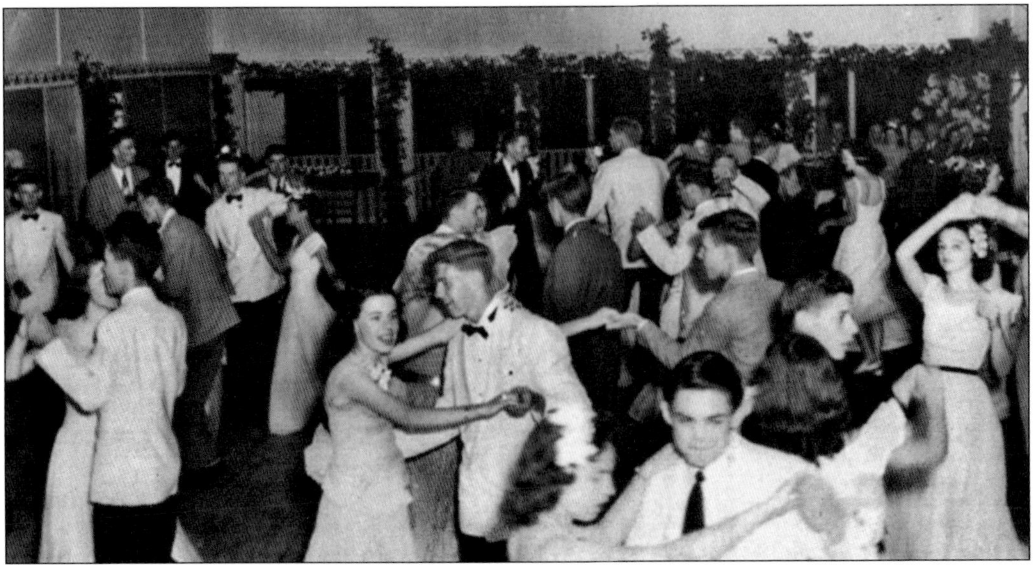

R&B great Fats Domino plays in the 1960s at the Gayla Room, a club on Third Avenue and State Street in Pine Bluff. Unlike some Delta cities closer to the Mississippi River that had full-fledged entertainment districts, Pine Bluff had a different dynamic. Its clubs and juke joints offering live music were dispersed throughout the city, with a cluster in the Third Avenue and State Street area, others on Dollarway Road, some on University Avenue (Cedar Street), and the remainder scattered around the city. (Courtesy of Special Collections Department, University of Arkansas.)

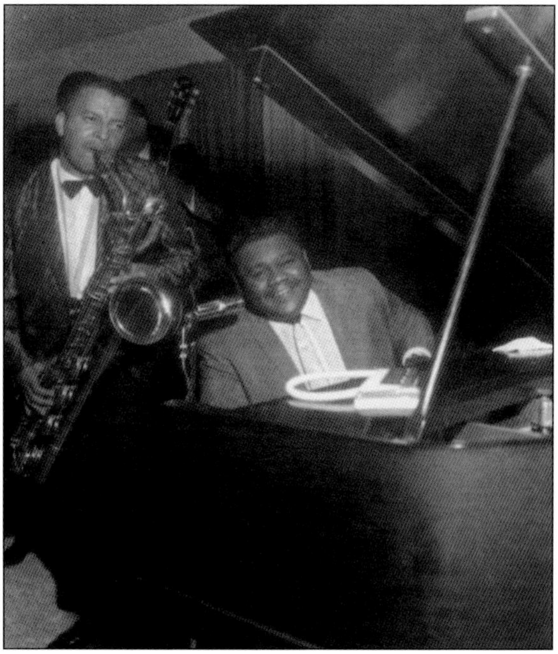

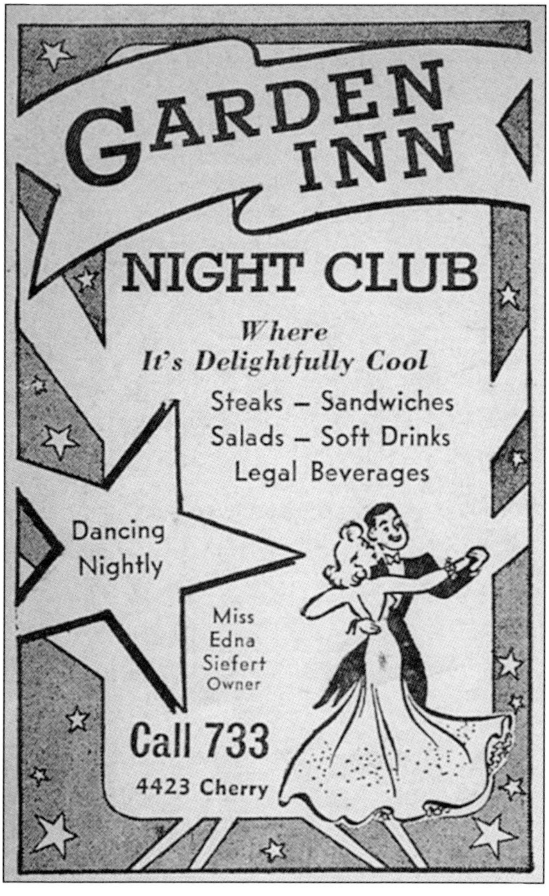

The Garden Inn was a Pine Bluff entertainment spot for live music in the 1940s. It became popular among GIs returning from World War II. The club brought small local bands playing a variety of music. Other comparable clubs/honky-tonks included the Dew Drop Inn, the American Legion Club, the Casino, the Canteena Club, the Diamond Club, the Plantation Club, Sam's Place, and others. (Courtesy of Paul Perdue.)

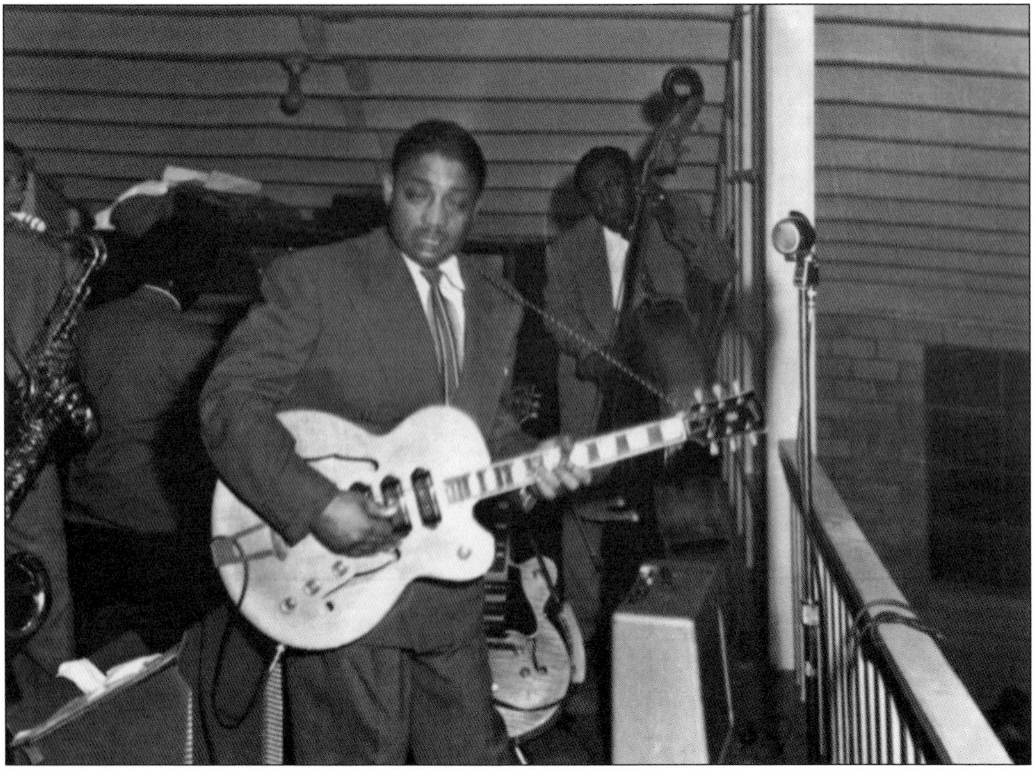

Popular blues guitarist and songwriter Lowell Fulson plays at the Townsend Park "Big Rec" Center in the 1950s. A multipurpose facility, the Big Rec was home to many concerts and dances in Pine Bluff. Stars like Ike and Tina Turner, Bobby Rush, Big Joe Turner, Little Milton, Johnny Taylor, and Tyrone Davis performed there. Rush first heard blues legend Howlin' Wolf and rock 'n' roll legend Little Richard there in the mid-1950s. (Courtesy of Special Collections Department, University of Arkansas Libraries.)

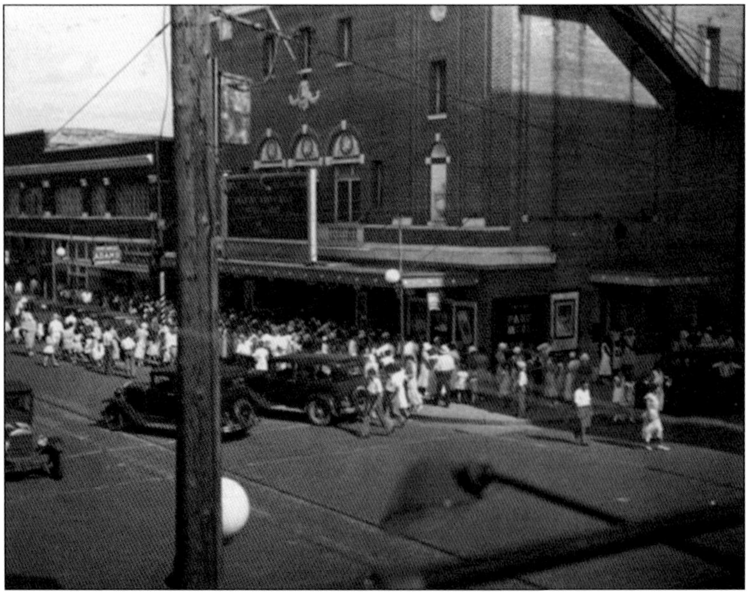

The Saenger Theater, called "The Showplace of the South," opened in 1924. It cost $200,000 when built and seated 1,500 people. The theater showcased people like Harry Houdini, Roy Rogers, producer D.W. Griffith, and practically every touring Broadway show of the era. At far right, black patrons enter through a side door to access the balcony in the era of Jim Crow segregation laws. (Benny Goodwin.)

A popular feature at Pine Bluff's Saengar Theater was its "Coke Shows," in which children could gain admission to select movies or shows on Saturdays if they brought an empty pop bottle. This promotion lasted through the 1970s. (Courtesy of Paul Perdue.)

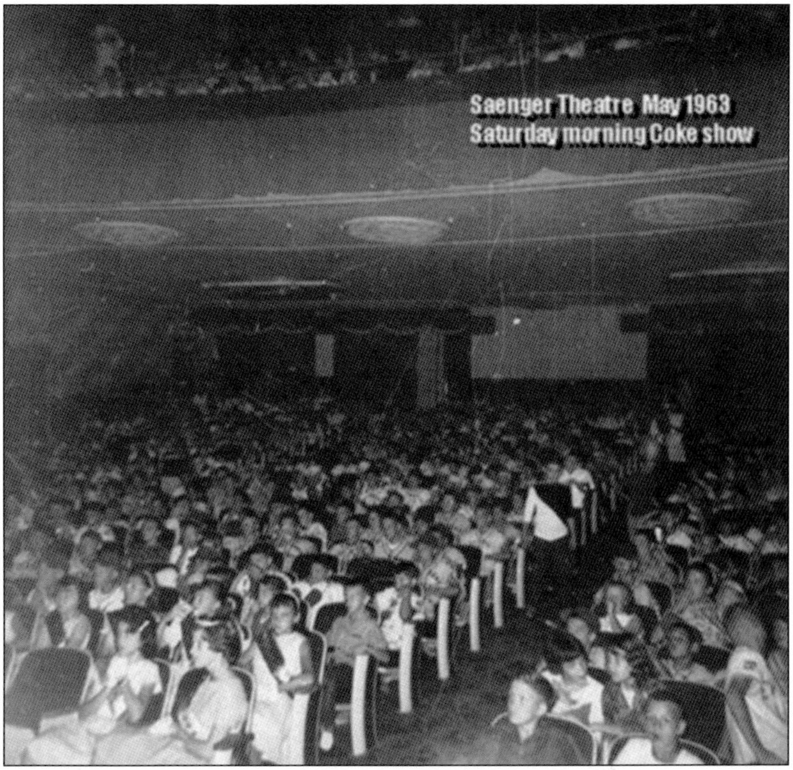

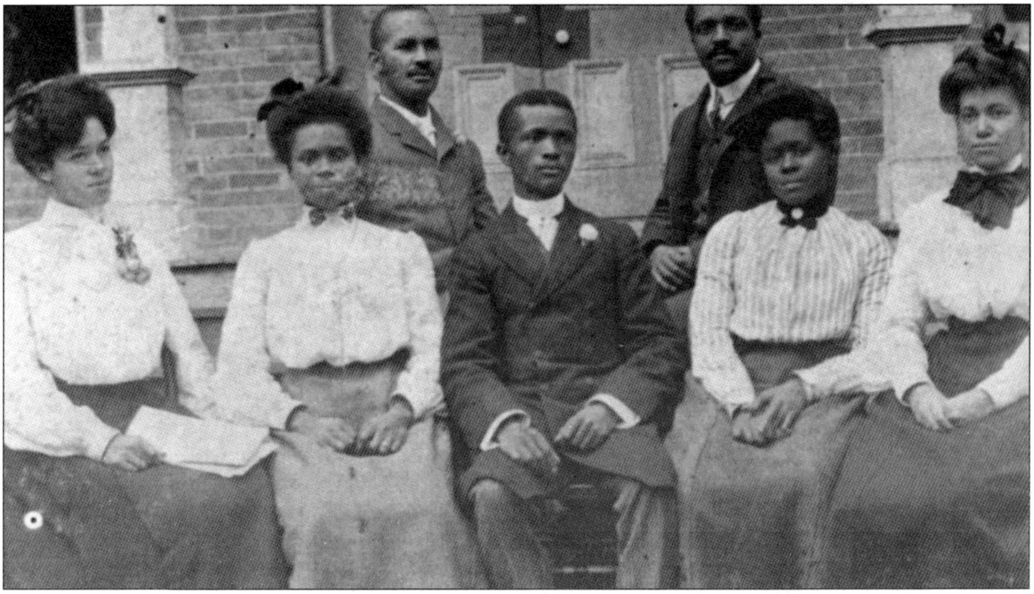

Isaac Fisher (seated, center), president of Branch Normal College (UAPB), was also the 1908 co-owner of a tent venue in Pine Bluff that featured "moving pictures." *Exhibition, The Film Reader* notes that local whites were quite unhappy with this pleasure blacks had afforded themselves. This tent venue may have been an early partnership with Dr. John Parker Sr., another local black professional who was listed in 1915 as a co-owner of the "Moving Picture Theater." (Courtesy of Arkansas History Commission.)

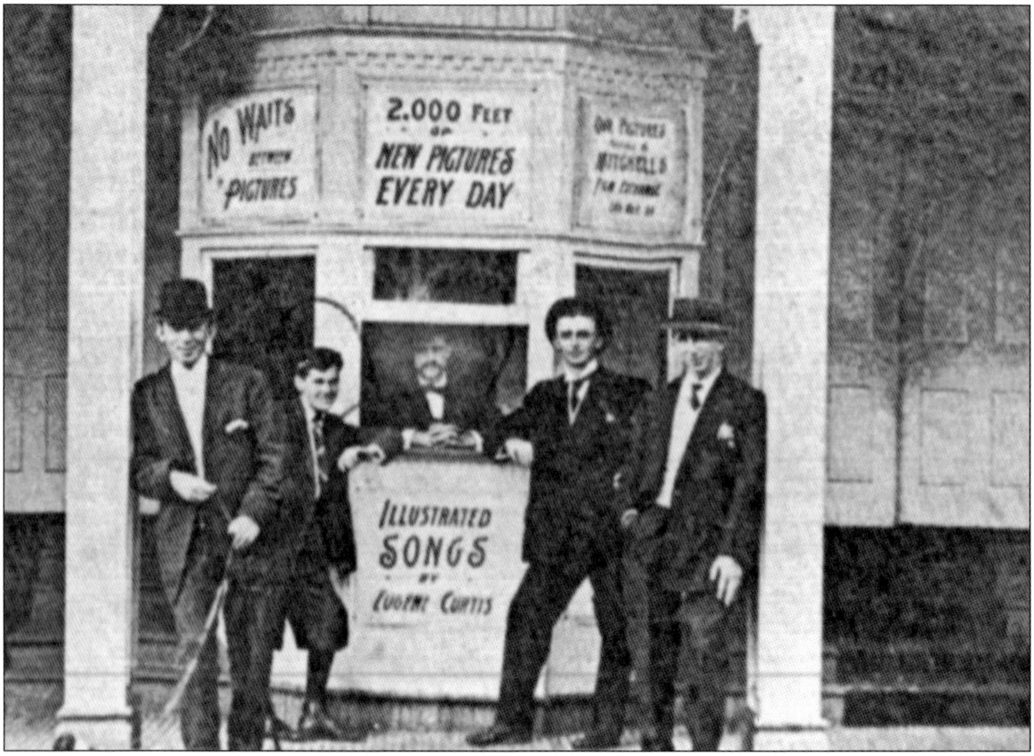

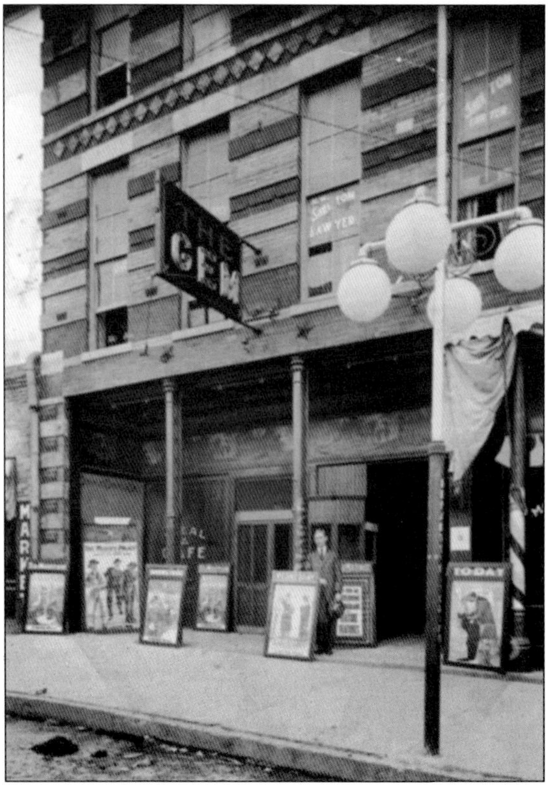

When the Theatorium opened in February 1907, it was the first dedicated movie theater in Pine Bluff and the Delta Lowlands (though the Elks Theater was the first to show a movie in Pine Bluff in January of that year). It was first housed on the corner of Sixth Avenue and Main Street, on the top floor of the Central Pharmacy building. The theater later moved to Second Avenue. (Courtesy of James Leslie Collection.)

The Gem Theater in Pine Bluff, owned by Otto C. Hauber, opened in 1914. It became the Miller Theater in 1917 and, later, the Strand Theater. It had a seating capacity of 500. Like most other theaters in Pine Bluff, the Gem was located on Second Street, the area's early theater district. (Courtesy of Rotary Club of West Pine Bluff.)

Owner O.C. Hauber stands in front of his A-Muse-U Theater around 1915 in Pine Buff. Hauber also later opened the Hauber Theater, which was a movie and vaudeville show venue. (Courtesy of Rotary Club of West Pine Bluff.)

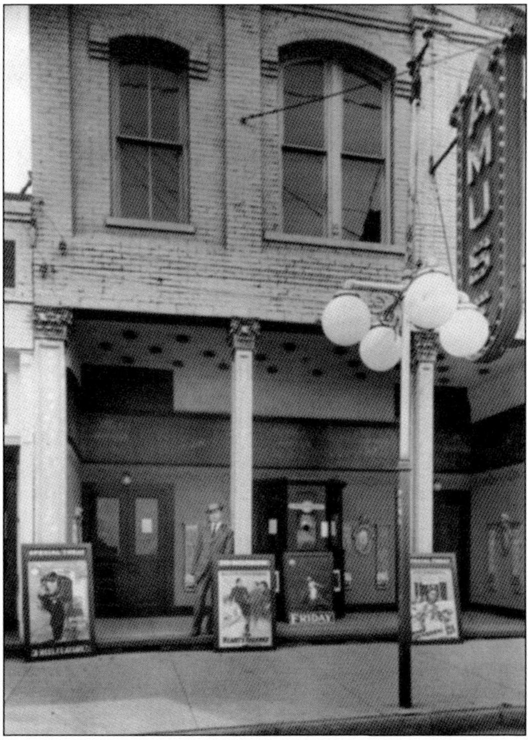

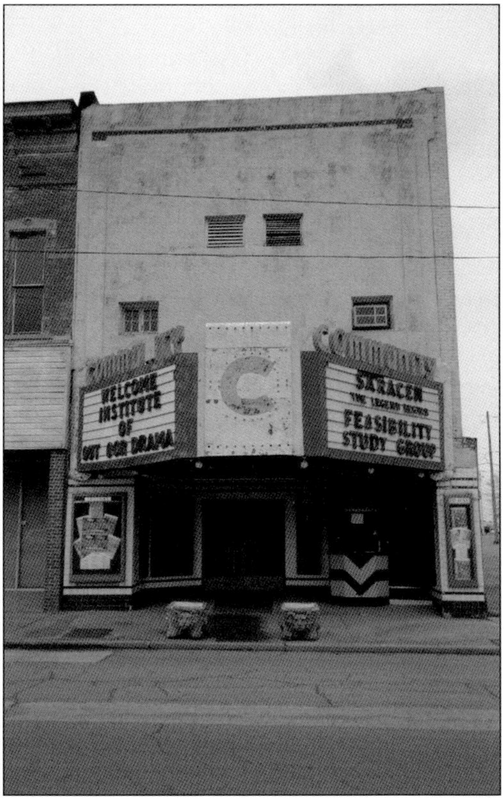

The Community Theater is one of Arkansas's oldest one-screen theaters in existence. It is housed in a Pine Bluff building that was constructed in 1889 and served as the home of the S.H. Kress five-and-dime store until 1918. The building was converted into a theater in 1922 and, by 1942, had become the Community Theater. It closed in 1963, but Old Towne Theater Centre, a local nonprofit, led restoration efforts that brought it back to full operation by 2013. (Courtesy of Paul Sableman.)

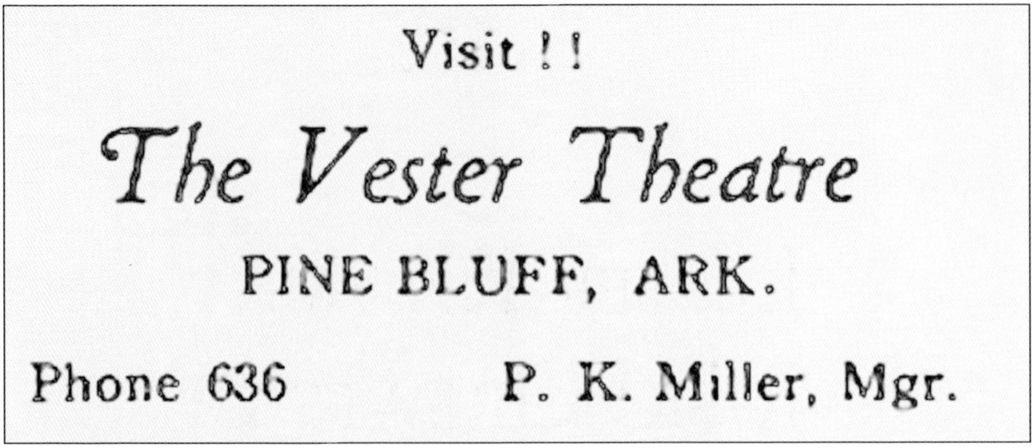

An advertisement for Pine Bluff's Vester Theatre beckons 1940s moviegoers. The downtown theater, owned by African American funeral home director P.K. Miller, provided movies and entertainment for blacks during segregation. (Courtesy of Allen Leslie.)

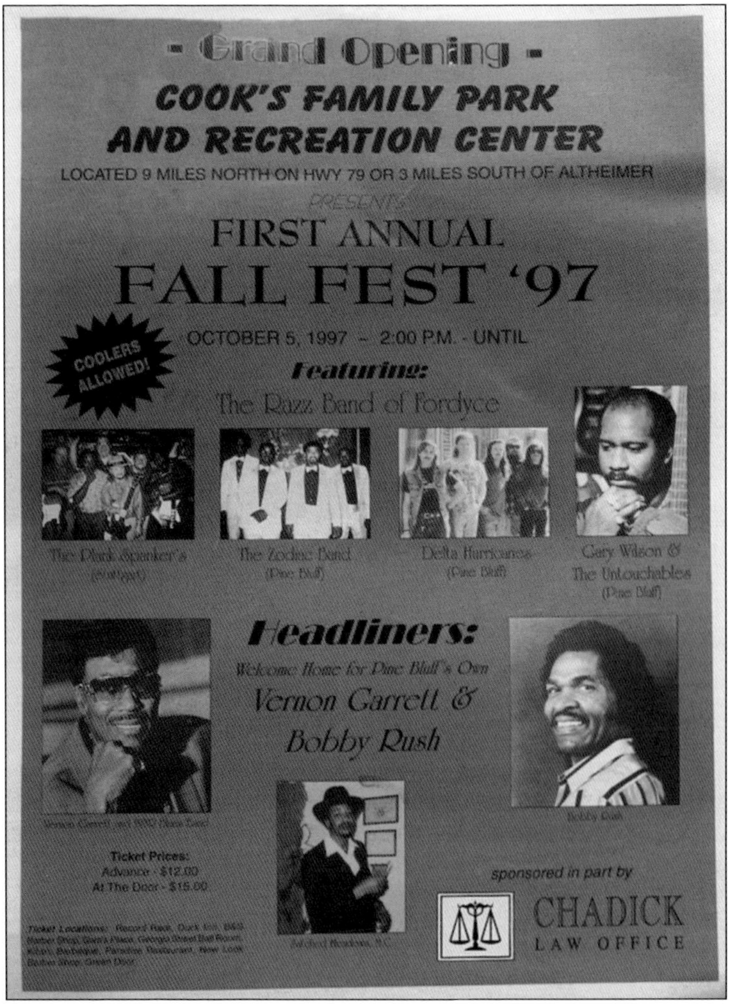

A poster advertises a 1997 fall music festival, which later evolved into the Pine Bluff/Altheimer Blues Festival, held annually at Cook's Family Park. The park is named after the tireless Sam Cook, a local concert promoter who brought every conceivable blues and Southern soul act to appreciative Jefferson County audiences from the 1970s to the 1990s. Cook worked in the tradition of past promoters from the area, like T.L Bradley, Jerry Townsend, Bert Maiden, Bob Hall, Eddie Johnson, and Al White. (Courtesy of Jimmy Cunningham Jr.)

Six

Lesser-Known Music Greats of the Delta Lowlands

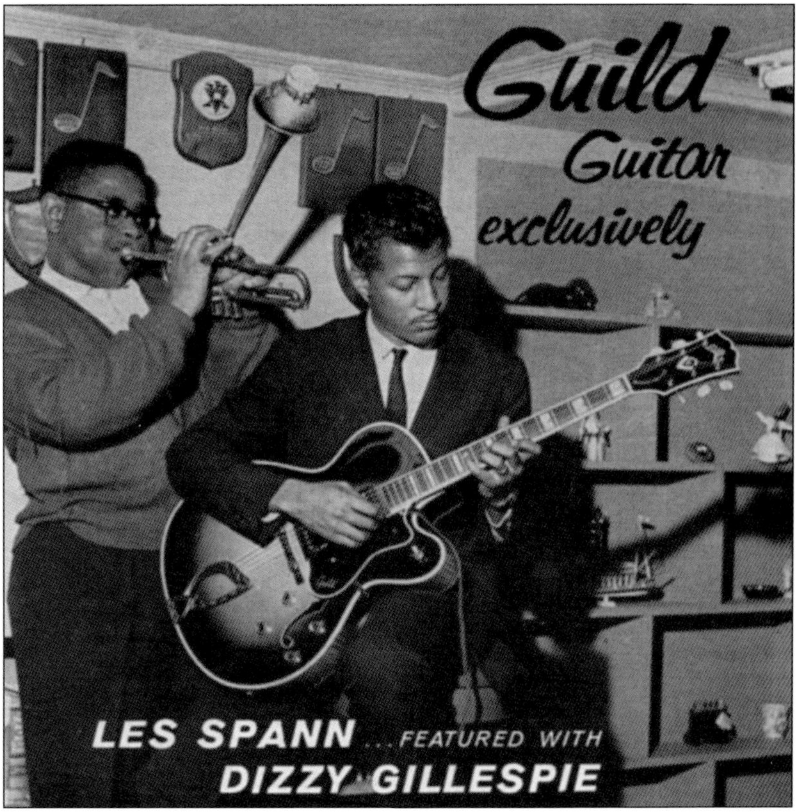

Les Spann (right), shown here with Dizzy Gillespie, was a self-taught guitarist and flutist from Pine Bluff who played with jazz legends like Quincy Jones, Duke Ellington, Ella Fitzgerald, and Natt Adderly, according to the *Virgin Encyclopedia of Jazz*. While he only recorded one album of his own, he appears on over 100 jazz albums. Sadly, Spann died while living on the streets of New York after a series of personal struggles in the 1980s. (Courtesy of Guild Guitar.)

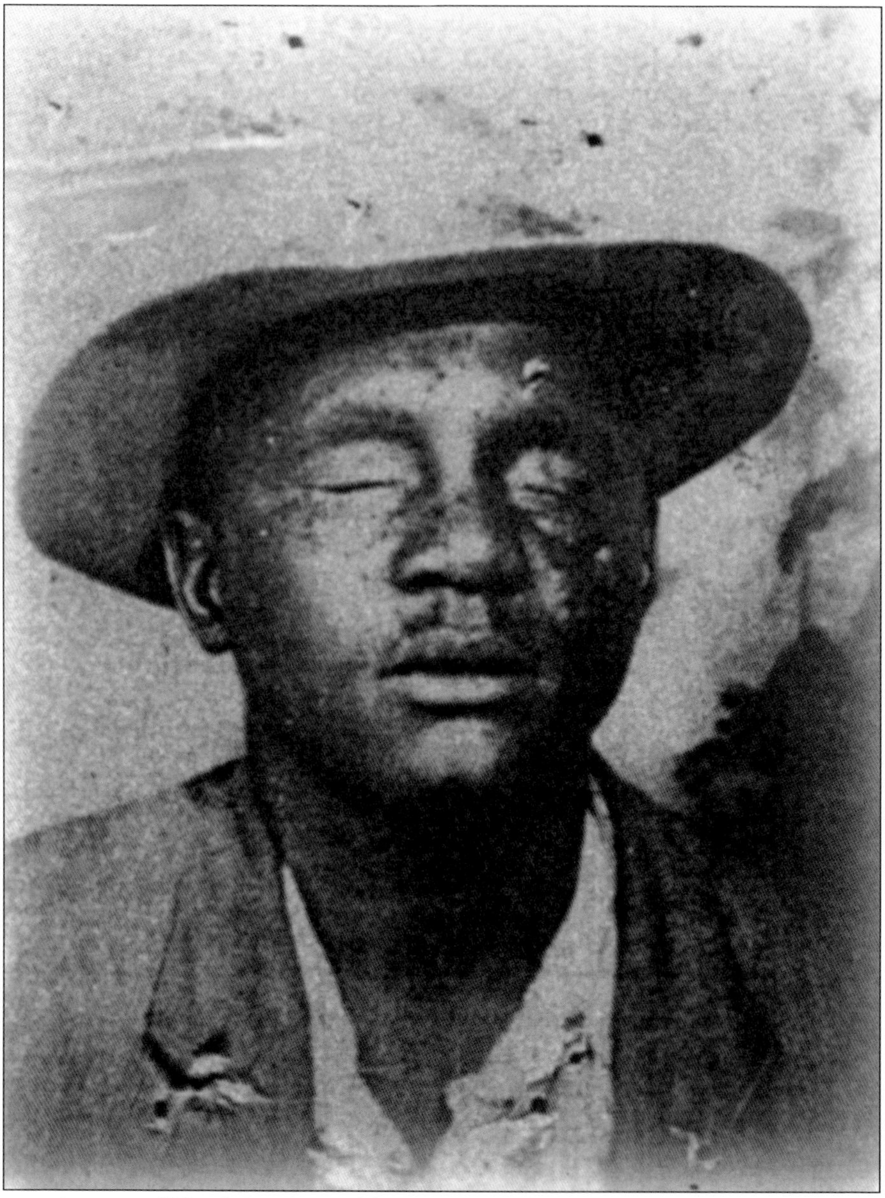

Blues singer/guitarist "Blind" Joe Reynolds was reportedly born in Talullah, Louisiana, though his death certificate lists an Arkansas birth. A fight in his 20s left him blinded after a shotgun blast to the face. Throughout his life, he often found himself in trouble with legal authorities and remained in constant flight. In the 1930s, he "resided" in the Delta Lowlands, at Cummins Prison, serving time for reasons unknown. Reynolds played juke joints and street corners in Pine Bluff; Greenville, Mississippi; Shreveport, Louisiana; and other area cities, always keeping an alias, according to *Chasing that Devil Music: Searching for the Blues*. He recorded singles in the 1920s and 1930s, some of which were covered by guitar legend Eric Clapton in the 1960s. Clapton's covers of his songs helped introduce the world to Reynolds's music. However, record company officials could not contact Reynolds for royalties, because his use of aliases made him impossible to track. He died in the late 1960s, before he ever knew his work had reached a national audience. (Courtesy of Jimmy Cunningham Jr.)

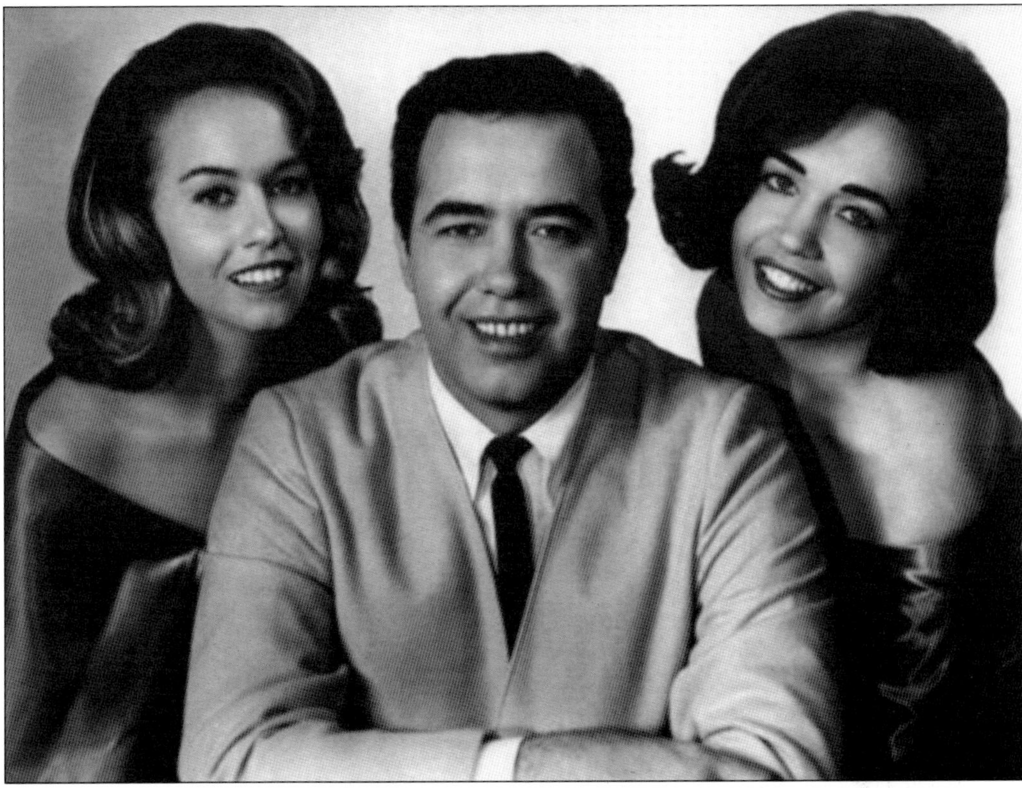

The Harden Trio, from England, Arkansas, was a 1960s country music group comprised of siblings Arlene (left), Bobby (center), and Robbie. Launching their career, they played a circuit of country music radio programs like Little Rock's *Barnyard Frolics*, Springfield, Missouri's *Ozark Jubilee*, and Nashville's *Grand Ole Opry*. They found success when their song "Tippy Toeing" peaked at number two on the country music charts in 1966. Several other songs charted from 1966 to 1968. (Courtesy of *Billboard* magazine.)

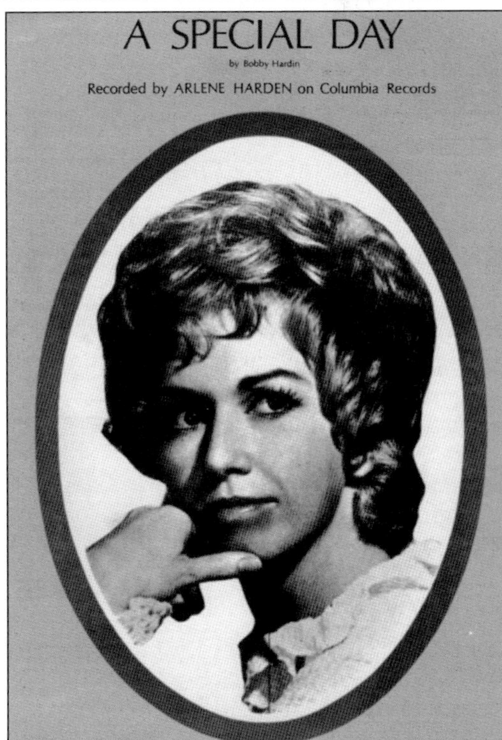

Arlene Harden of England continued with a solo career after the Harden Trio broke up. She recorded largely as a solo act from 1967 to 1978 with her success yielding 18 singles on the country music charts. One of her best known chart-topping songs, "True Love Is Greater than Friendship," was specifically written for her by legendary singer/musician Carl Perkins and was used on the 1970 movie sound track (though covered by Johnny Cash) for Robert Redford's *Little Fauss and Big Halsy*. (Courtesy of Two Rivers Music.)

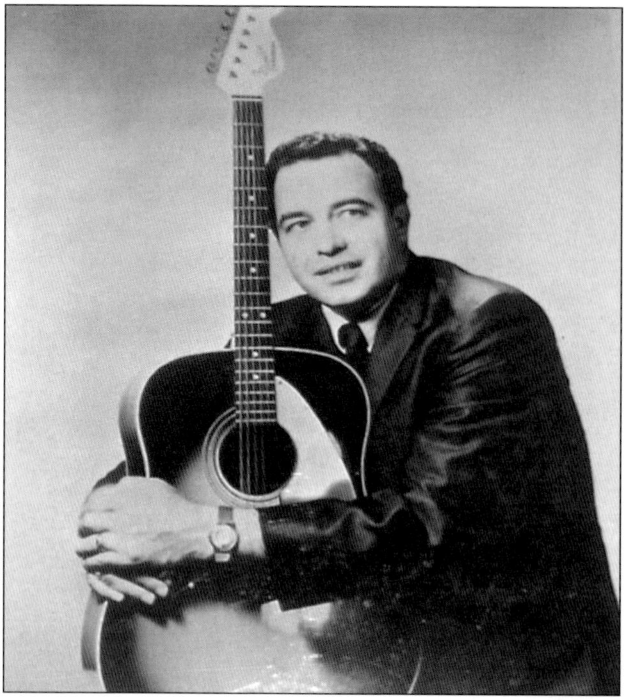

England's Bobby Harden pursued a career in singing after the break-up of the Harden Trio, though he found more success as a songwriter. From the 1970s until his death in 2006, Harden penned top-10 songs for Loretta Lynn ("Home"), Reba McEntire ("Today All Over Again"), and Mark Chestnutt ("Too Cold at Home" and "Old Country"), along with other songs for Kenny Rogers, Conway Twitty, George Jones, Gene Watson, and a host of country artists. (Courtesy of Royal Press.)

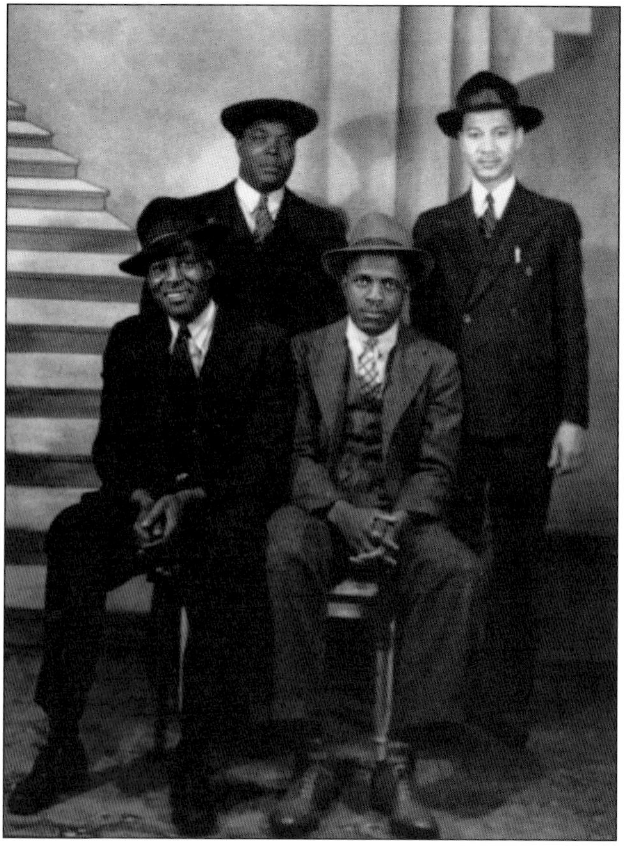

Joshua Altheimer (standing, right) of Altheimer, Arkansas, described as "the greatest blues pianist on records" in the *1956 Guide to Jazz*, was Big Bill Broonzy's primary pianist. He also played for greats like Sonny Boy Williamson I, "Washboard Sam," Jazz Gillum, and Lonnie Johnson. Altheimer appears in over 70 blues compilation albums. He died in his prime at age 30 in 1940 after a bout with pneumonia. This is the only known picture of him. (Courtesy of Michael Ochs Archives/Getty Images.)

Sherrill-born Leonard "Wine" Gill was one of the most sought-after blues bass players on the West Coast from the 1970s to the 1990s. Gill played for and/or recorded with many blues and R&B legends, including B.B. King, Johnny Taylor, Little Milton, John Lee Hooker, and Otis Rush. Gill accompanied Luther Allison on his 1997 Grammy-nominated blues album *Reckless*. Gill's work is noted in *60 Years of Recorded Jazz, 1917–1977*. (Courtesy of Jim O'Neal.)

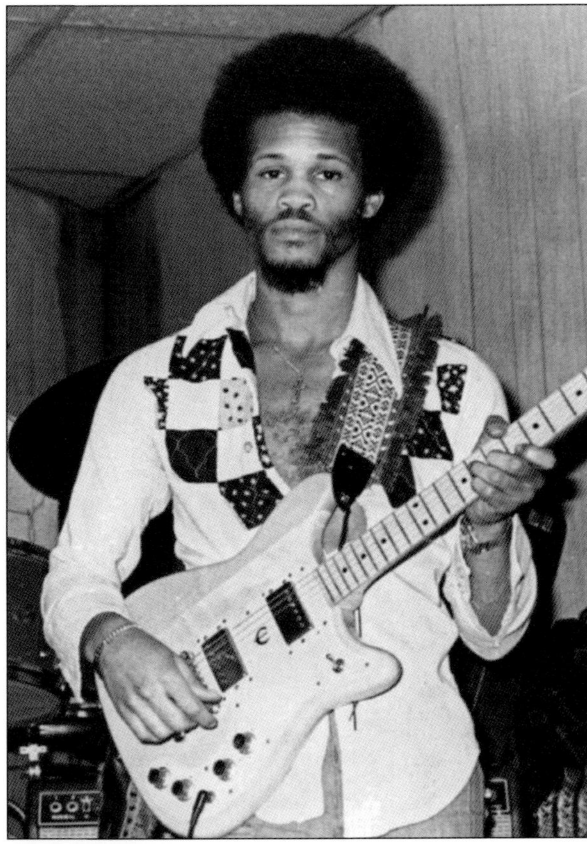

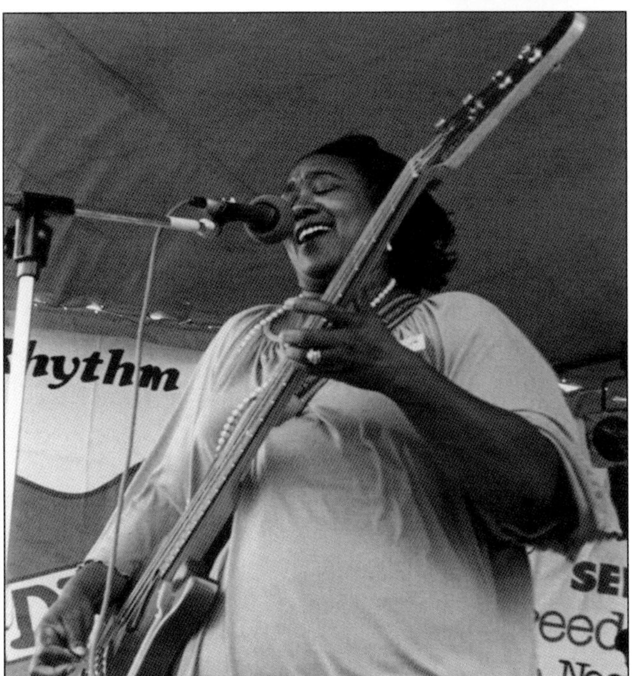

"Queen" Sylvia Embry, born in Wabbaseka, grew up around her blues-loving grandmother, who wanted her to play only gospel on the piano as a child. Young Embry, however, loved boogie-woogie. Embry later became leader of her own Chicago-based blues band and a bass player. *The Encyclopedia of Blues* described her work as "powerful" and said she was "one of the most interesting blues women in the post–World War II era." She played often with bluesmen like her husband, Johnny Embry, and veteran Lefty Dizz. She later recorded her own albums for Alligator Records. Embry appeared in two blues documentaries: *Big City Blues* (1986) and *Hubert Sumlin: Livin the Blues* (1988). (Courtesy of Blues Collection, University of Mississippi.)

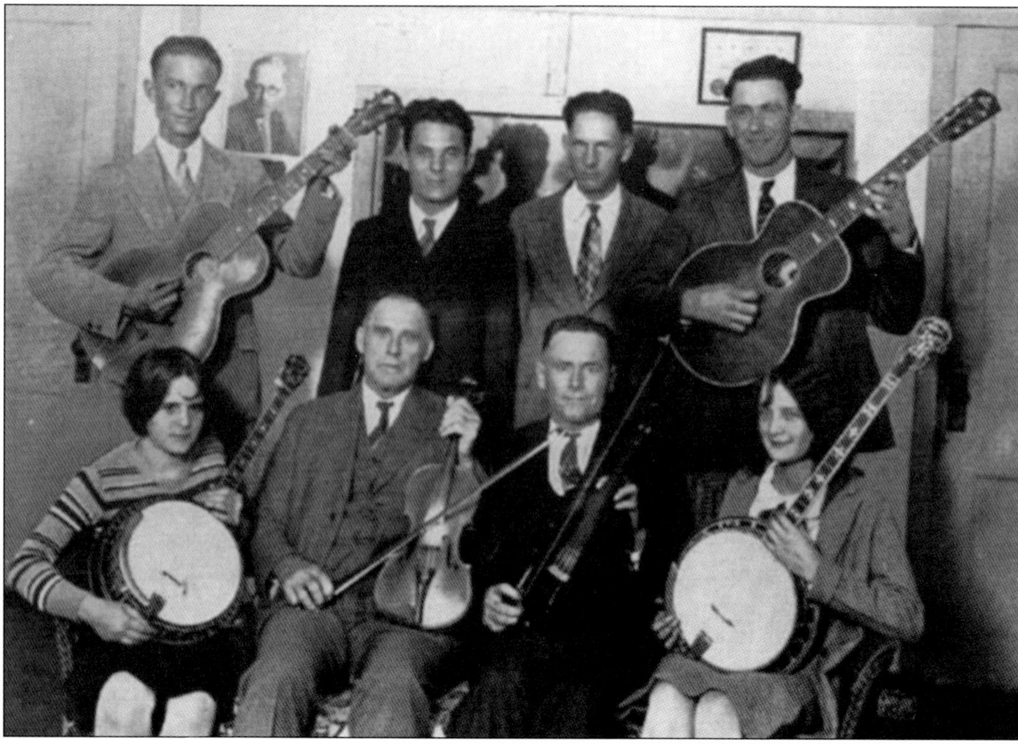

"Fiddlin'" Bob Larkin (seated, second from left) was an early-1920s pioneer fiddler in country music. Born in New York, he moved to Lonoke County as a young man. He recorded as a bluegrass bandleader but was more popular on live radio. He was famous for his 1930s group the Music Makers, who regularly played for a live national radio audience, as detailed in *Country Music Originals: The Legends and the Lost*. He was voted the champion fiddler in Arkansas in 1927 and 1928. (Courtesy of the Larkin family.)

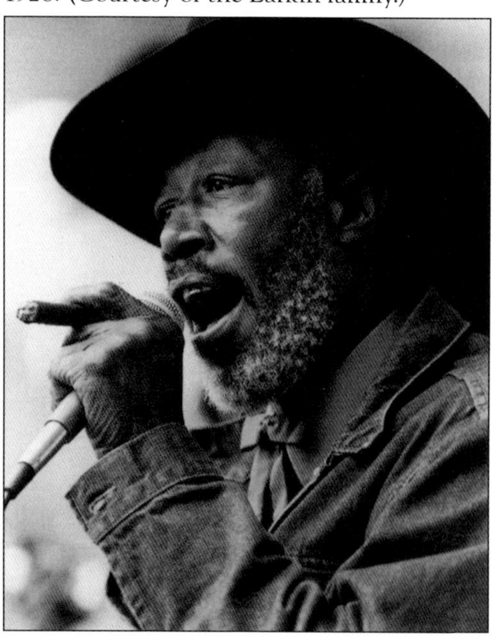

James "Tail Dragger" Jones, nicknamed by legendary blues singer Howlin' Wolf, continues to entertain crowds. Born in Altheimer, he moved to Pine Bluff, where he first heard his idol, Howlin' Wolf, perform in the 1950s. After following Wolf from juke joints to house parties, Jones developed his own vocal style. He has performed worldwide, has been on the ballot for a Grammy nomination, and has recorded several albums. He has also appeared in three movies (see page 126). *Today's Chicago Blues* cites his work. (Courtesy of James Fraher.)

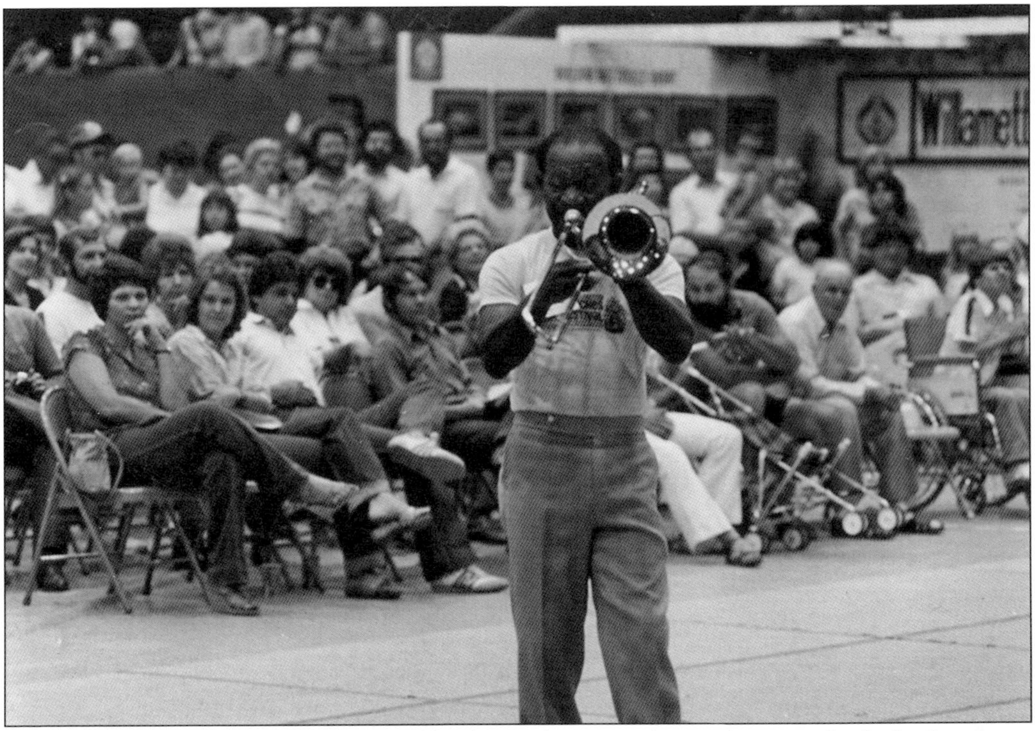

Leon "Pee Wee" Whittaker, a blues/jazz/rock trombonist and an inductee in both the Louisiana Hall of Master Folk Artists and the Delta Music Museum, was a Newellton, Louisiana, native who moved as a youth to Lake Village, Arkansas. He played with childhood friend and blues legend Louis Jordan in the Rabbit Foot Minstrels Show. Whittaker later formed his own band, touring internationally and recording. His work is referenced in *Ragged but Right: Black Travelling Shows, Coon Songs, and the Dark Pathway to Blues and Jazz.* (Courtesy of Don Sepulvado.)

Isaac Scott was one of the West Coast's most prominent blues guitarists in the 1970s and 1980s. Born in Pine Bluff, he moved as a youth to Seattle, Washington. Scott toured briefly with the Five Blind Boys of Mississippi, then turned to blues. His riveting performances and acclaimed albums earned him induction into the Washington Blues Society Hall of Fame. Israbox.com called him the "King of Seattle Blues." He is noted in *Blues: A Regional Experience.* (Courtesy of Jim O'Neal.)

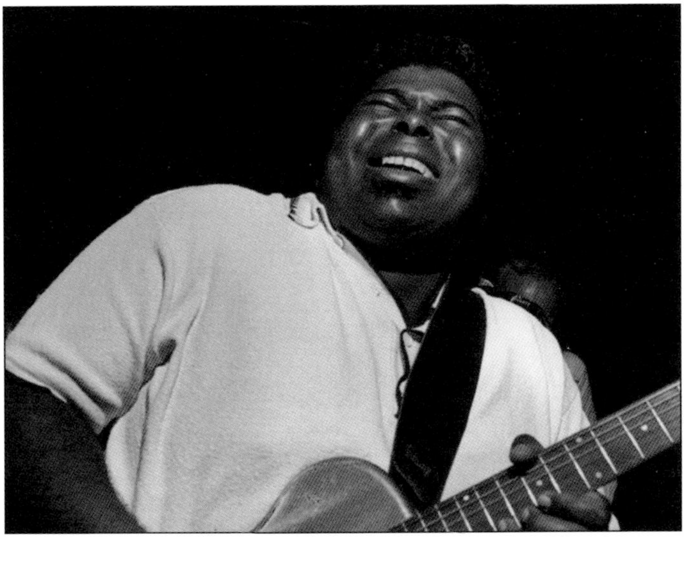

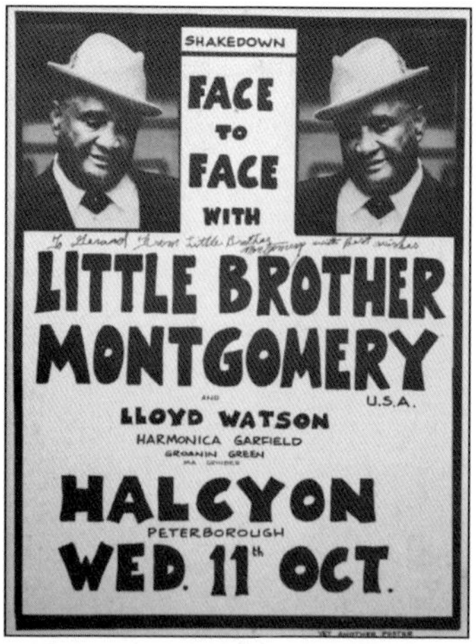

Blues Hall of Fame member Eurreal "Little Brother" Montgomery, extolled in a 1940 *Downbeat* magazine article as "the greatest pianist that ever invaded Dixie," was born in Kentwood, Louisiana, in 1906. He left home, wandering through Mississippi and settling in the Eudora, Arkansas, area for a period. Accounts in *The Blues Line: Blues Lyrics from Lead Belly to Muddy Waters* tell of his formative years in Arkansas, playing with piano greats like "Burnt Face Jake" Fakey, George "Son" Young, Walter Lewis, Joe Martin, and "Skinny Head Pete" in Eudora, Lake Village, and Arkansas City. (Courtesy of Jimmy Cunningham Jr.)

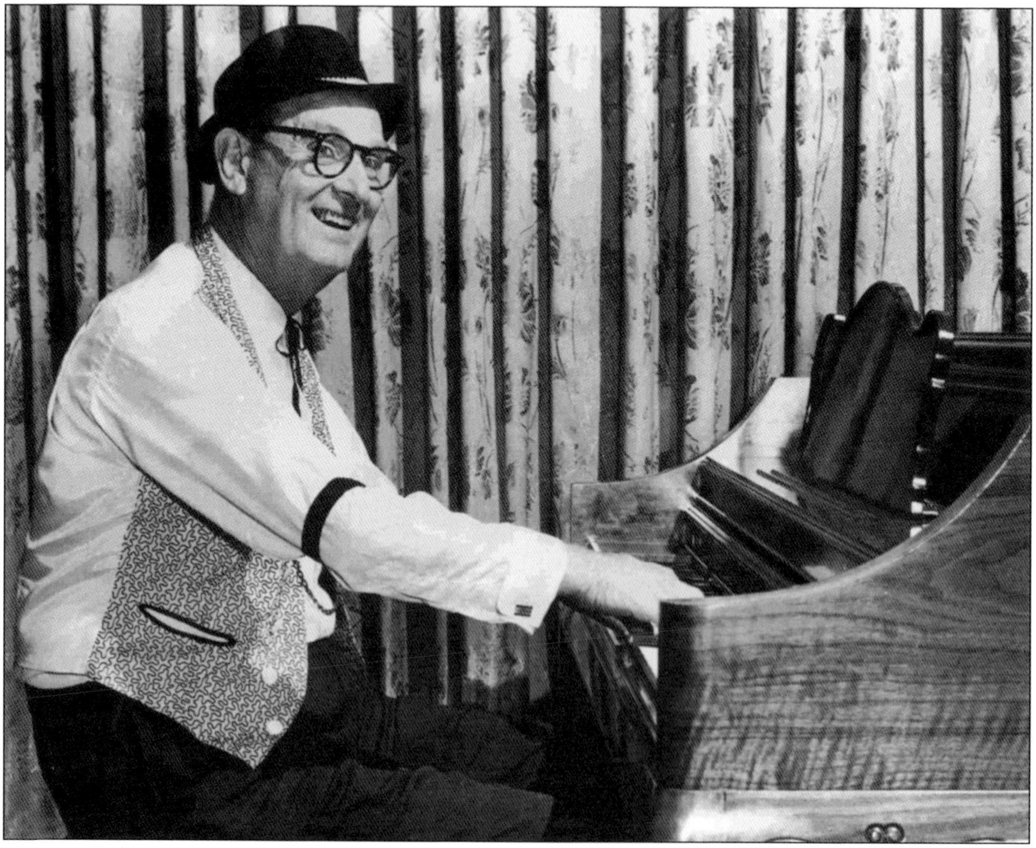

"Poppa" John Gordy, a Pine Bluff native and renowned pianist, was known as the "Father of Honky-Tonk." A ragtime and New Orleans–style jazz musician in the 1920s and 1930s, he added country music to his repertoire by the 1940s, recording sessions with greats like Chester Atkins and Homer & Jethro. Gordy recorded his own albums in the late 1940s and 1950s and went on to record scores of sessions with other country artists in Nashville. He was a major influence in the development of legendary pianist and Country Music Hall of Fame member Hargus "Pig" Robbins. His signature song, "Salty Dog Rag," became a chart-topper for country star Red Foley in 1952. His work is referenced in *This Is Ragtime*. (Courtesy of William Poe.)

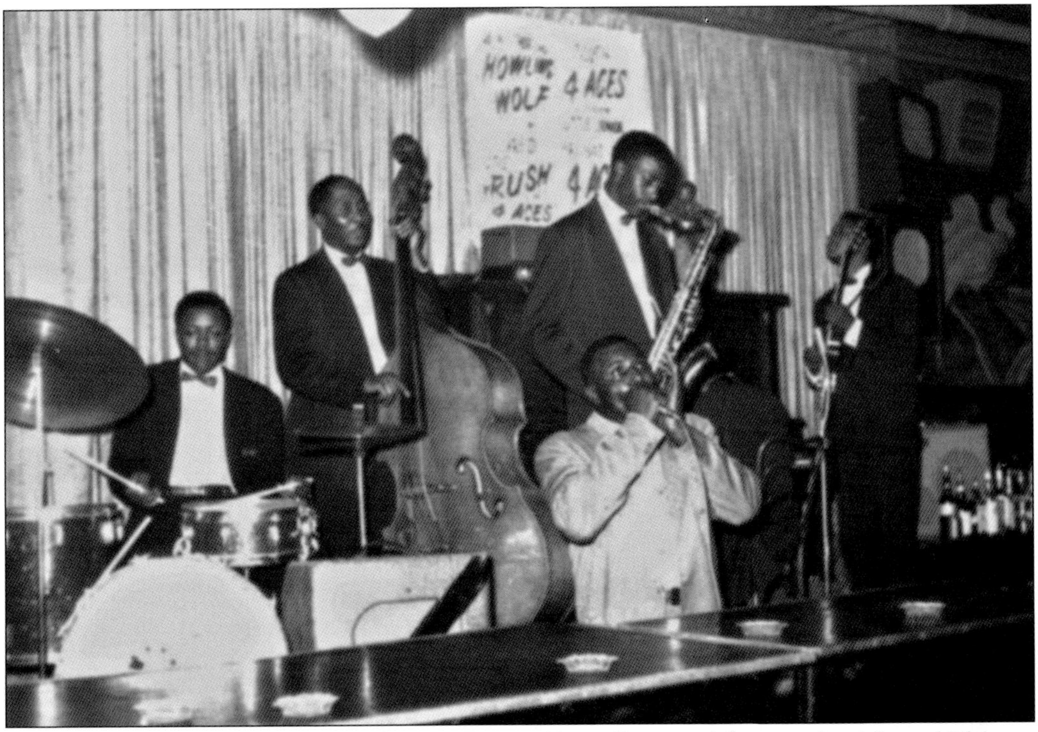

Alfred Elkins (second from left) was born in Jerome, Drew County, Arkansas. A celebrated Chicago blues bass player from the 1930s to the 1950s, Elkins recorded and played with blues greats like Sonny Boy Williamson I, Big Maceo, and Memphis Minnie. He was also a session player with Chess Records. Elkins is best known for his 1950s recordings with Howlin' Wolf (kneeling at center), including the classic hit "Sitting on Top of the World." Elkins's work is noted in *Chicago Blues: The City and the Music*. His music can be heard in several documentaries, including *Martin Scorsese Presents the Blues: A Musical Journey* (2003). (Courtesy of Yannick Bruynoghe Collection.)

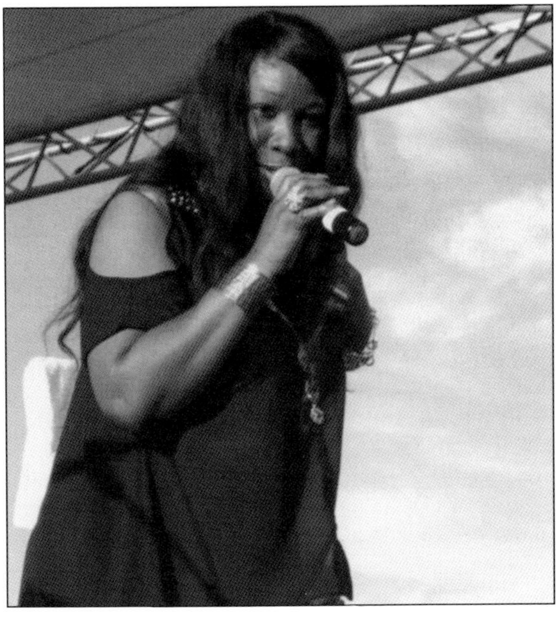

A rising new Southern soul artist is Pine Bluff's Karen Wolfe. As a backup singer for soul/blues legend Denise LaSalle, Wolfe was encouraged by LaSalle to start a solo career. With three album releases since 2006, she has won regional acclaim and has become a popular staple on the Southern soul circuit. Music scholar and author David Whiteis said her voice "both smoldered and glinted with steel" in her regional hit "Man Enough." Wolfe's work has been highlighted in *Southern Soul Blues*. (Courtesy of Karen Wolfe.)

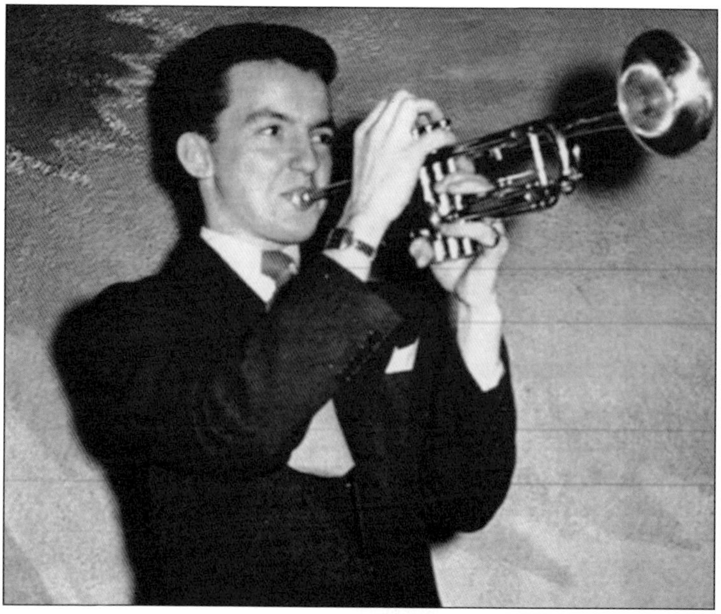

Pine Bluff native and jazz trumpeter William "Bitsy" Mullins was an accompanist for jazz greats like Count Basie, Lena Horne, Mel Tormé, Louis Armstrong, Duke Ellington, Tommy Dorsey, and Buddy Rich. From 1955 to 1975, he played in house bands in Las Vegas with people like Sammy Davis Jr., Dean Martin, and George Burns. Mullins was inducted into the Arkansas Jazz Hall of Fame in 1995 and appears in *American Big Bands.* (Courtesy of Dave Cooper.)

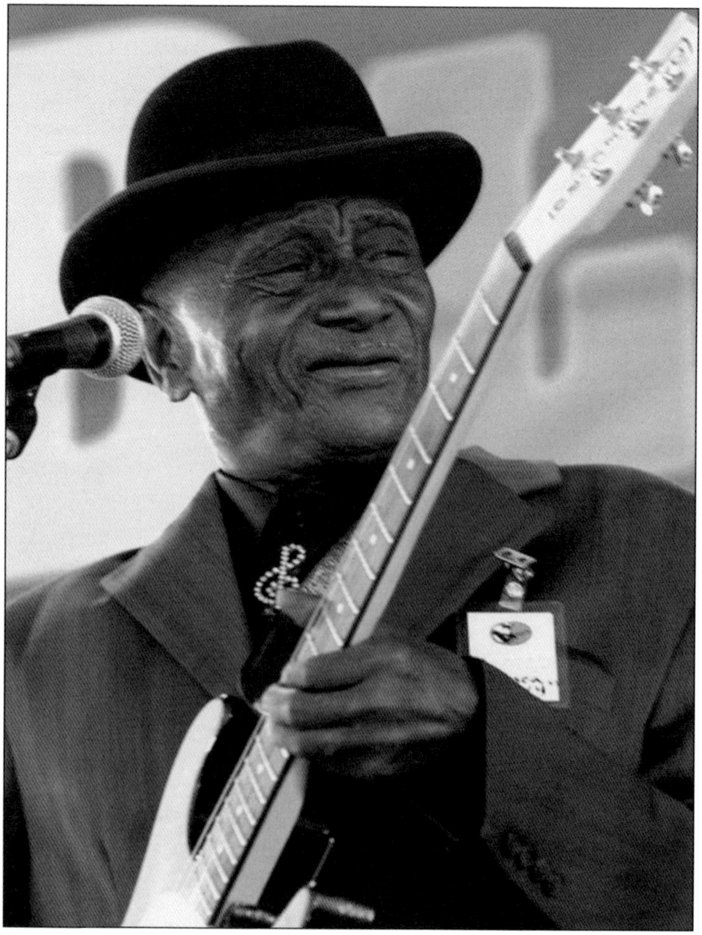

Hosea Leavy, called "The Grandaddy of the Blues," was a native of Altheimer, a vocalist, guitarist, bass player, drummer, and pianist. He worked the club/juke-joint scene throughout Arkansas and the Delta with his brother, Calvin. The duo found success with their 1970 *Billboard* hit "Cummins Prison Farm." Hosea later moved to California and began recording as a solo act after the release of his highly praised *Greasy Greens* album. He is included in *The Encyclopedia of Blues.* (Courtesy of Hans Labuser.)

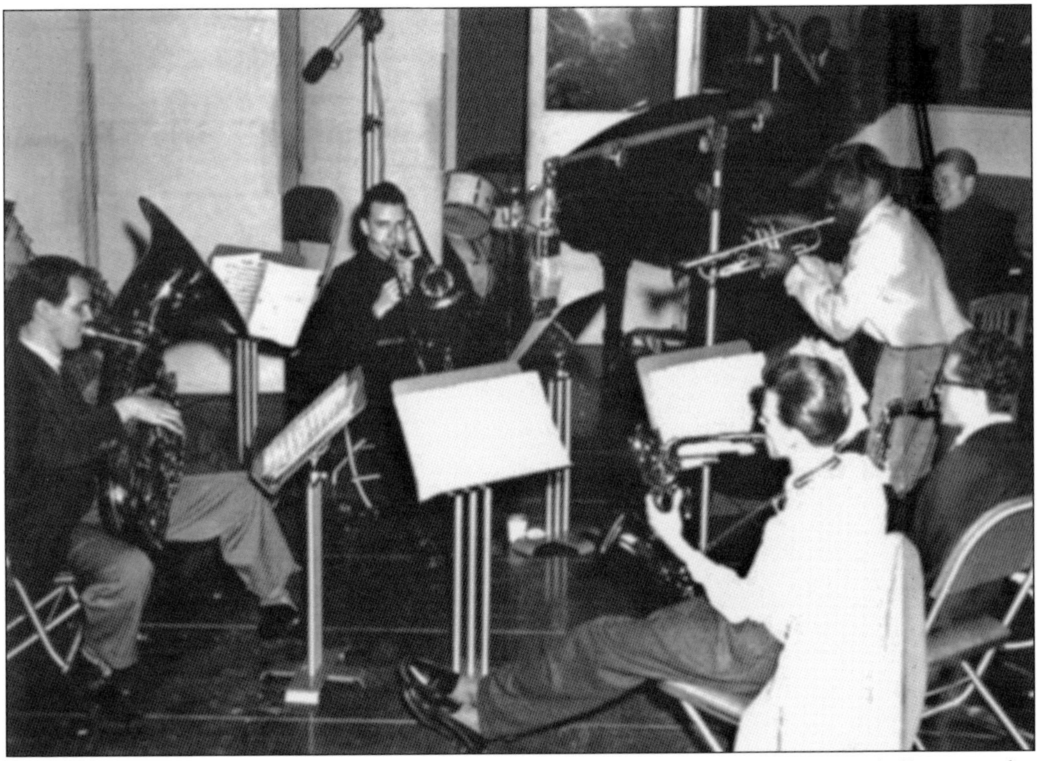

Addison "Junior" Collins (far left), an American French horn player, was a Pine Bluff native who was a member of the famous Miles Davis nonet that appeared on the groundbreaking album *Birth of the Cool* in 1957. He was also a member of Glenn Miller's Army Air Force Band and Claude Thornton's Orchestra. Collins later played and recorded with greats Charlie Parker, Max Roach, Cole Porter, and Gerry Mulligan. He is noted in *The Penguin Jazz Guide*. (Courtesy of Frank Driggs Collection.)

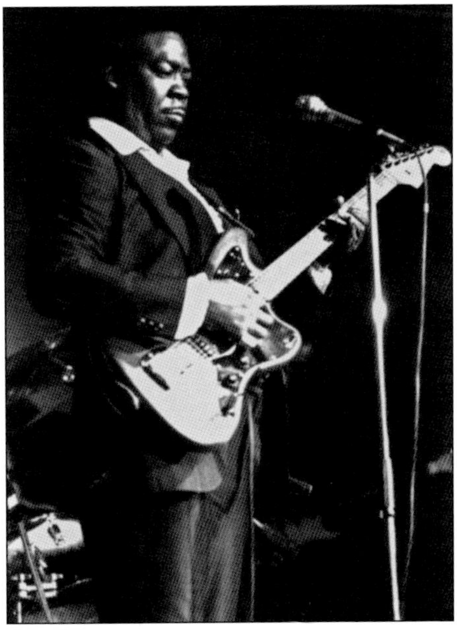

Blues guitarist and singer Larry "Totsie" Davis started professionally in the 1950s, eventually playing with Albert King. He later wrote and recorded the song "Texas Flood," which became a 1980s hit for Stevie Ray Vaughn, as noted in *The Grove Press Guide to Blues*. A cover of "Texas Flood" was also included in the popular music video game *Guitar Hero* in 2005. Davis went on to record several award-winning blues albums and traveled internationally. While his birthplace is unclear (he told researchers that he was born in Kansas City, Missouri, and Pine Bluff, Arkansas), sources state that he was raised in England, Little Rock, and Pine Bluff. (Courtesy of Lionel Decoster.)

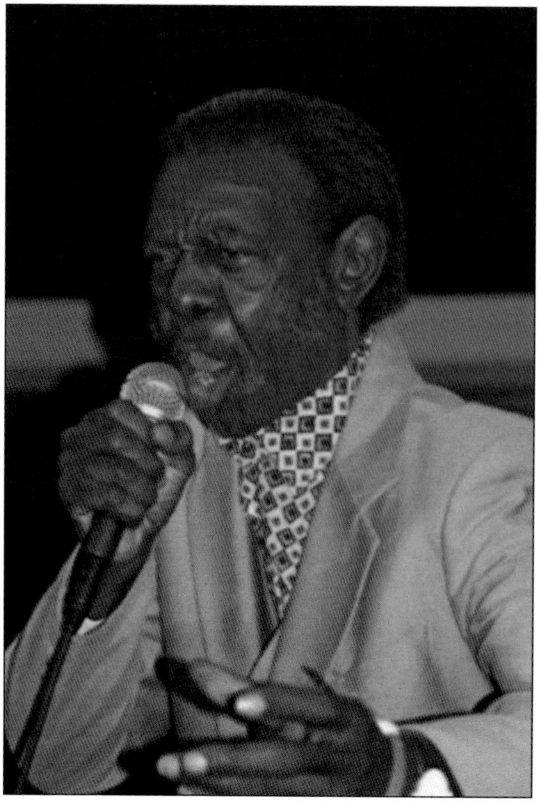

"Lil" Aaron Mosby of Pine Bluff first began playing bass for the legendary Sonny Boy Williamson II after moving to East St. Louis in the 1950s. Subsequently, he played for Chuck Berry for 13 years, then with Albert King for another 13 years. He later formed his own band and recorded, culminating with his 1962 hit "Going to East St. Louis." His career spanned almost 50 years, and he played with a virtual who's who of blues greats. He is cited in *Blues: A Regional Experience*. (Courtesy of Jocelyn Richez.)

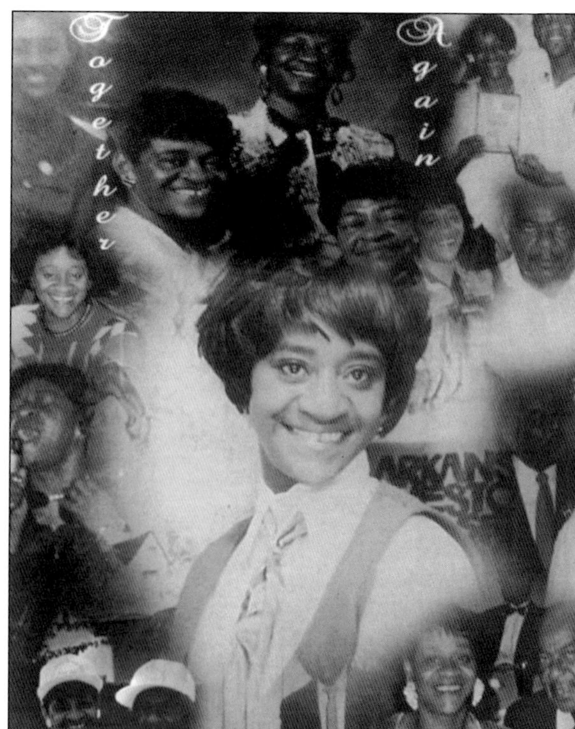

Former R&B singer Minnie Epperson-King (center), from Pine Bluff, is shown in a memorial family tribute. In 1968, *Billboard* magazine predicted that her soulful single "Grab Your Clothes" would be an R&B hit. Epperson-King toured with the Ike and Tina Turner Review, Bobby "Blue" Bland, and O.V. Wright, while releasing her own singles. Her music was arranged by Al Green's legendary producer, "Papa" Willie Mitchell. Epperson-King's songs are referenced in *House of Hits: The Story of Houston's Gold Star/Sugar Hill Recording Studio*. (Courtesy of Dornetta Hobbs.)

Joe Pitts, a blues-rock guitarist/vocalist, continues the tradition of talented Delta Lowlands artists. The Pine Bluff native, influenced by soul, jazz, rock, and blues, has blended these genres in his eight previous albums. He has played with Bobby "Blue" Bland, Cedell Davis, Larry McCray, and other blues greats. His album *Ten Shades of Blue* reached number five on the Roots and Blues national charts. He is as a member of the Arkansas Blues Hall of Fame. (Courtesy of Joe Pitts.)

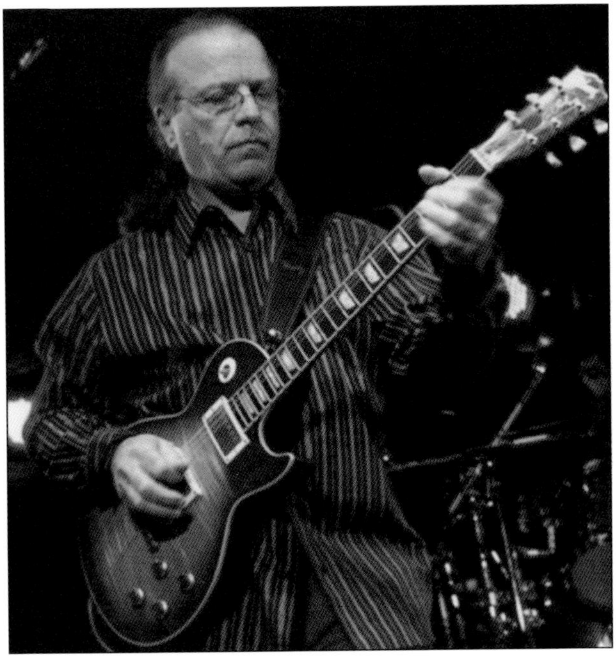

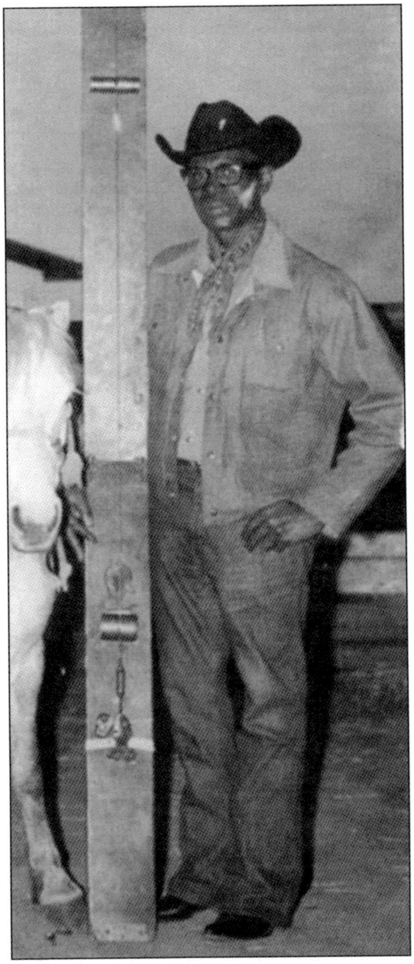

The one-string guitar some called the "didley bow" or the "unitar" harkens back to blues' origins in the late 1800s. By the 1940s and 1950s, almost all blues guitarists had switched to six strings, except for a few, like Willie Joe Duncan, likely from Plum Bayou in Jefferson County, based on research by historians Bob Eagle and Eric LeBlanc in *Blues: A Regional Experience*. Duncan is shown here with his unitar, made from an amplified seven-foot wooden plank and one string of wire. He played with blues star Jimmy Reed in Chicago and later recorded with Specialty Records. (Courtesy of Tom Mazzonlini.)

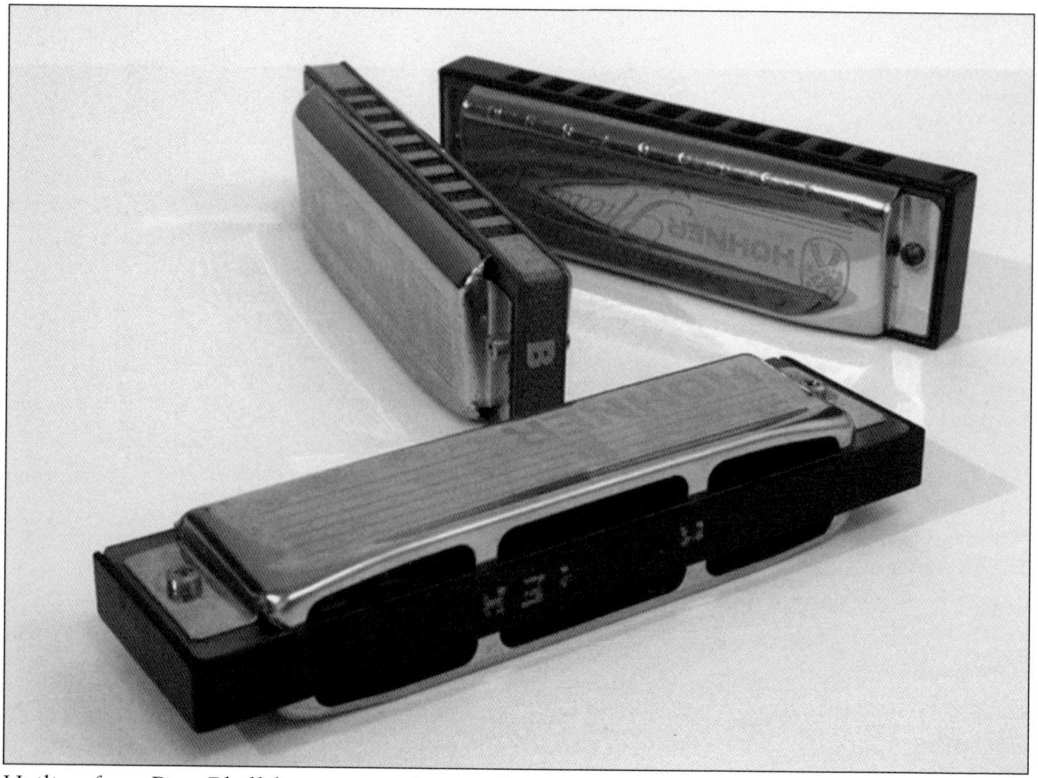

Hailing from Pine Bluff, harmonica player "Sleepy" Otis Hunt (so named because of his naps during poker games) was also a vocalist and drummer. When, as a young man, he discovered that Howlin' Wolf was having an affair with his wife, Hunt angrily confronted him. The two almost drew guns one night, but another blues legend, "Little Walter" Jacobs, intervened. Wolf and Hunt later became friends while Little Walter taught Hunt to play harmonica. Hunt played in Chicago in the 1950s with blues giants Freddy King and Elmore James, among others. His recorded work is cited in *The Encyclopedia of Blues.* (Courtesy of Crane Lize.)

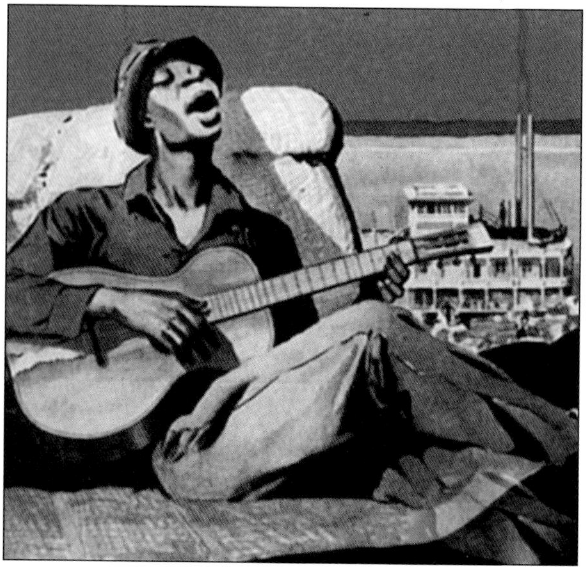

This blues guitarist plays much like Elmon "Driftin Slim" Mickle of Keo, Arkansas, may have while growing up near the Arkansas River. A harmonica player, drummer, and guitarist, Mickle was mentored by Sonny Boy Williamson I; he later helped Sonny Boy Williamson II start his radio career. In the 1950s, Mickle recorded with the Pine Bluff trio of Junior "Cripple Red" Brooks, Sunny Blair, and Edgar "Babyface" Turner. In the 1960s and 1970s, Mickle began playing in a one-man-band format. *The Encyclopedia of Blues* cites his work. (Courtesy of Victor Records.)

James "Jimmy" McKissic, internationally acclaimed pianist, was a product of Pine Bluff. He began playing the piano at the age of three and eventually performed for three US presidents, multiple heads of state, and at venues of all kinds, including 29 appearances at Carnegie Hall. He recorded one album and is referenced in the music anthology *Our Own Sweet Sounds*. He was the subject of the PBS documentary *How Do You Get to Carnegie Hall*. (Courtesy of Pine Bluff Commercial.)

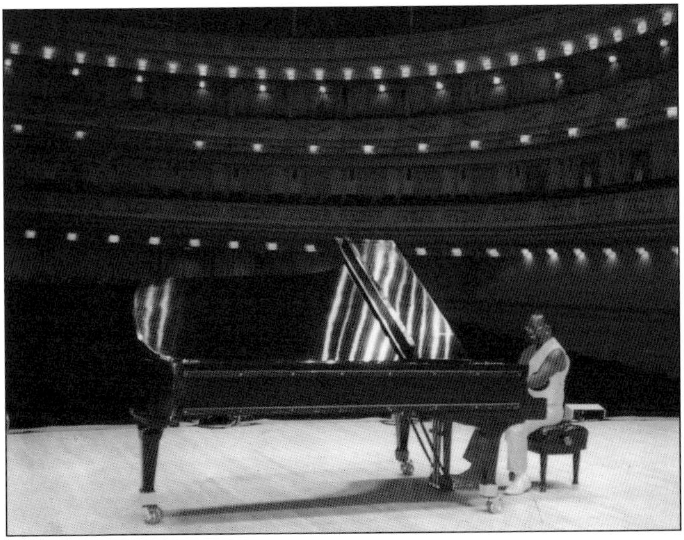

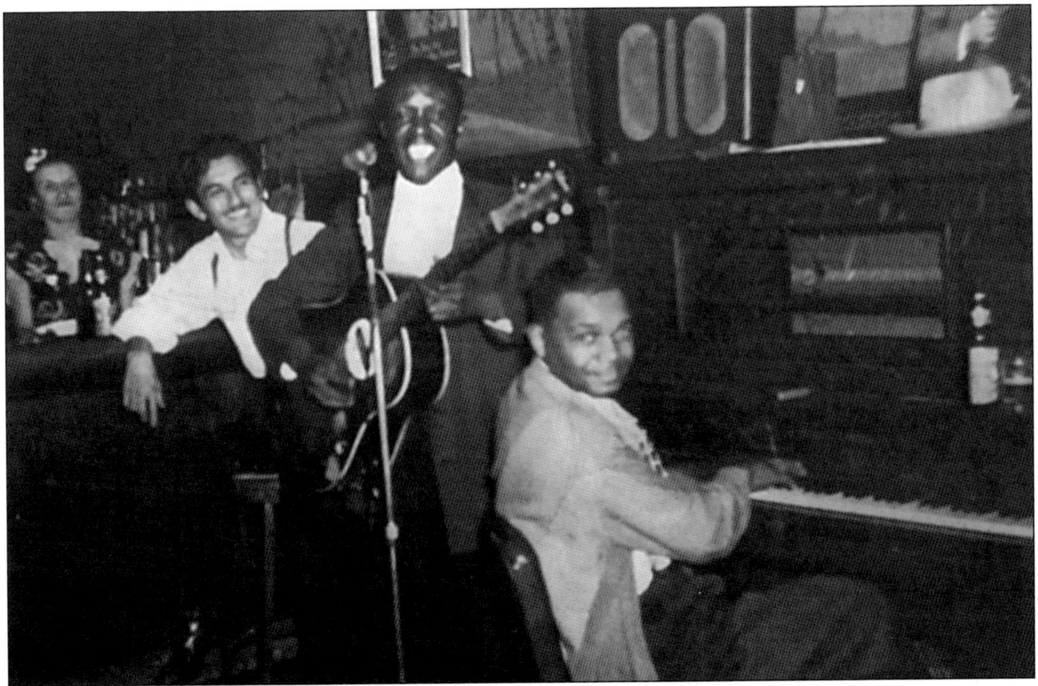

Jimmy Deberry (standing, center), a veteran blues guitarist, pianist, vocalist, and recording artist, was from Gumwood, Lonoke County, according to *Blues: A Regional Experience*. He played in clubs and juke joints throughout the Delta and recorded in St. Louis, Memphis, and Jackson, Tennessee, from the 1930s to the 1970s. He recorded with harmonica player "Big Walter" Horton on the classic hit "Easy," which *The Blues Encyclopedia* called an "instrumental masterpiece." Deberry is included in 17 blues compilation albums. (Courtesy of Jimmy Cunningham Jr.)

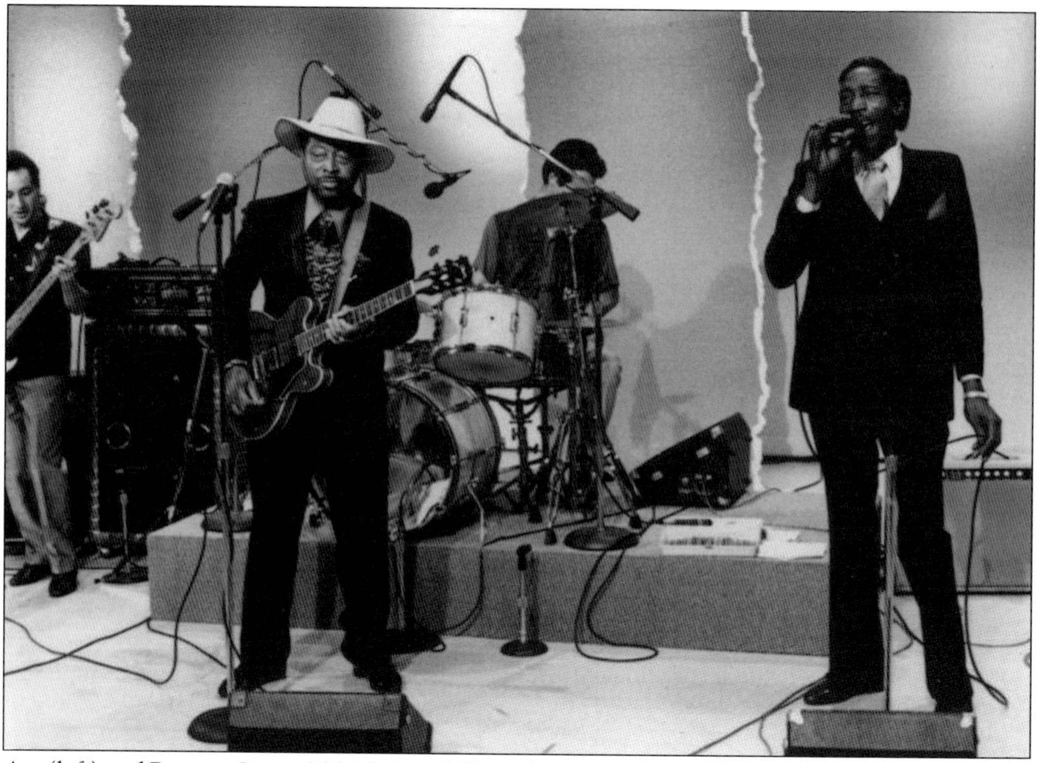

Art (left) and Roman Griswald (right) could have been called the "Blues Brothers." Born in Tillar, Desha County, the siblings later moved to Toledo, Ohio, according to *The Blues Encyclopedia*. Both brothers sang vocals, with Art also playing guitar and Roman handling keyboards and harmonica. They began playing backup for music greats like Freddie King and Jimmy McCrackin in the 1950s. The brothers formed their own blues band in the mid-1960s, recording albums and touring internationally. Both brothers appeared with B.B. King, Bobby "Blue" Bland, John Lee Hooker, and others in the documentary *The Hines Farm Blues Club* (2003). (Courtesy of Jim O'Neal.)

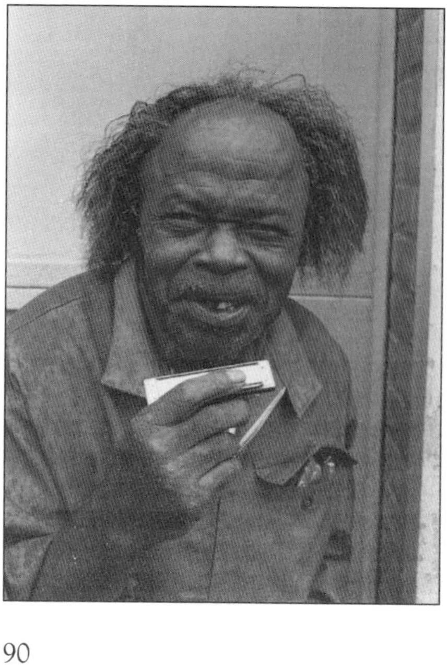

Blues harmonica player "Little Walter" Mitchell, born in Pickens, Desha County, acquired his nickname due to his small stature long before the more celebrated "Little Walter" Jacobs popularized the name. Mitchell began recording in the 1940s, largely in the Detroit-Toledo area, and continued to do so through the 1980s, according to *The Blues Encyclopedia*. He was known as the "Father of Toledo Blues." The Little Walter Mitchell Award is presented each year in Toledo to the area's best blues artist. (Courtesy of John Rockford.)

Though Faith Taylor and her group, the Sweet Teens, never made it big, the Dumas-born 1950s doo-wop singer made a splash. Taylor (far right) started performing at the age of four, winning a talent contest in Little Rock. Her family moved to Chicago, where she played in several combos, most notably with Muddy Waters. By the time Taylor was nine, the Sweet Teens had formed. They cut several singles, toured, and received generous reviews from national media outlets. Taylor is chronicled in *Girl Groups: Famous Females Who Rocked the World*. (Courtesy of Federal Records.)

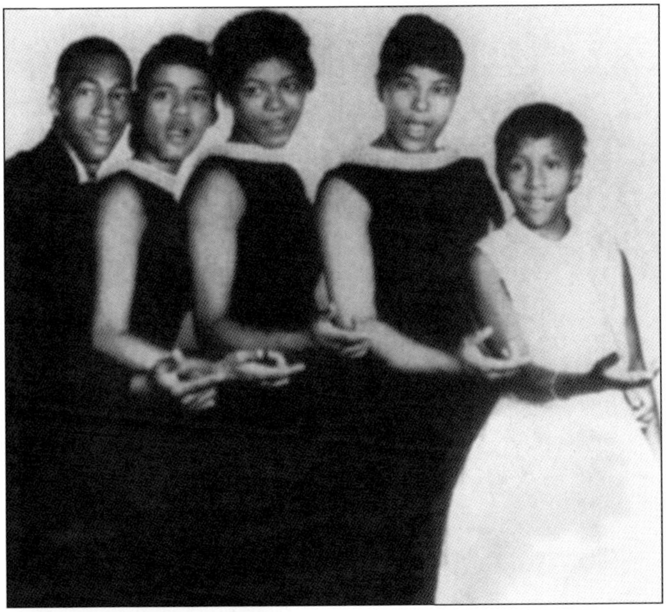

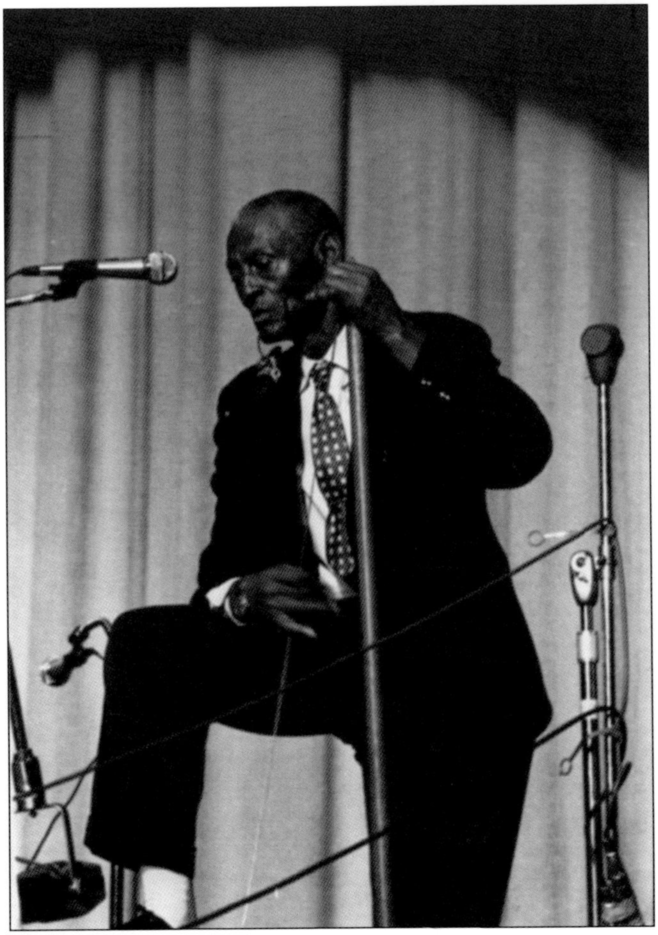

Dewey Corley, one of the most revered jug band members of his era according to *The All Music Guide to the Blues*, was born in Halley, Desha County, Arkansas. He was a harmonica player, washtub bassist, kazoo and jug player, and leader/founder of the famous Beale Street Jug Band, which started in the 1930s. He was also a member of Will Shade's legendary Memphis Jug Band in the 1920s. Jug bands ruled in Memphis and the rural South during the early 20th century. They combined hokum-style music, folk ballads, and early blues. Corely's playing and recording years span the 1920s to the 1970s. (Courtesy of Jim O'Neal.)

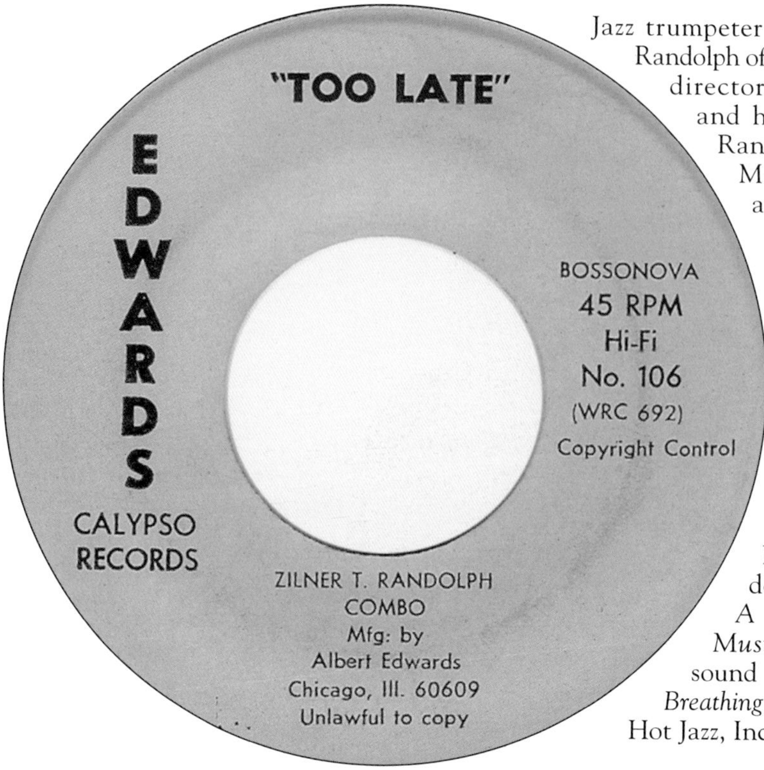

Jazz trumpeter and songwriter Zilner Randolph of Dermott was the musical director for Louis Armstrong and his band in the 1930s. Randolph's song "Old Man Mose" became famous after Armstrong's 1935 recording. In the 1940s, Randolph recorded with his own quartet and contributed arrangements to the bands of Earl Hines, Duke Ellington, and others. *Who's Who of Jazz: Storyville to Swing Street* cites his contributions. Randolph appears in the documentary *Bluesland: A Portrait in American Music*. His music is on the sound track for the movie *Still Breathing* (1997). (Courtesy of Red Hot Jazz, Inc.)

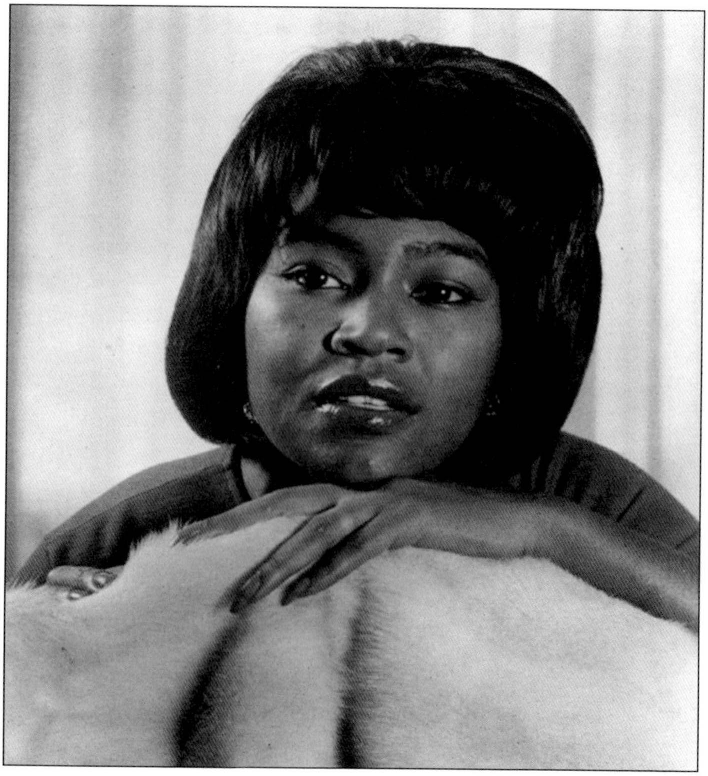

The music of soul singer Jackie Day has grown in popularity since her death. She was born in Eudora, later moving to Shreveport, Louisiana. Davis recorded her first single in 1965 with the label of Johnny Cochran Sr. (father of the famous lawyer). By 1970, she had recorded songs with various labels. Her records have become prized items among British soul music enthusiasts. A rare copy of "Before It's Too Late" was auctioned for $4,000 in 2004. A compilation album of her music was released in 2011. She is referenced in *Blues: A Regional Experience*. (Courtesy of Bill Lazerus.)

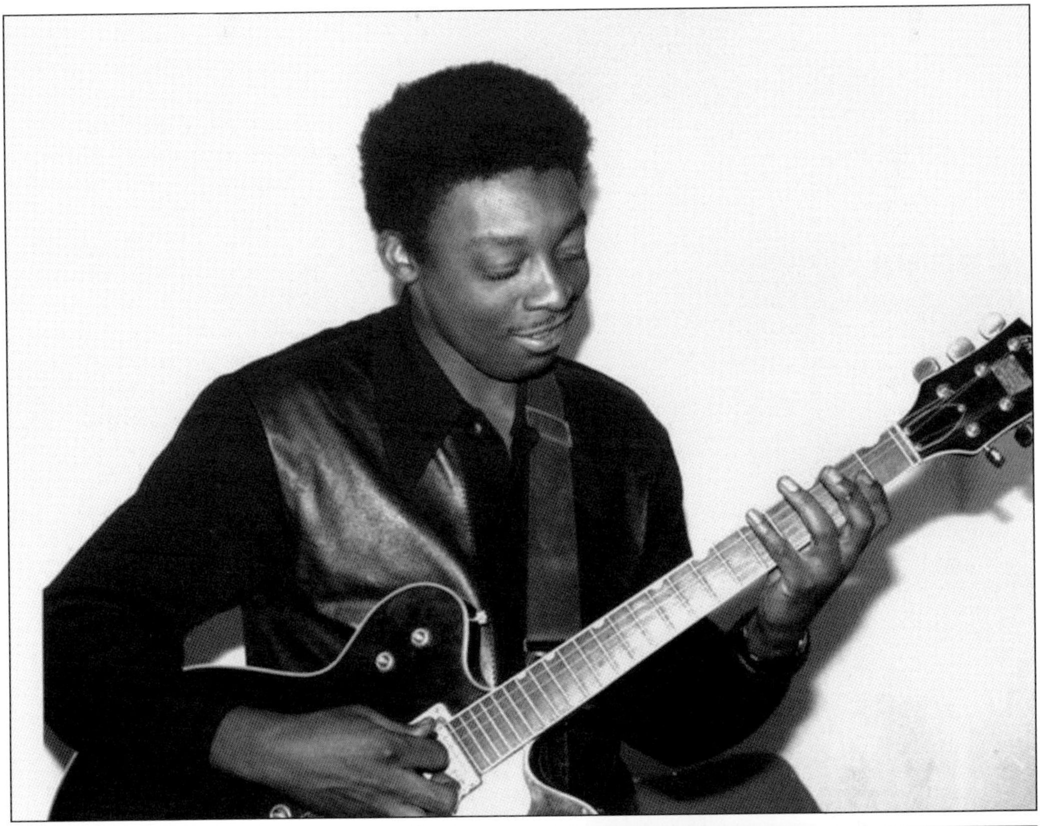

Bobby King, Chicago blues singer and guitarist, was born in Jefferson County, Arkansas, according to *Blues: A Regional Experience*. King recorded as a sideman with blues legends Freddy King, Bobby "Blue" Bland, and many others from the 1960s through the early 1980s. He also recorded several singles of his own. Hailed by many in the 1970s as the next up-and-coming blues great, his life was tragically cut short when he died at age 42 after complications from a brawl in a Chicago club. (Courtesy of Jim O'Neal.)

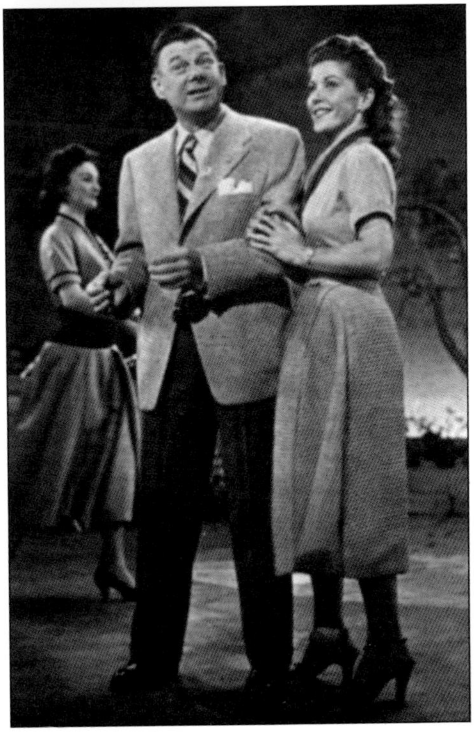

Janette Davis, born in Memphis and raised in Pine Bluff, is shown with 1950s television star Author Godfrey. She was the popular lead vocalist and, later, producer for Godfrey's popular program, *The Arthur Godfrey Show*, which ran from 1949 to 1957. She sang pop, jazz, country, and Western swing ballads, recording albums with Godfrey and as a solo act. Davis's celebrity status landed her on several covers of *TV Guide*, *Radio Mirror*, and *Downbeat* magazines. Her work is chronicled in *The Encyclopedia of American Radio*. (Courtesy of Ray Hagen.)

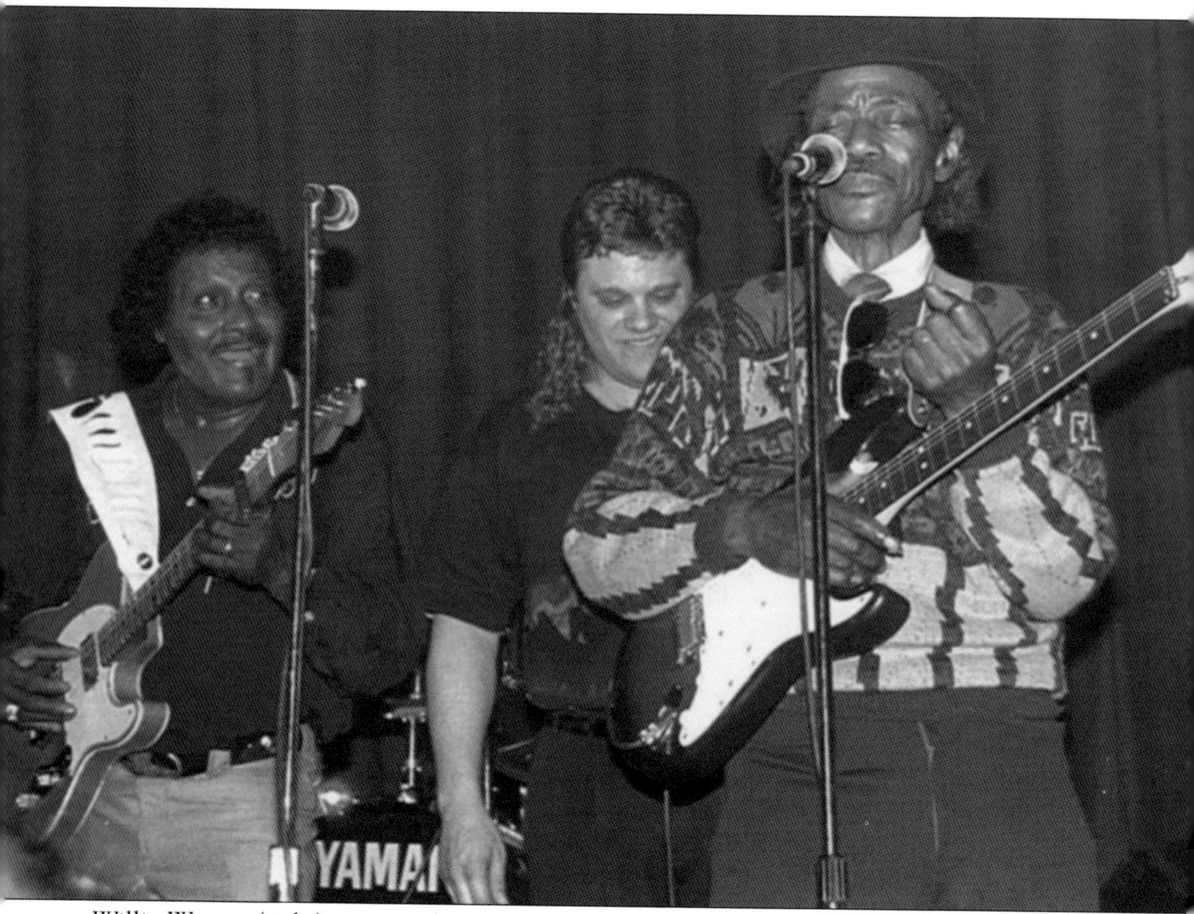

Willie Warren (right), a singer, bass player, and guitarist, was raised in Lake Village (not to be confused with the Lake Village blues artist Willie "Wineheaded" Williams, who was also later based in Chicago). Here, he is shown with blues legend Albert Collins (left). Playing in Chicago and Detroit, Warren worked with Jimmy Reed, Otis Rush, Freddie King, and others. He is credited with teaching Blues Hall of Fame legend Eddie "Guitar Slim" Jones to play guitar in 1948 when the young bluesman joined his band in Lake Village. Blues enthusiasts state that Warren first popularized the electric bass while playing in local clubs in the early 1950s by tuning down the four low strings on his guitar. Months later, Fender came out with the first mass-produced electric bass. Otis Rush, in an interview with T.E. Mattox, said: "We ran our strings down, the bass strings, giving it a bass sound, different from the guitar tuning. We ran it down and we was the hottest thing in Chicago. Musicians . . . stars was coming by to see where we was getting this sound from. So, about 6 months later everybody had it." Warren recorded on his own in the 1970s, as detailed in *The Encyclopedia of Blues.* (Courtesy of Mike Boulan/No Cover Productions.)

Seven

Select Gospel Quartets and Groups in the Delta Lowlands

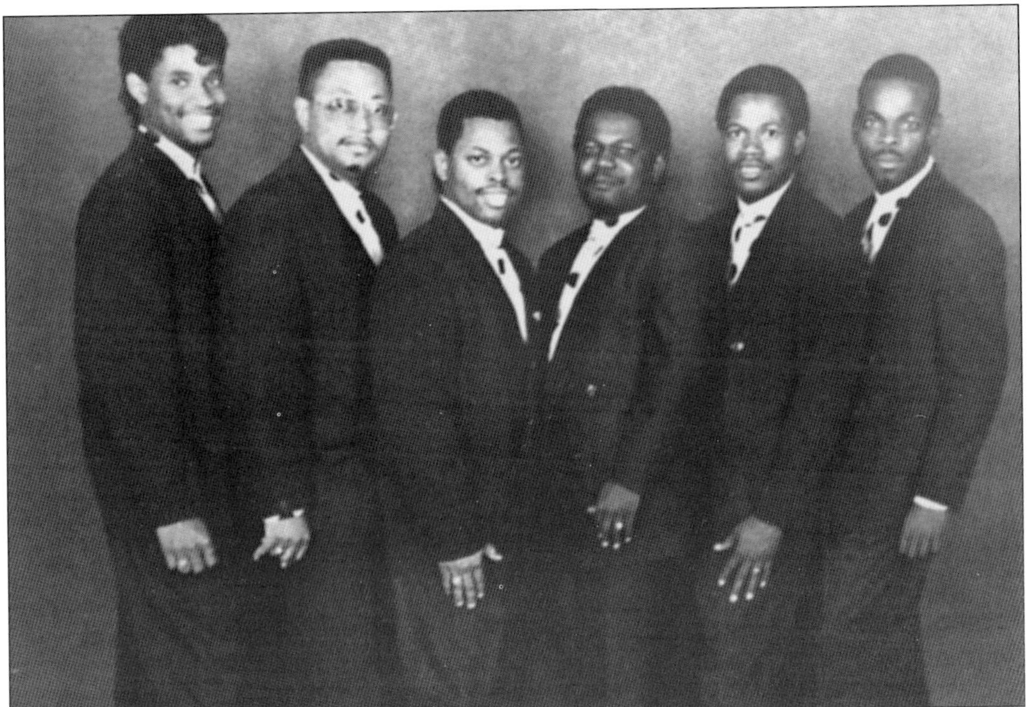

The Racy Brothers Quartet of Dumas is one of the most well-known contemporary recording quartets in Arkansas. Originating in a family steeped in gospel music, the members organized their singing group in the 1980s, around the time this photograph was taken. The quartet has recorded seven albums and has traveled throughout the United States to play for its scores of fans. *Billboard* magazine called the quartet's music "an exuberant classic gospel sound reveling in . . . traditional roots while readily adding a contemporary edge." The appear in the concert video film *Living Legends of Gospel: The Quartets* (1998) with such greats as the Fairfield Four, the Mighty Clouds of Joy, Luther Barnes, Lou Rawls, and many others. (Courtesy of Walter Witherspoon.)

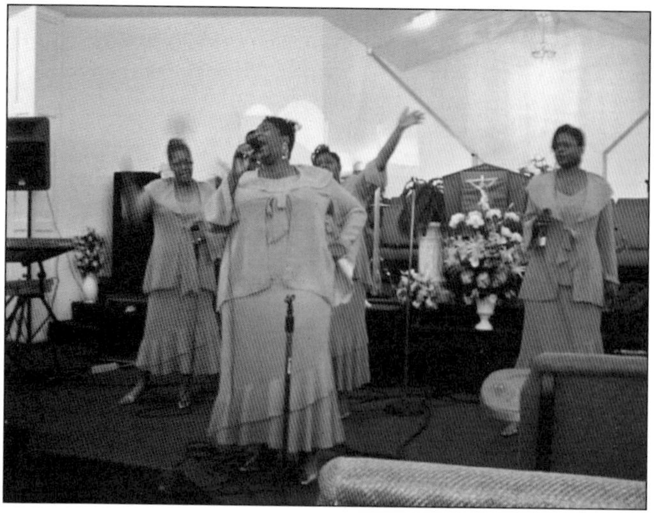

The Williams Singers of Pine Bluff began with the mother-father duo of U.Z. and Jessie B. Williams in 1960. They traveled throughout the South, playing with Sister Rosetta Tharpe, Brother Joe Mays, Clara Ward, and others. Their gifted children, some of whom are shown here, continued the family tradition of gospel artistry. The Williams Singers recently celebrated their 54th anniversary of musical excellence as a group. (Courtesy of Carol Williams Rankin.)

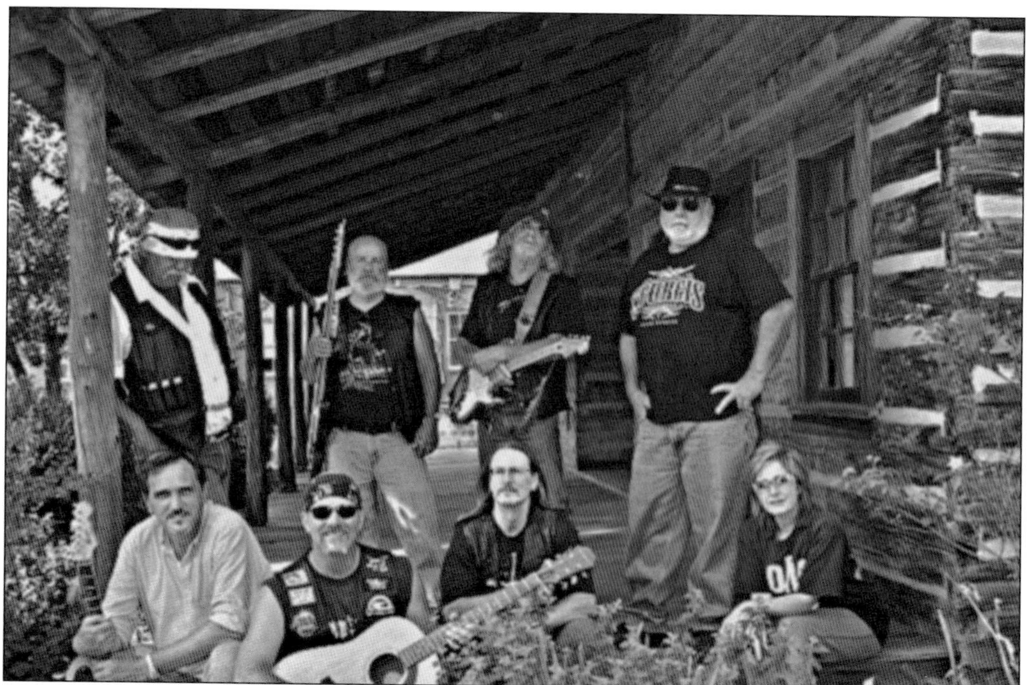

The Gospel Outlawz, a Christian-based music group, was started around 2000 by Ed (standing second from right) and Pat Ashcroft (seated far right) of Lonoke. Influenced by their love of the music of their youth, but passionate about a calling to share the gospel, they formed a band that incorporates rock, blues, country, pop, and reggae in all of their songs. They largely write their own lyrics and music, performing often in central Arkansas but occasionally in out-of-state venues. (Courtesy of Steven Braud.)

Rev. R.L. LaVeaux, (aka "Mr. Gospel"), a disc jockey and gospel concert promoter, poses in the 1960s, possibly at Pine Bluff's KCAT radio station. His daughter, Naomi LaVeaux Summerville, remembered that, when she was a child, music legends would come to her Pine Bluff home to eat meals prepared by her mother after performances. Among the visiting artists were Shirley Caesar, the Mighty Clouds of Joy, the Swan Silvertones, Edwin and Walter Hawkins, the Five Blind Boys, James Cleveland, and the Staple Singers. (Courtesy of Naomi LaVeaux Summerville.)

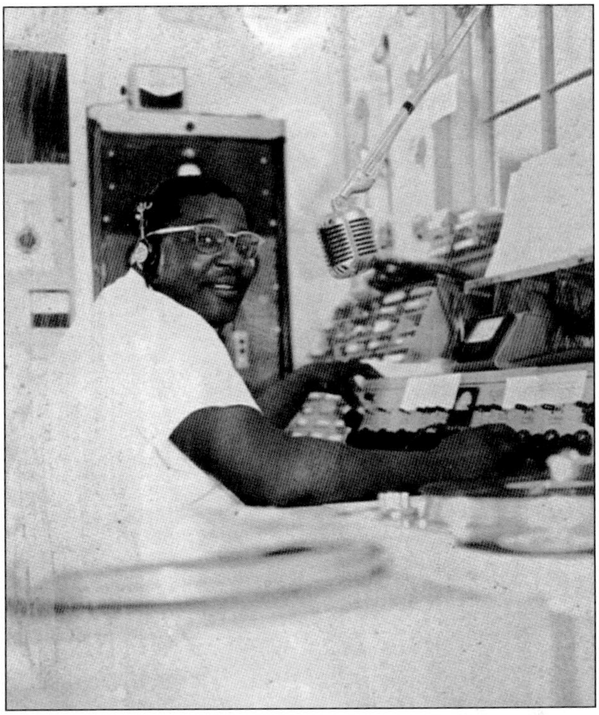

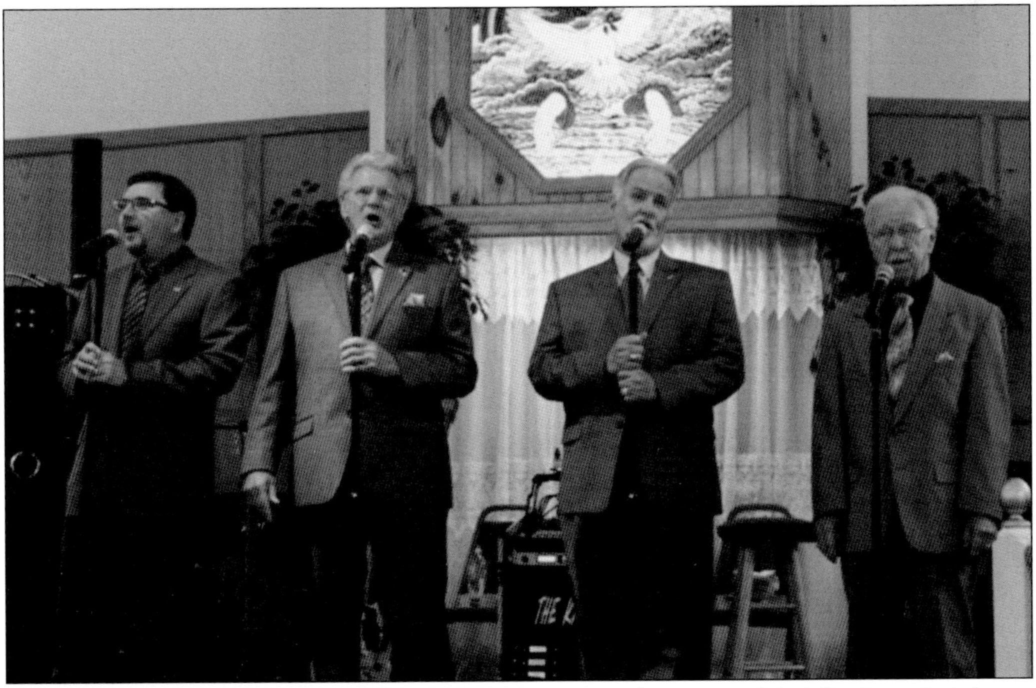

In 1985, talented brothers Gary and Pat Newton met up with a cousin, Mark Little, at their home to form the Kinsmen, a gospel quartet. The group later included Bill Hankins and Gerald Williams (an inductee in the Southern Gospel Music Association Hall of Fame). Since that time, the Pine Bluff group has performed throughout Arkansas, Louisiana, and Mississippi, sharing the stage with notable groups like Gold City, the Hoppers, and the Melody Boys. (Courtesy of the Kinsmen.)

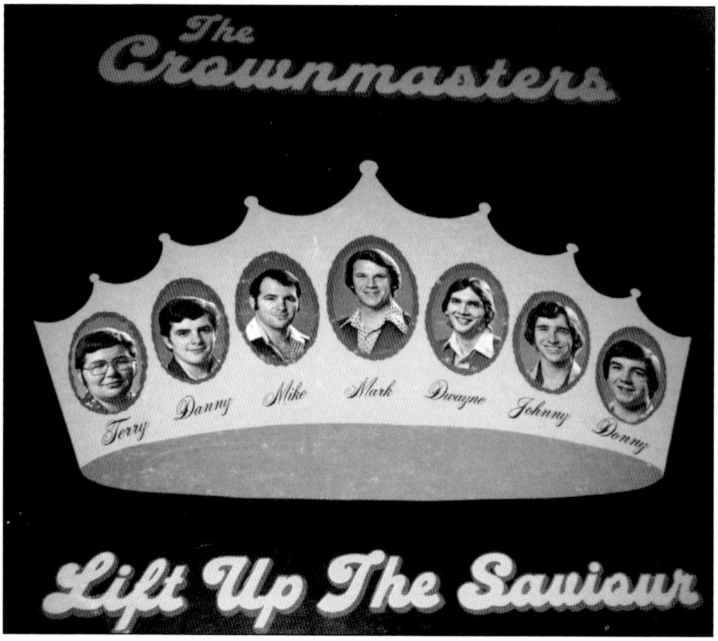

The Holcomb Brothers Quartet of Pine Bluff is one of the great veteran Southern gospel quartets of the Delta Lowlands. They formed over 40 years ago. Shown here is their first album, entitled *The Crownmasters*. They have produced several albums since then and continue to sing in area churches and venues of all kinds. Members include, from left to right, Terry, Danny, Mike, Mark, Dwayne, Johnny, and Donny. The late Tommy Holcomb, a former member, is not pictured. (Courtesy of Rep. Mike Holcomb.)

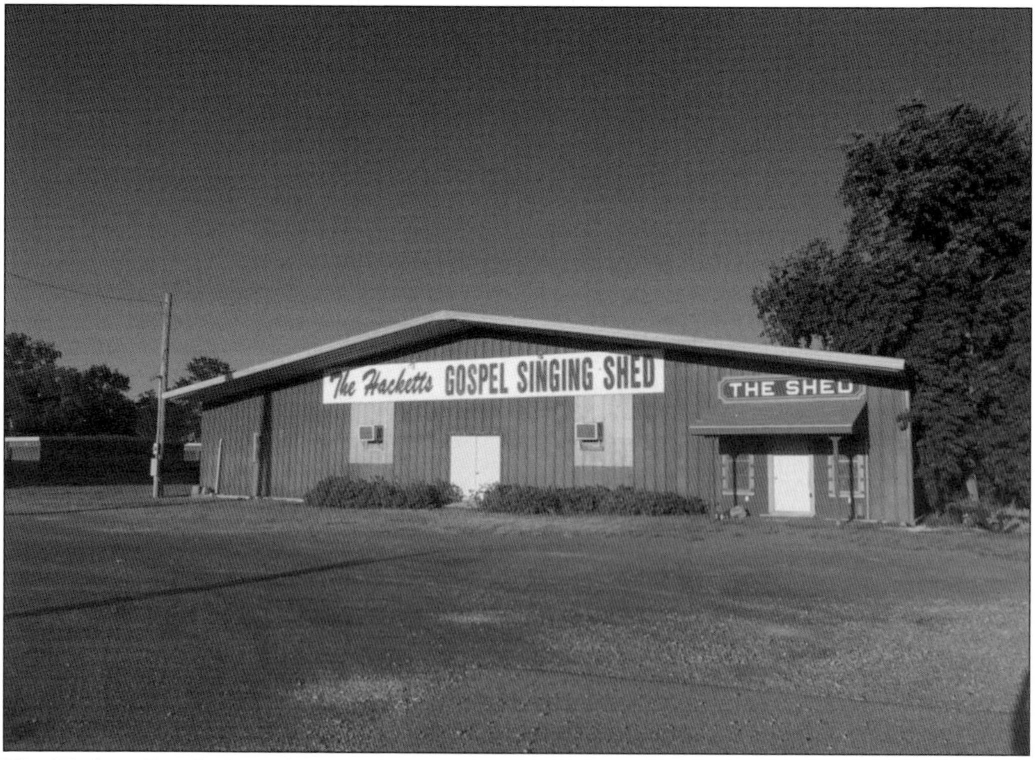

The Hackett Family Gospel Singers, a group that has been singing and recording (14 albums) since the late 1960s, owns the Shed, a gospel-music venue located just outside of Dermott. Situated on the edge of a 122-acre cotton farm, it was originally a tractor shed. The group converted into a performance hall. With 200 vintage theater seats providing comfort, the Shed provides space for all kinds of foot-stomping Southern gospel programs. (Courtesy of Henry Hackett.)

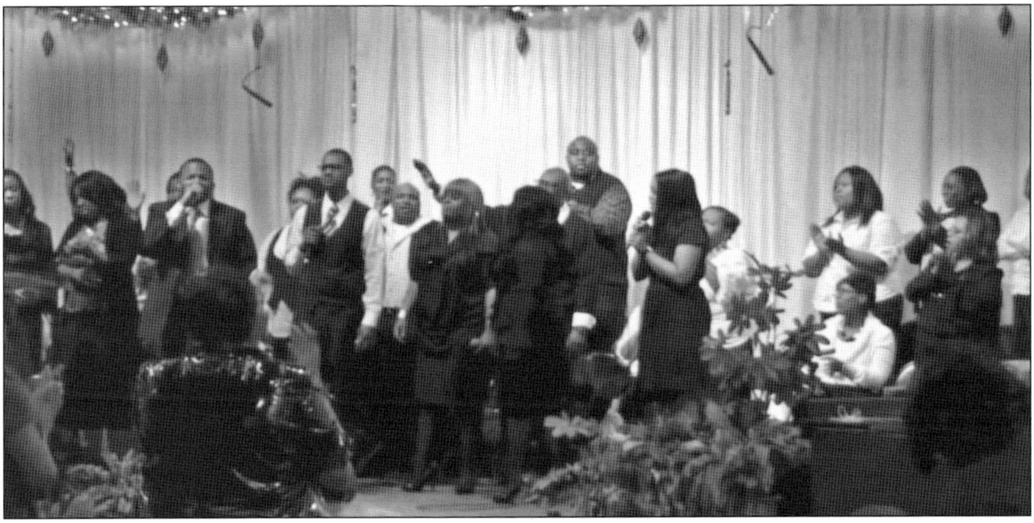

Dedrick Jones (third from left) is a Pine Bluff songwriter, producer, and director. In 2001, he formed a gospel group, Dedrick Jones and Chosen Praise. Since that time, its recorded music has been heard on radio stations across the country. The group has appeared on *The Bobby Jones Gospel Show* and the Victory Television Network. Chosen Praise has worked with gospel giants Kim Burrell, Dorinda Clark Cole, Vickie Winans, and others. (Courtesy of Dedrick Jones.)

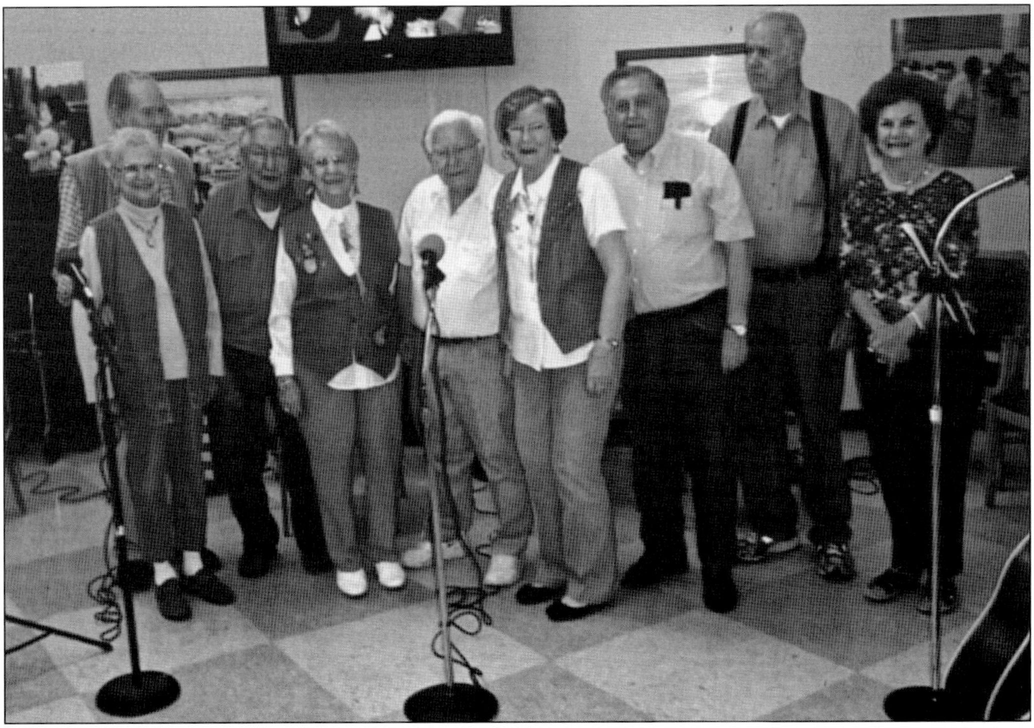

The Blue Sky Country Music Band is a Pine Bluff group that performs all music genres, including gospel music. The group, made up of retirees, has largely entertained audiences in nursing homes and assisted living facilities since the 1990s. Members include (from left to right) Bobby and Gerri Henderson, Jim and Reba Torres, Carlton and Lynn Thompson, Earl Gober, Bud Casion, and Juanita Sinks. (Courtesy of Earl Gober.)

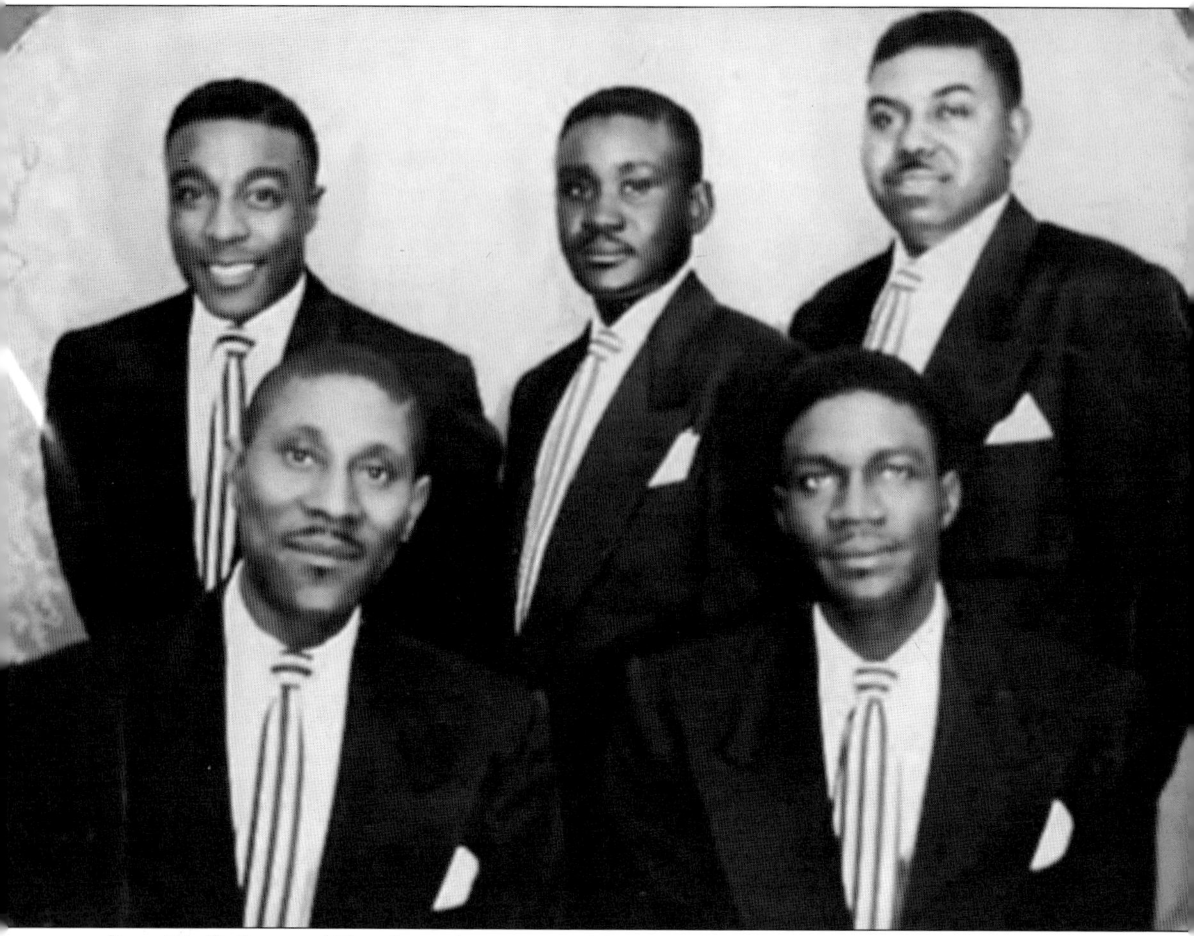

Pine Bluff's Spiritual Five formed in 1938 and became the standard for Delta quartet excellence. The United Quartets of America, a national gospel talent association, chose them as the top quartet in Arkansas in the 1950s. The group, made of numerous members over the years, performed throughout the South. They also backed up Blues Hall of Famer and gospel great Rosetta Tharpe several times and performed in concert with the Dixie Hummingbirds, the Staple Singers, the Soul Stirrers, the Pilgrim Travelers, and others in their 50-plus years of singing. Local lore suggests that the Soul Stirrers heard the Spiritual Five around 1950 or 1951 in Pine Bluff and asked member Washington Ficklin to join them as a permanent member. However, Ficklin declined because of the recent birth of his children and a new local job. The Soul Stirrers soon after extended the invitation for the slot to legend Sam Cooke, who sang his first public performance with them in Pine Bluff not long after Ficklin's declination. Spiritual Five members in this 1950s photograph include, from left to right, (first row) Curtis Rice and George Monk; (second row) Washington Ficklin Sr., Theo Rodgers, and Willie McClendon. (Courtesy of Wanda Ficklin Walker and Colette Ficklin.)

Eight

Film and Television in the Delta Lowlands

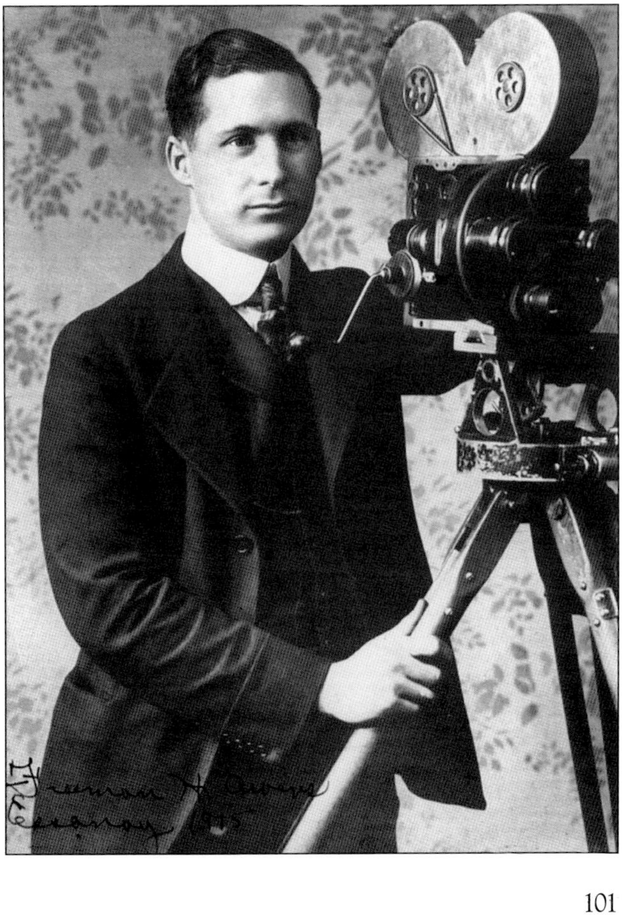

Freeman Harrison Owens, born in Pine Bluff, was one of the most important cinematographers and inventors in the 20th century. In 1922, he began working professionally with the "Father of Radio," Dr. Lee de Forest. Owens invented and filed a patent for Phonofilm, the first synchronized sound and film apparatus. However, de Forest also filed a patent for Owens's invention. The courts decided in de Forest's favor, because Owens was employed by him at the time of the invention. Historians, however, credit Owens with the technological milestone. Owens, using his new apparatus, was also the cinematographer for the first commercial dramatic film shot as a talking picture, *Love's Old Sweet Song* (1923). He designed the Nielsen Ratings system for television and had 11,812 inventions with over 200 patents. (Courtesy of Arkansas Entertainers Hall of Fame.)

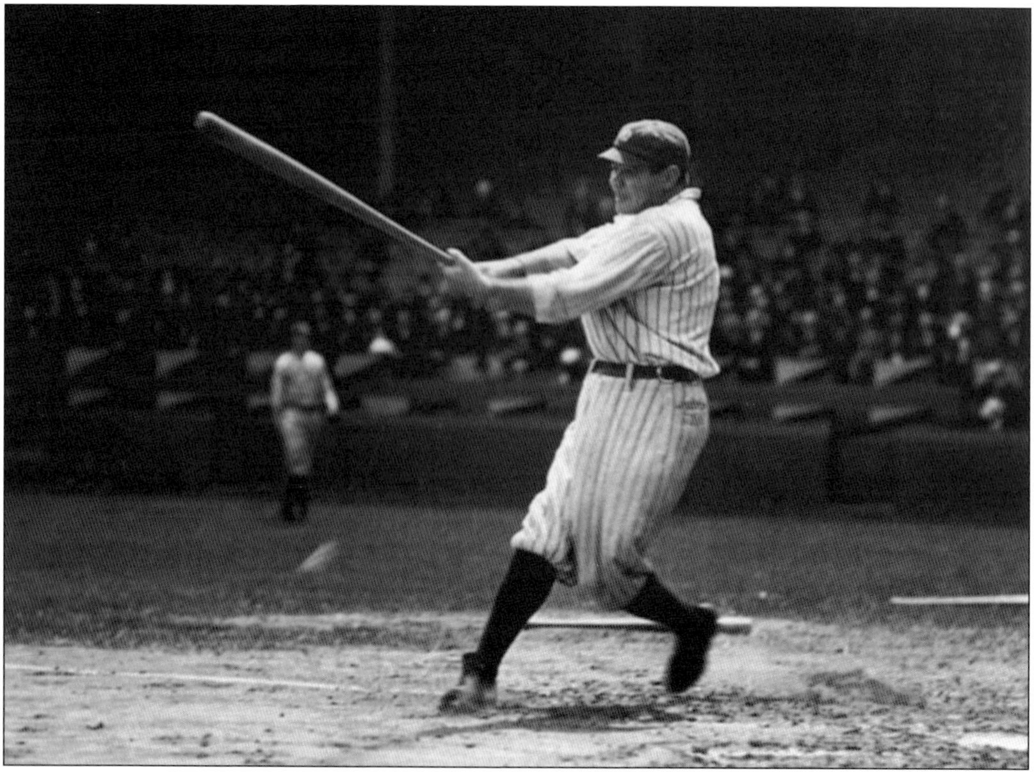

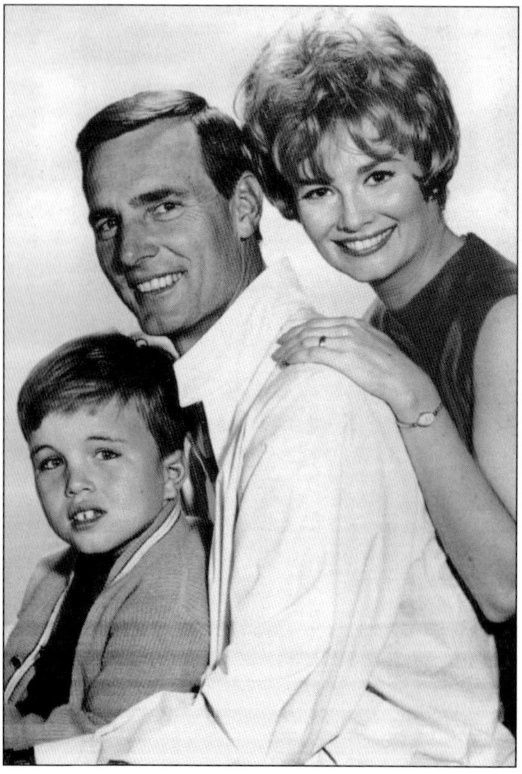

How Babe Ruth Hits a Home Run was a short, but monumental, documentary clip (about 30 seconds long) by Pine Bluff's cinematic genius, Freeman Harrison Owens. In the clip, shot on August 17, 1920, Owens introduced the world to slow-motion film, capturing the iconic Babe Ruth hitting a home run, according to *The Encyclopedia of Arkansas History and Culture*. Reportedly, Ruth sued Owens for revealing his batting technique in slow-motion footage. (Courtesy of Library of Congress.)

Beth Brickell (right), a cast member of the 1967 television series *Gentle Ben*, poses with costars Dennis Weaver (center) and Clint Howard. Born in Camden but raised in Pine Bluff and Brinkley, Brickell is an actress, producer, and director. With appearances in over 100 television shows, she has received Emmy nominations for appearances on episodes of *Hawaii Five-O* and *Bonanza*. She has directed popular television shows and has had roles in several movies, including *Posse* (1975), playing opposite Kirk Douglas. (Courtesy of Ivan Tors Productions.)

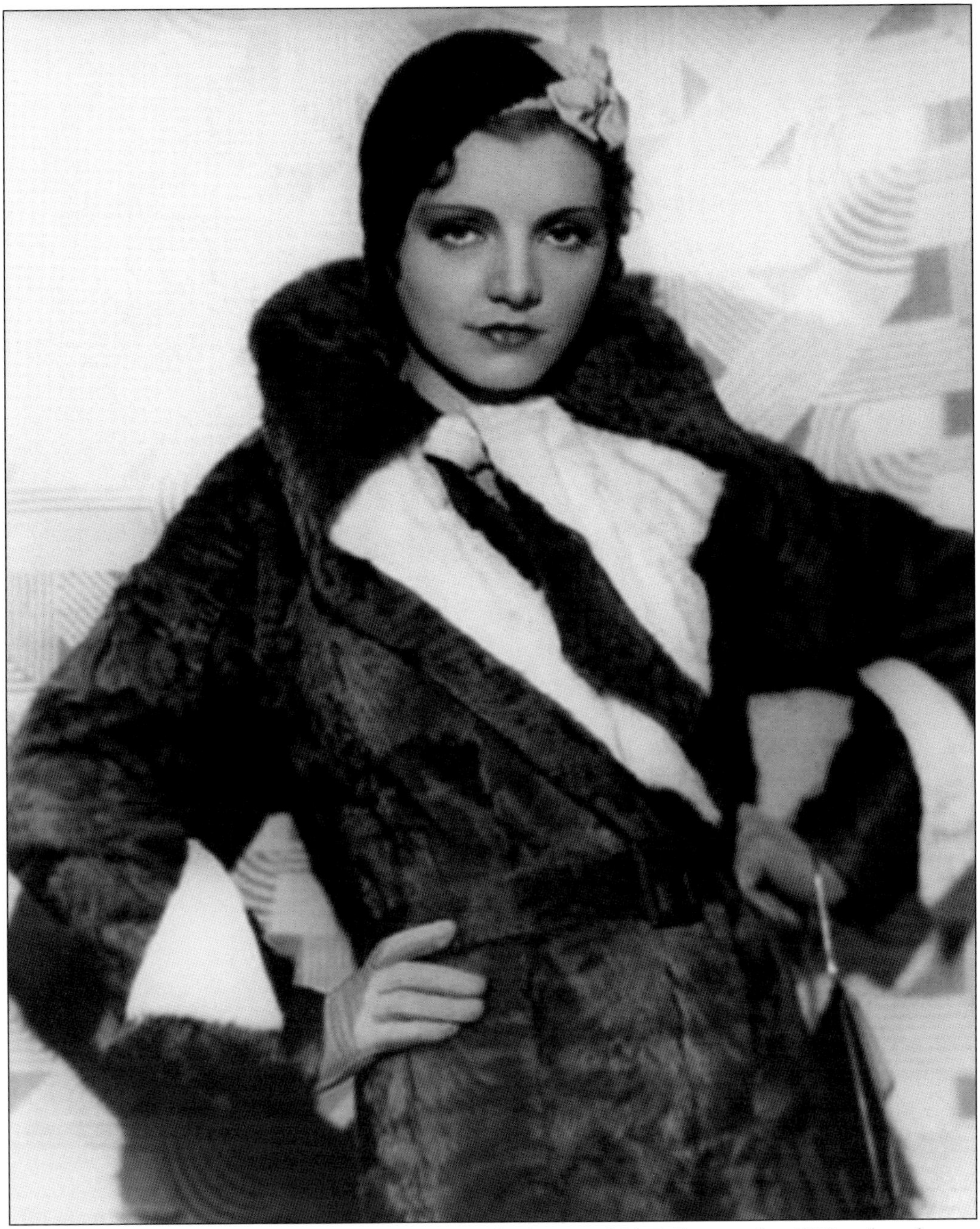

Pine Bluff's Peggy Shannon began dancing with the Ziegfeld Follies in the 1920s, then began appearing in films around 1931 with Spencer Tracy, Ronald Reagan, and others. With numerous starring B-movie roles and serious consideration for a part in *Gone with the Wind* by the late 1930s, she was predicted to be the next major starlet. However, alcoholism increasingly hampered her dependability, and her roles practically stopped coming by 1940. In 1941, her husband came home from a trip and discovered her dead in a kitchen chair, a result of the effects of alcoholism. She was only 32 years old. Distraught, he committed suicide three weeks later in the same chair in which he had found her. (Courtesy of Sergio Leeman.)

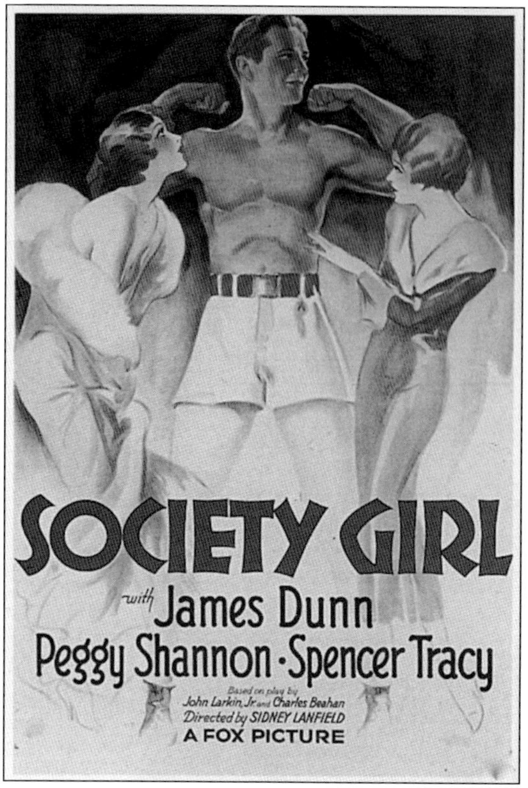

Society Girl was a 1932 moving starring Peggy Shannon, Spencer Tracy, and James Dunn about a boxer training for a championship fight. His romantic interest with a society debutante threatens his athletic pursuits. (Courtesy of Fox Pictures.)

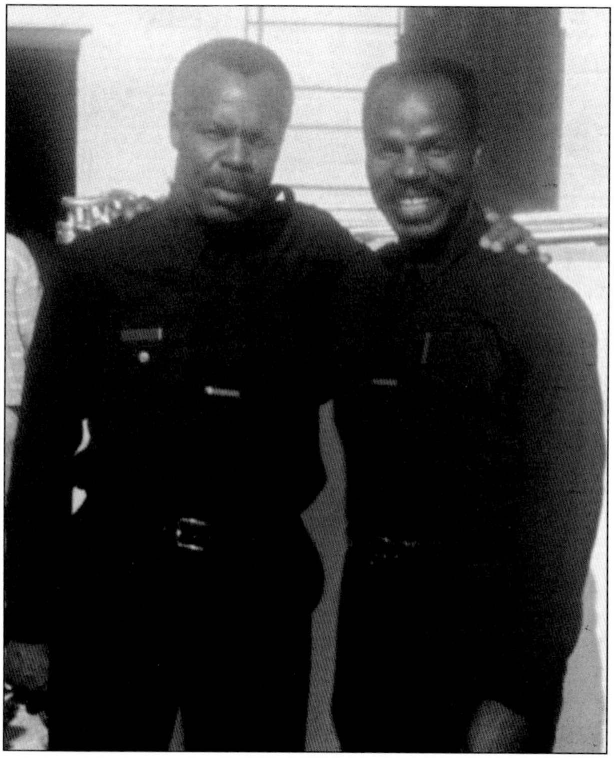

Roy Lee Jones Sr. (right), pictured with actor Danny Glover, was born in Humphrey, Jefferson County. He studied acting with veteran actress Beah Richards and has appeared in several television and film productions, including *Harlem Nights* (1989), *NYPD Blue* (television series, 2001), *Daredevil* (2003), *Girlfriends* (television series, 2005), and *True Grit* (2010). When not engaged in stage and screen exploits, Jones also sings blues, soul, and gospel music professionally. (Courtesy of Roy Lee Jones Sr. via IMDB.)

Broncho Billy Anderson, born in Little Rock but raised in Pine Bluff and St. Louis, Missouri, achieved fame as America's first star in the Western film genre. From 1900 to 1926, he wrote for, produced, directed, or appeared in more than 450 movies. Through his film company, Essanay Studios, Anderson produced the 1915 movie *The Tramp*, in which Charlie Chaplin's iconic persona came to full maturity. Essanay also produced the first American Sherlock Holmes movie in 1916. Anderson's 1921 movie *A Lucky Dog* was the first film to include both members of the classic comedy team of Stan Laurel and Oliver Hardy. In 1958, Anderson received an honorary Oscar award. (Courtesy of Library of Congress.)

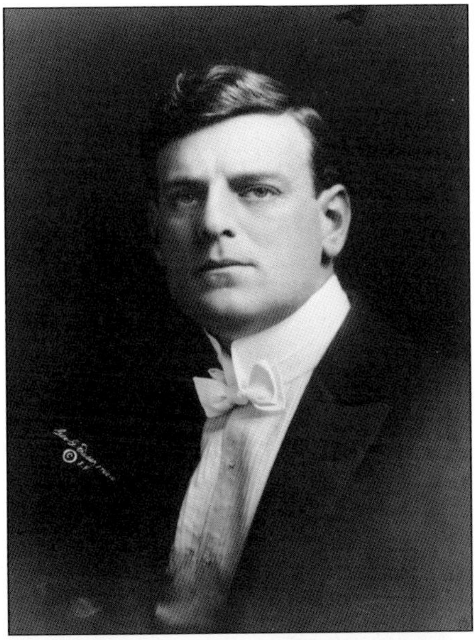

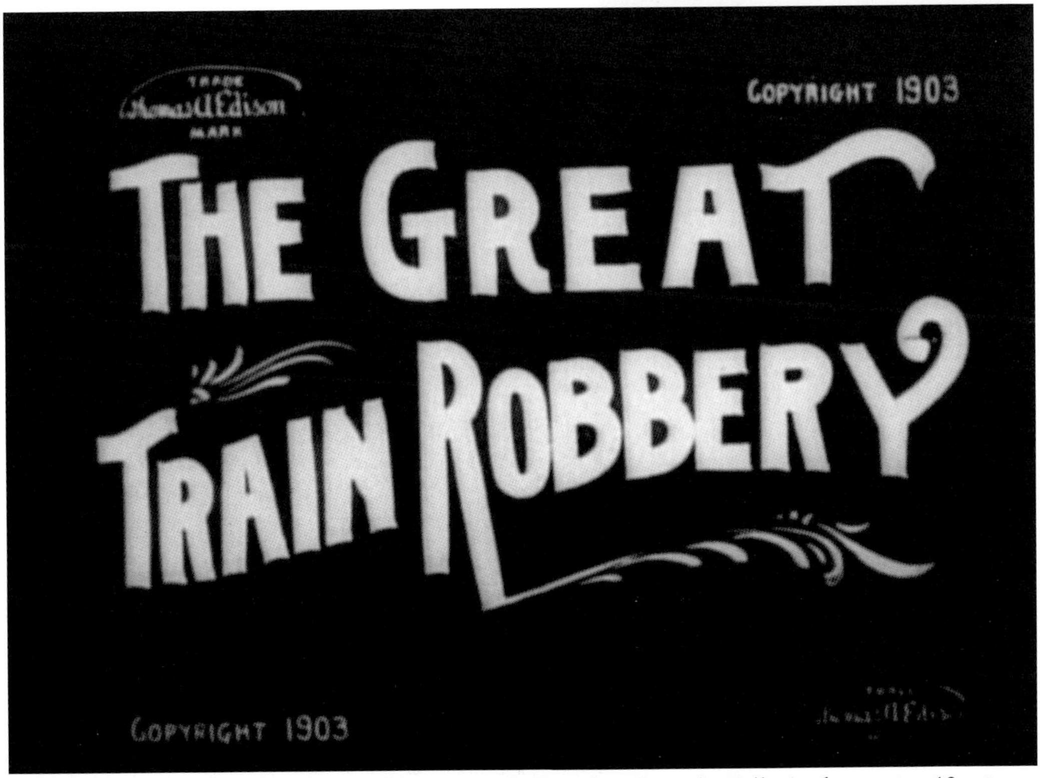

The Great Train Robbery, featuring former Pine Bluff resident Broncho Billy Anderson, is a 10-minute silent movie made in 1903 and considered a milestone in American film history. The movie used a number of innovative techniques, such as on-location filming, camera movement, crosscutting, and composite editing. While the movie's budget was only about $150, it had tremendous box-office success and is considered one of the first cinematic blockbusters. Its producer was inventor Thomas Edison. (Courtesy of Library of Congress.)

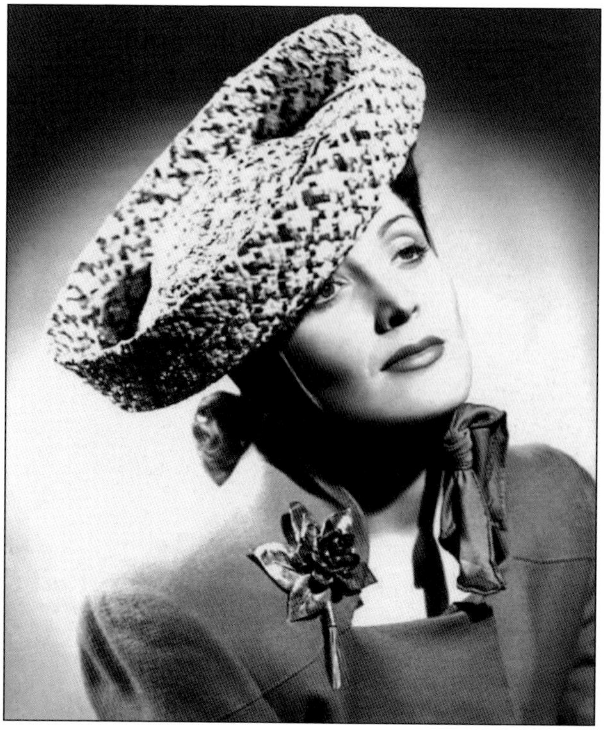

Kaye Linaker (also known as Kate Phillips), a native of Pine Bluff, acted in a range of 1930s and 1940s movies, including several Charlie Chan films. Her filmography includes 56 credits. However, her greatest role in Hollywood came as the coscreenwriter for the 1958 science-fiction cult classic hit *The Blob*, starring Steve McQueen. Linaker coined the movie's title. In spite of the millions the movie made, Linaker was only paid $125 for her work, though she was promised a 10-percent gross of receipts, which she never saw, according to the *Los Angeles Times*. (Courtesy of Sergio Leeman.)

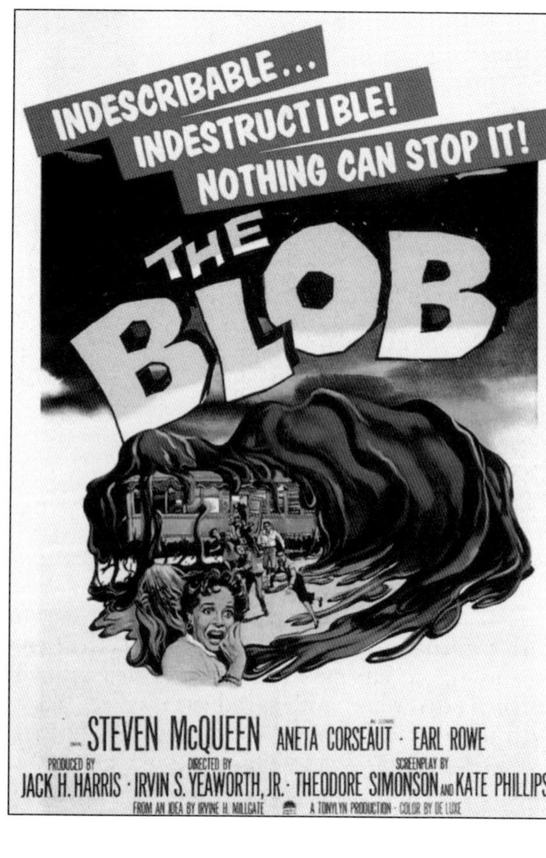

The Blob was a 1958 sci-fi thriller about a mysterious space protoplasm that threatens a small Pennsylvania town. The movie was Steve McQueen's debut lead role. The movie's coscreenwriter was Pine Bluff's Kaye Linaker. It was made on a $100,000 budget, and film historian Tom Weaver estimates the film's gross revenue was about $40 million. It has become a cult classic and inspired a remake in 1988. *Paste* magazine rates it in the top 100 B movies of all time. (Courtesy of Paramount Pictures.)

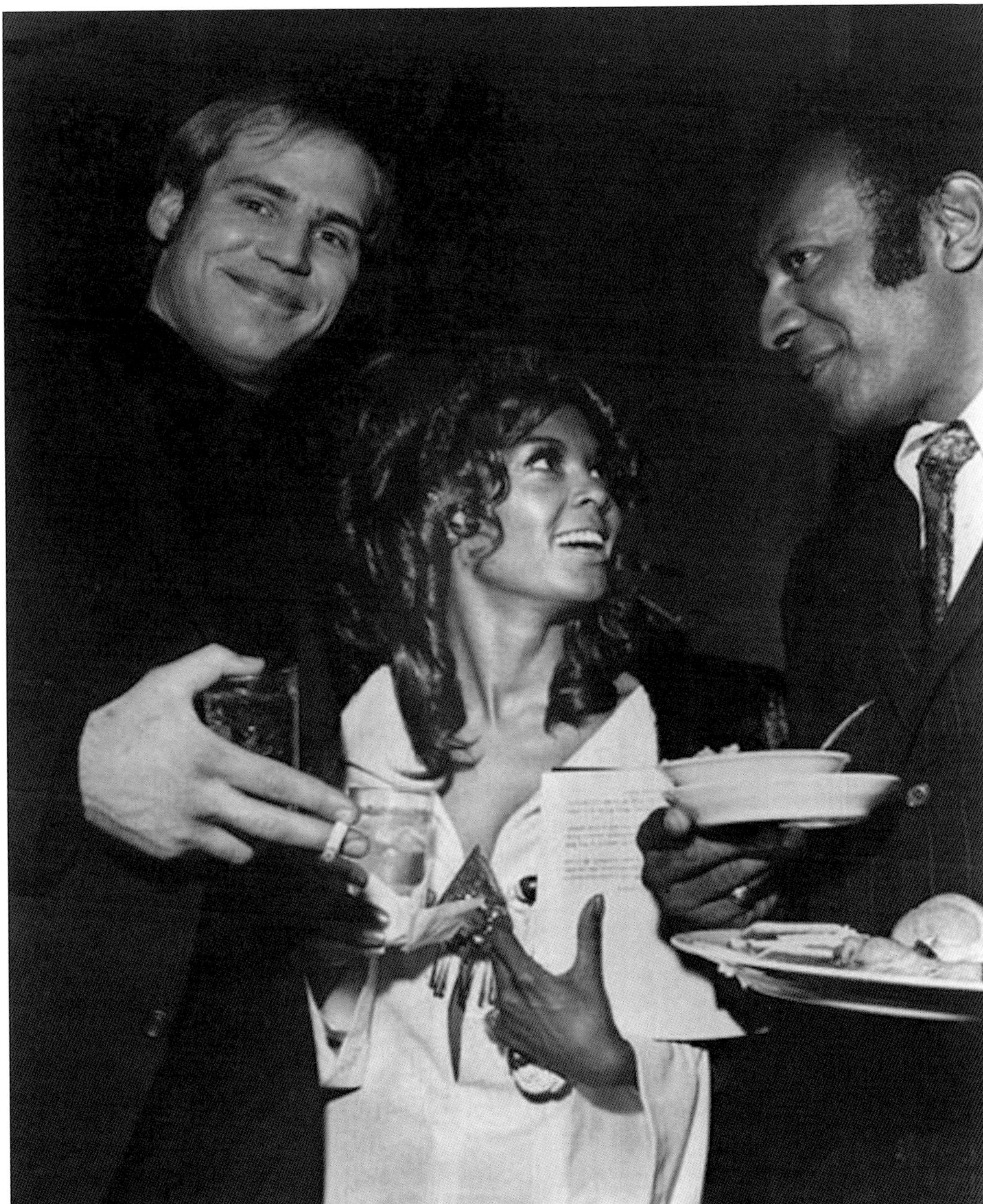

Ena Hartman (center), pioneering actress from Moscow, Arkansas, stands with actors Don Stroud (left) and Raymond St. Jaques. Hartman was the first African American to sign a talent contract with a major television network and was the first black actress to be contracted with NBC-TV. According to *Glamour Girls of Sixties Hollywood*, Hartman, Judy Pace, and Mimi Dillard are the three women who most "paved the way" for black female stars of the 1970s. Hartman played in such popular 1960s shows as *Bonanza*, *It Takes a Thief*, *Ironside*, *Star Trek*, and several movies by the 1970s. (Courtesy of Holdman Photos.)

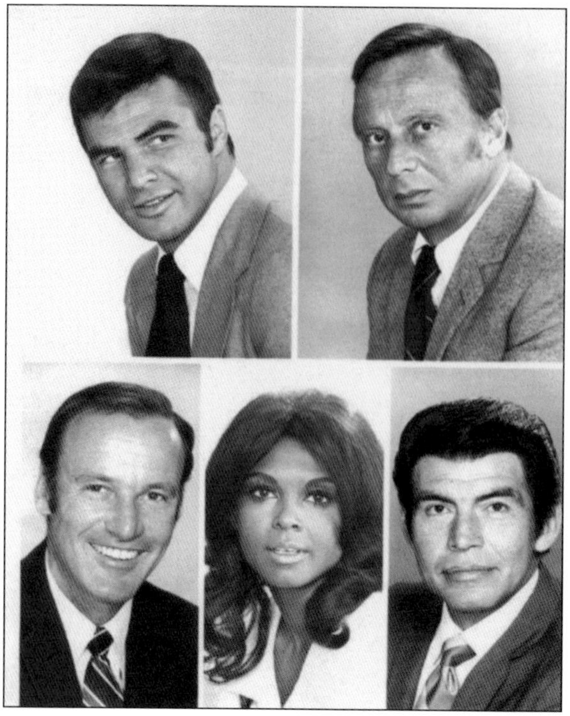

Dan August was a police detective show that aired on ABC from 1970 to 1971. Moscow's Ena Hartman (bottom row, center), who played Katy Grant, is shown with other cast members, including popular film and television star Burt Reynolds (upper left). (Courtesy of ABC Television.)

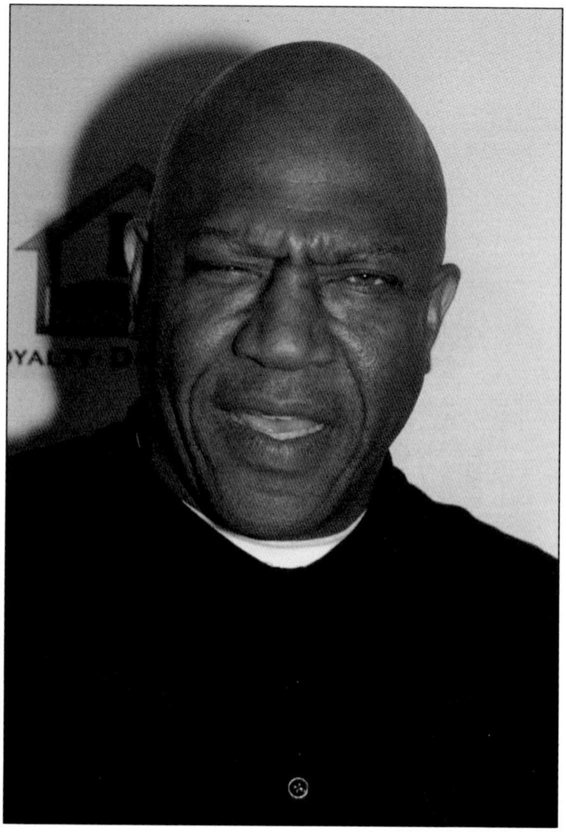

Numerous media sources and publications credit Pine Bluff as the birthplace of actor Tom "Tiny" Lister, stating that he moved as a young toddler to Compton, California, where he grew up. However, Lister's own biographical information omits Pine Bluff, emphasizing his California roots. His official birth records were not available for verification by the time of this publication. With over 80 credits in television and film, Lister has appeared in movies like *Thin Line Between Love and Hate* (1996), *Austin Powers in Goldmember* (2002), and *The Dark Knight* (2008), to name a few. However, he is most well known for his role as the bully, Deebo, in rapper Ice Cube's 1995 movie *Friday*. (Courtesy of Glenn Francis, www.pacificprodigital.com.)

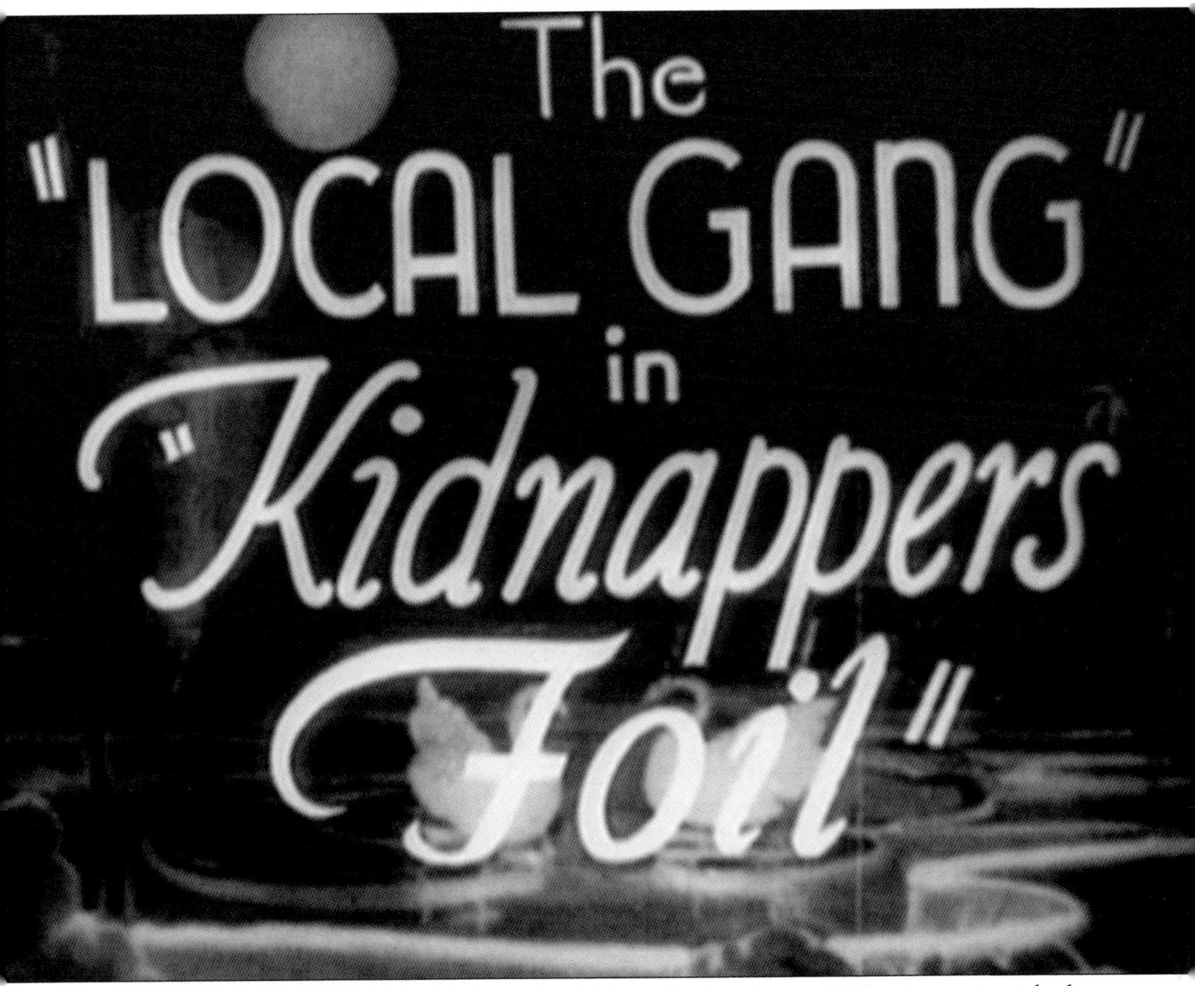

From the 1930s to the 1950s, Texas filmmaker Melton Barker shot a children's movie with the same plot and title, *Kidnappers Foil*, in scores of cities across the nation, including Pine Bluff. Using different local youth in each town and incorporating area music talent, the plot always involved a local gang of youth saving a kidnapped girl named Betty Davis. Though Barker made hundreds of these movies, only 16 survived, including the Pine Bluff version. In 2012, the Library of Congress deemed these surviving films to be historically significant, including them in its prestigious National Film Registry. With only 625 total movie inductions in the National Film Registry's history, *Kidnappers Foil* joins classic productions such as *Gone with the Wind*, *Stormy Weather*, *The Wizard of Oz*, and others in recognition of cultural importance. (Courtesy of the Texas Archive of the Moving Image.)

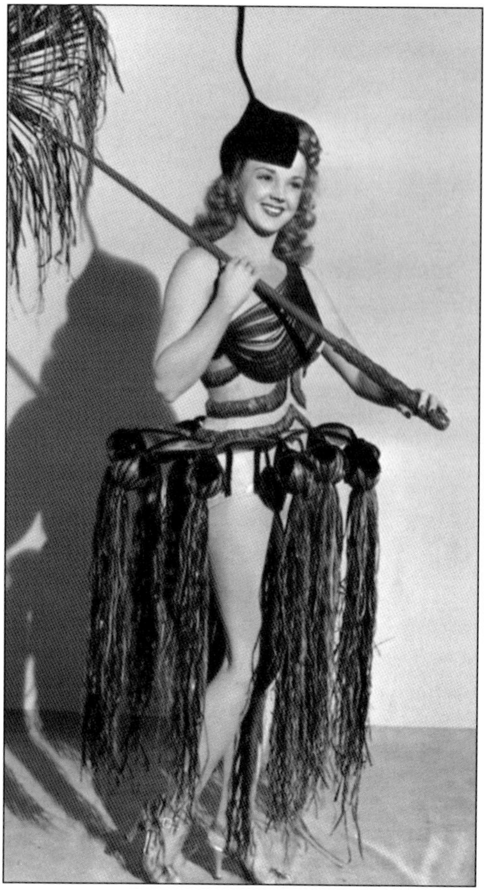

Helen Seamon, born in Dermott and raised in Pine Bluff, was an actress who began as a child singer in matinees at a local theater. She sang her way to Hollywood, scoring roles in the television show *The Lone Ranger* (1949), movies like *Strike Up the Band* (1940) and *Ball of Fire* (1941), and on Broadway. However, her most notable role was a small part in *The Wizard of Oz* (1939). (Courtesy of Magnolia Wesson Images.)

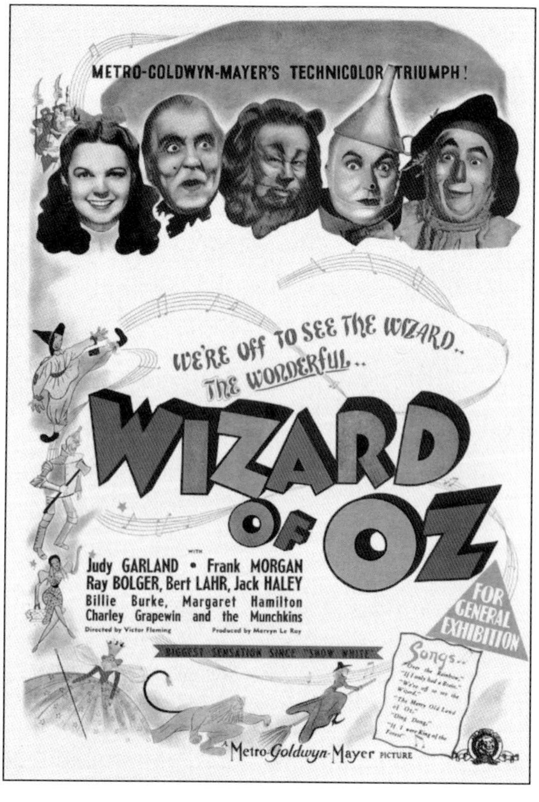

Helen Seamon had an uncredited but memorable role in *The Wizard of Oz* as the beautifully adorned Emerald City citizen holding a Siamese cat. In the scene, her cat catches the attention of Dorothy's dog, Toto, as the Wizard is leaving Emerald City in his balloon. (Courtesy of Metro Goldwyn Mayer.)

Actress Janet Chandler (Lillian Guenther-Barrett) was born in Pine Bluff. A popular model as a teenager, she was also a junior hostess during the 1932 Olympics. She landed roles in 12 movies from 1921 to 1935. Some of her movies include *Cowboy Holiday* (1934), *House of Danger* (1934), and *The Golden West* (1932). (Courtesy of Classic Cinema Gold.)

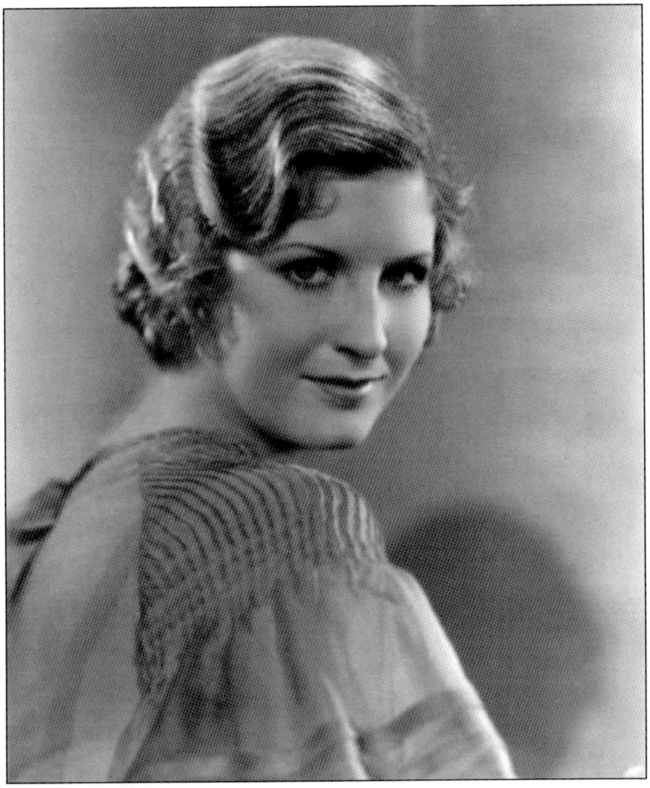

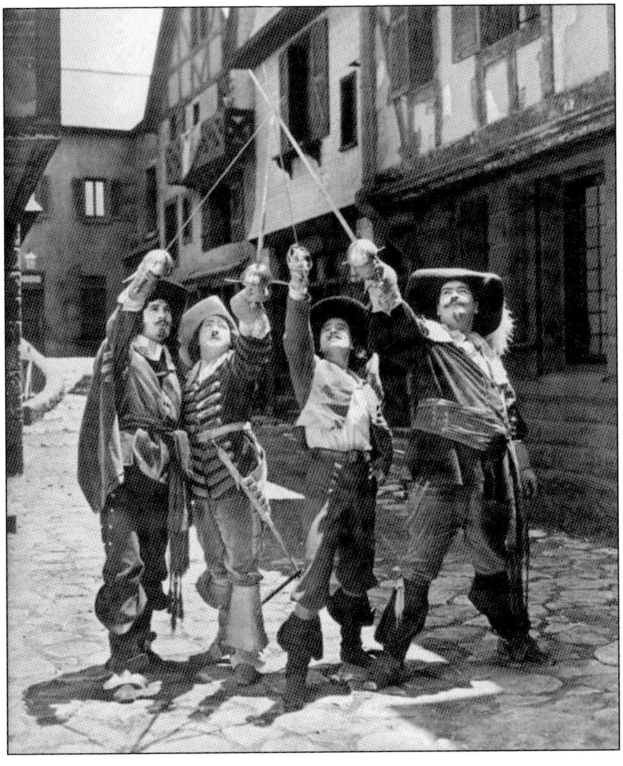

The Three Musketeers, a classic silent film featuring movie legend Douglas Fairbanks Sr., gave Pine Bluff–born Janet Chandler her screen debut. She had an uncredited role as a young child in the popular production, which helped her gain other acting projects. (Courtesy of United Artists.)

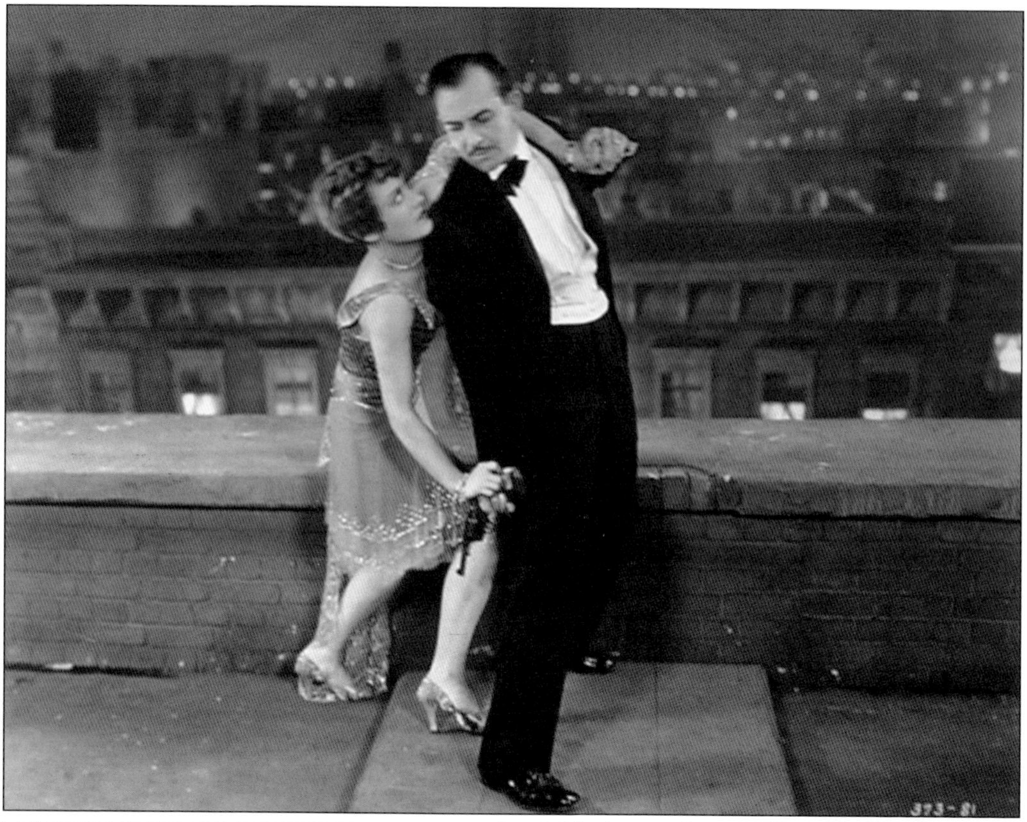

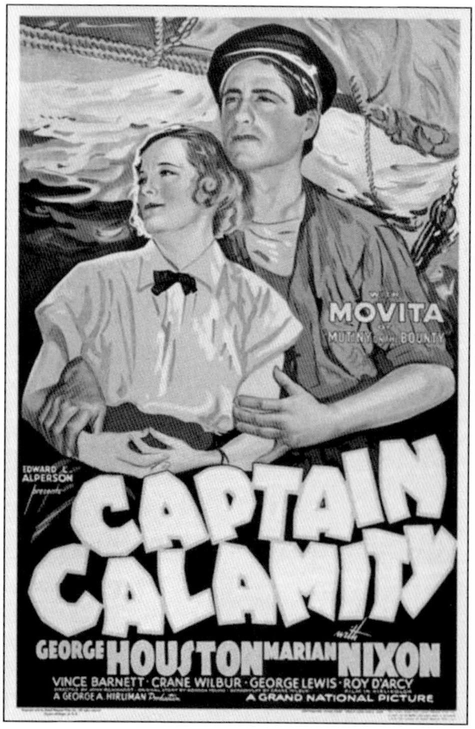

Louis Natheaux, born in Pine Bluff, is shown here with Hollywood superstar Joan Crawford in the 1928 movie *Four Walls*. Natheaux, a character actor, appeared in about 80 movies between 1919 and 1942, ranging from dramas to comedies. (Courtesy of Metro-Goldwyn-Mayer.)

In *Captain Calamity* (1936), Pine Bluff's Louis Natheaux plays a greedy storeowner and local merchant who tries to swindle Capt. Bill Jones (played by George Houston) out of treasure that he has supposedly found. (Courtesy of Grand National Films.)

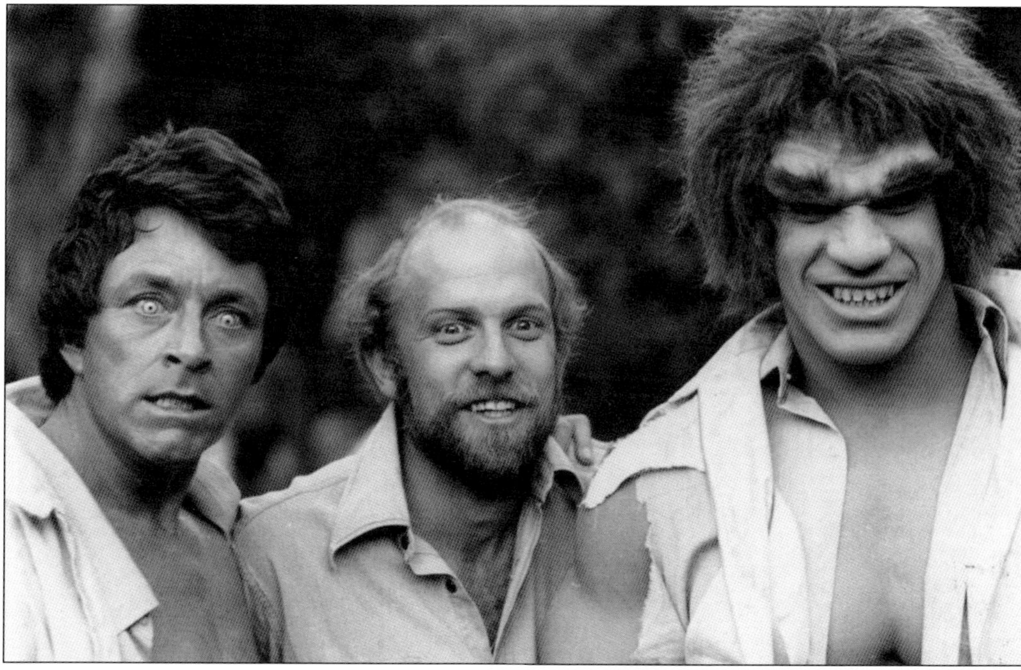

Pine Bluff–born Kenneth Johnson (center), a television writer, producer, and director, stands with cast members Bill Bixby (left) and Lou Ferrigno from the 1970s–1980s series *The Incredible Hulk*, for which he produced and wrote. Other television creations of his include *The Bionic Woman*, *The Six Million Dollar Man*, the original miniseries *V*, and *Alien Nation*. Johnson has garnered two Emmy nominations. (Courtesy of Kenneth Johnson.)

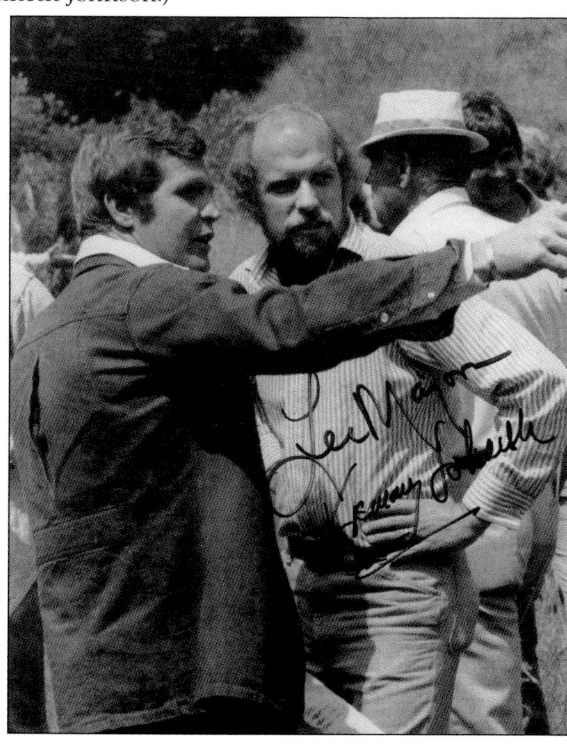

The Six Million Dollar Man, starring Lee Majors (left), was produced by Pine Bluff's Kenneth Johnson (right) and aired on ABC Television from 1974 to 1978. It was one of the most popular programs of the decade. The series was about a former astronaut who survived a crash and underwent surgery, in which his limbs were replaced with bionic parts, giving him superhuman strength. (Courtesy of Kenneth Johnson.)

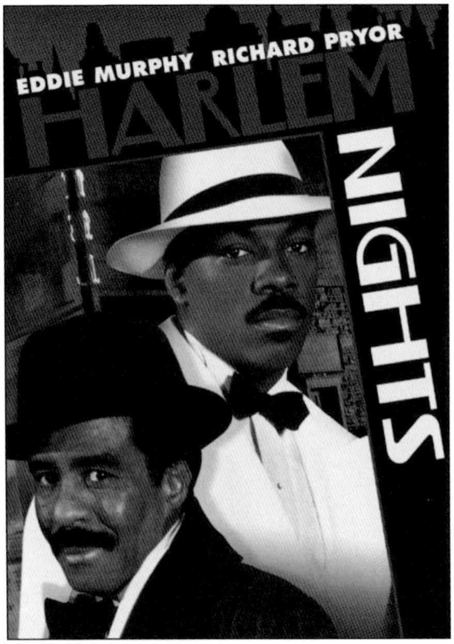

When legendary producer and musician Quincy Jones needed a skilled arranger, conductor, and orchestrator for the 1989 movie *Harlem Nights*, he turned to UAPB graduate Garnett Brown. Brown has numerous film and television credits, including *A Soldier's Story*, *A Hero Ain't Nothing But a Sandwich*, *Fat Man and Little Boy*, *Gilligan's Island*, *Hart to Hart*, *The Carol Burnett Show*, and *The Richard Pryor Show*. (Courtesy of Paramount Pictures.)

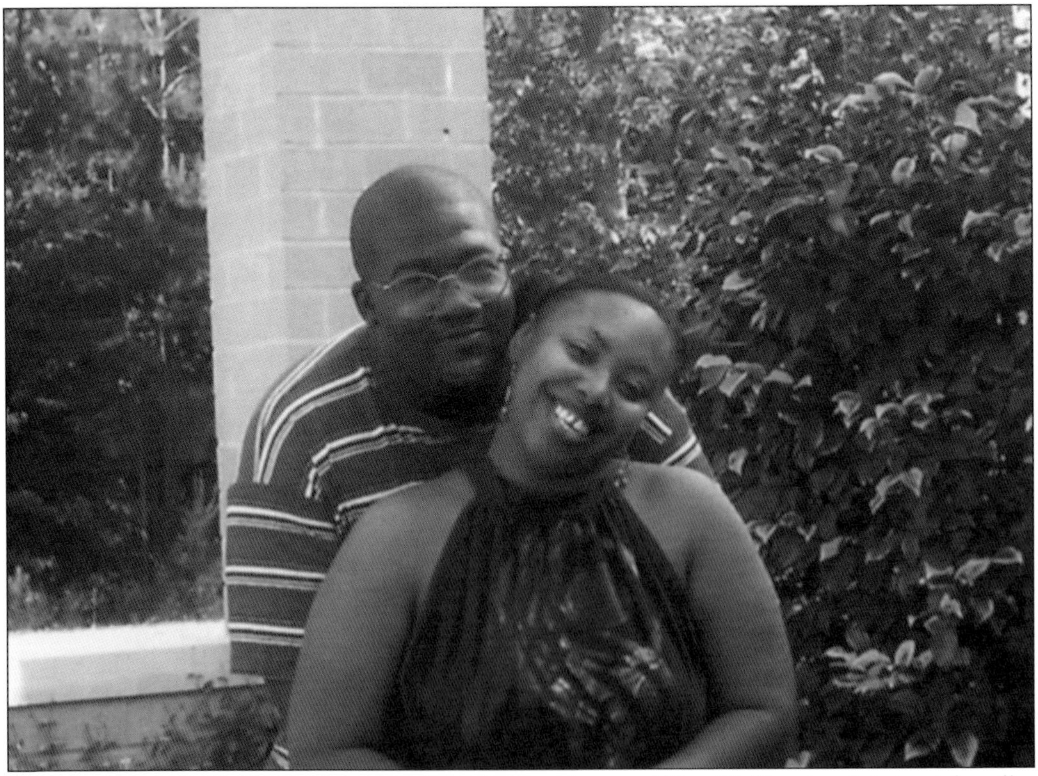

If Devlon Chandler Sr. (left), a longtime Pine Bluff resident, and Pine Bluff native Arinitra Chandler (right), continue with their pace of movie productions, the married couple could become Pine Bluff's dynamic duo of film. Since 2010, they have cowritten, coproduced, directed, and acted in eight short films and three feature movies. Fans have seen their work, including *Let's Go On A Date*, *Deal With It*, *Karma*, and others. (Courtesy of Devlon Chandler.)

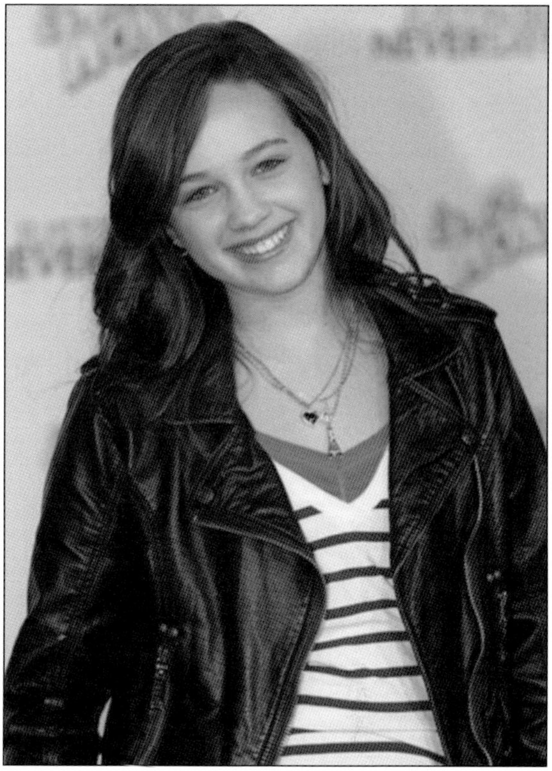

Mary Mouser, one of Pine Bluff's most talented and promising young actresses today, continues the area's film and screen traditions She was recently tapped to play Karen Grant on ABC's popular television series *Scandal*. Her work in film and television includes productions like *Medeas* (2013), *Frenemies* (2012) *Body of Proof* (2011), *Bride Wars* (2009), and *Monk* (2005), among others. She comes from a family of acting talent—her brother, Aaron Parker Mouser, has appeared in television shows and movies like *The Runaways* (2010), *Everbody Hates Chris* (2007), *Wristcutters: A Love Story* (2006), and others. (Courtesy of Mary Mouser via IMDB.)

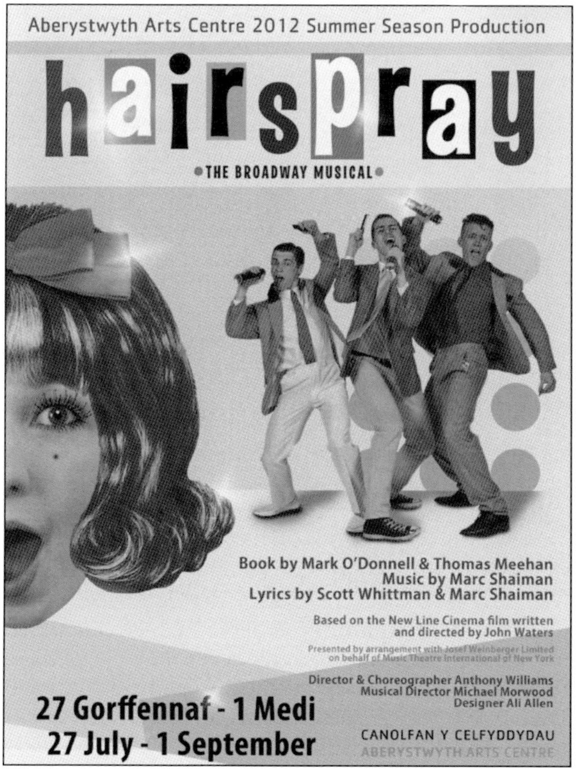

Hairspray, a Broadway musical and a 1988 cult movie about a teenage dance show, was loosely based on 35-year Pine Bluff resident Buddy Deane's actual Baltimore dance show, which aired from 1957 to 1964. The movie explores the lives of 1960s teen dancers and the manner in which parents and television executives reacted when confronted with integrating the show's cast. Deane made a cameo appearance in the movie. (Courtesy of Aberstwyth Arts Centre.)

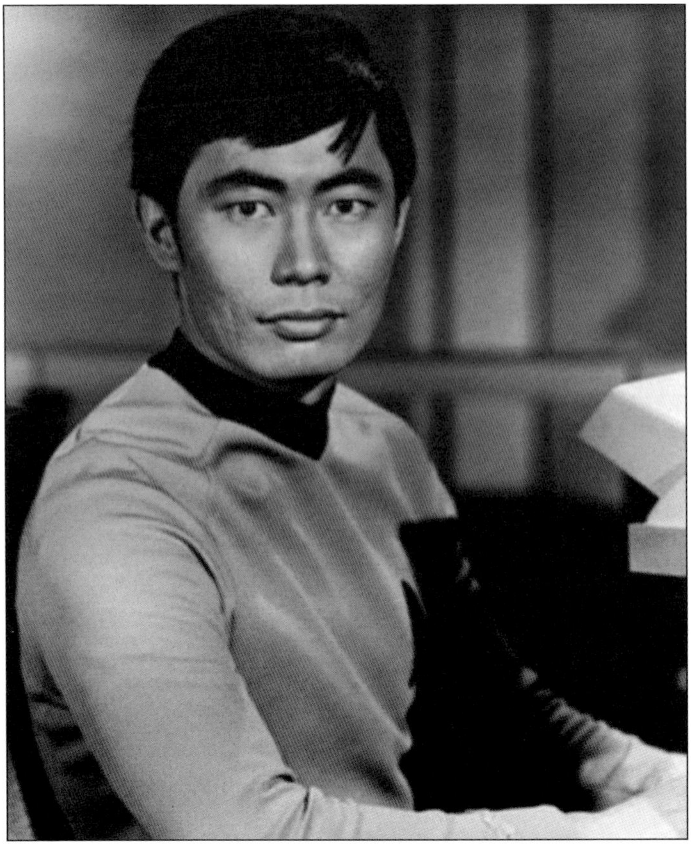

George Takei, actor, director, and author, best known as Lt. Hikaru Sulu of the USS *Enterprise* in the 1960s television series *Star Trek*, was born in Los Angeles. However, in 1942, when he was five years old, his family was forced to move to the Rohwer War Relocation Center in Rohwer, Desha County, for internment because of their Japanese ancestry. As an actor, Takei has starred in numerous other movies and television programs. (Courtesy of NBC Television.)

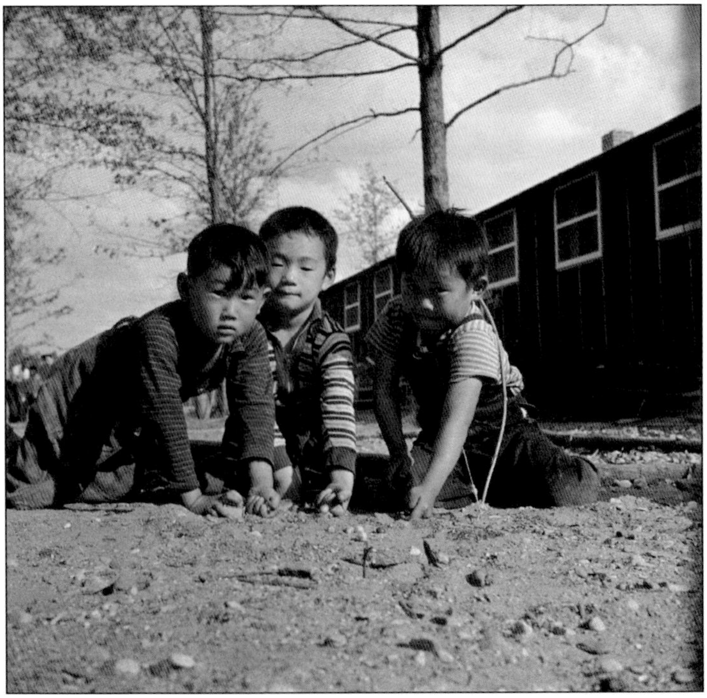

Japanese American boys play in an internment camp in Rohwer, Arkansas, around 1942. A 2005 PBS documentary, *A Time of Fear*, chronicled the plight of 16,000 Japanese Americans who were forced to relocate during World War II to two Delta Lowlands internment camps. Actor George Takei, future cast member of the 1960s television show *Star Trek*, and other former camp residents shared their painful memories of life in the camps. (Courtesy of Library of Congress.)

The 1973 movie *White Lightning*, filmed in Scott and Keo, was one of several Hollywood movies shot in the Delta Lowlands. Other motion pictures filmed in part or in full in the area include the following: *End of the Line* (1979), shot partially in Pine Bluff and Scott; *Shotgun Stories* (2007), shot partially in Keo and England; and *Mud* (2012), filmed partially in Dumas, Lake Village, and an island near Eudora. While the 1980 movie *Brubaker* was not filmed in Arkansas, it is based on actual efforts to reform Cummins and Tucker Prisons in the 1960s and 1970s. (Courtesy of United Artists.)

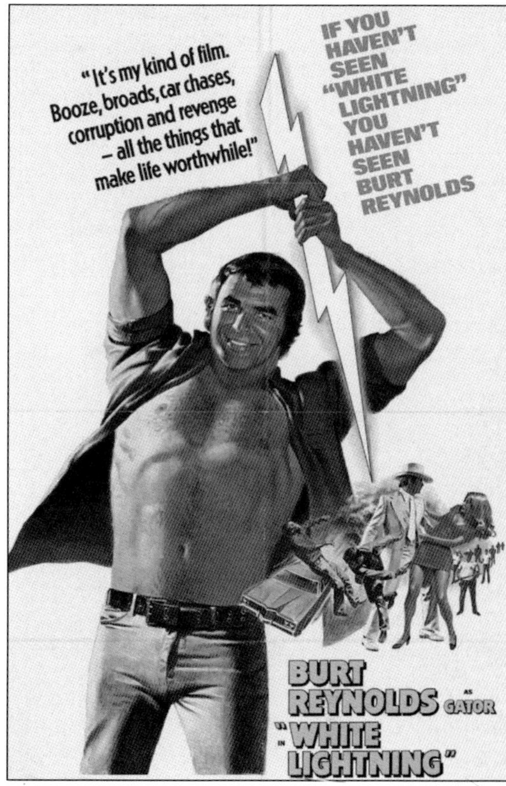

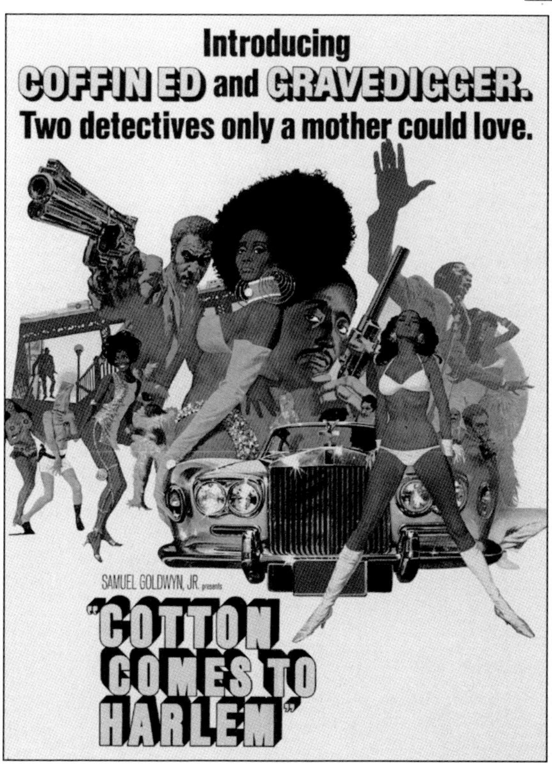

Cotton Comes to Harlem is a 1970 movie about the pursuit of a lost bale of cotton stuffed with money. The movie was adapted from the novel by award-winning author Chester Himes, a 1920s Pine Bluff resident whose literary work was profoundly impacted by the racism he experienced while living in the area. Actor Ossie Davis made his directorial debut in this film. Himes wrote three other novels that became movies: *Come Back Charleston Blue* (1972), *A Rage in Harlem* (1991), starring Danny Glover, and the television movie *Cosmic Slop* (1994). (Courtesy of United Artists.)

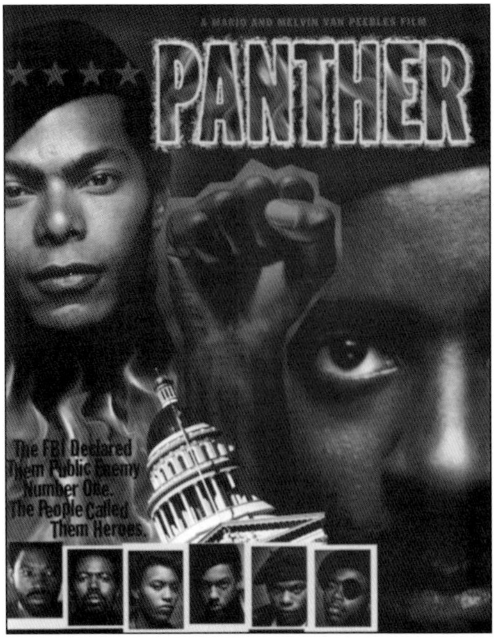

Panther (1995), directed by Mario Van Peebles, traced the story of the Black Panther Party's (BPP) founding in the 1960s, focusing on its internal and external struggles. The experiences of two Jefferson County natives and Black Panther icons are portrayed in the movie: Pine Bluff's Bobby Hutton, the first recruited BPP member; and Wabbaseka's Eldridge Cleaver, BPP minister of information and author of the best seller *Soul on Ice*. (Courtesy of TriBeCa Productions.)

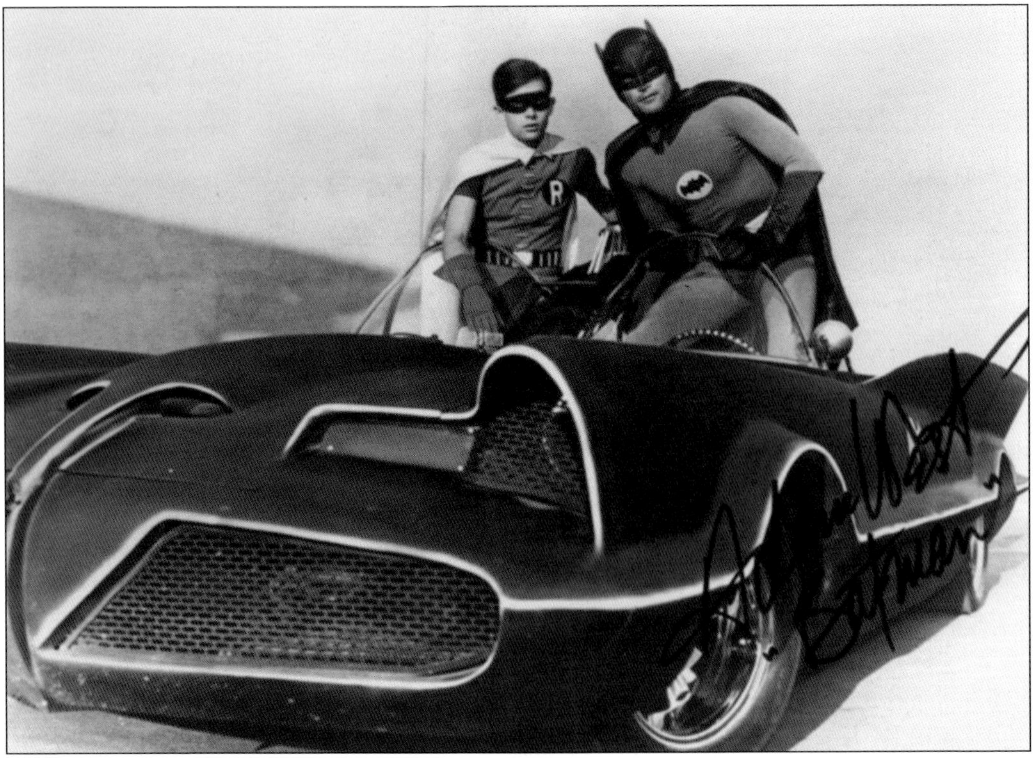

The 1960s *Batman* television series crew included Harold Wooley, a native of Pine Bluff, who served as its sound effects editor. Wooley was nominated for Emmy Awards for *Batman* (1966), the television movie *Brian's Song* (1972), and *The Legend of Lizzie Borden* (1975). Wooley was sound editor in several other popular series, like *The Green Hornet*, *Annie Oakley*, and *Dick Tracy*. (Courtesy of ABC Television.)

Bluesland: A Portrait of American Music is a 1993 documentary chronicling the complex history of blues and its impact on American music. Examining a cross section of the nation's most revered blues pioneers, it highlights Jefferson County's Big Bill Broonzy, who is also featured on the cover. (Courtesy of Toby Byron.)

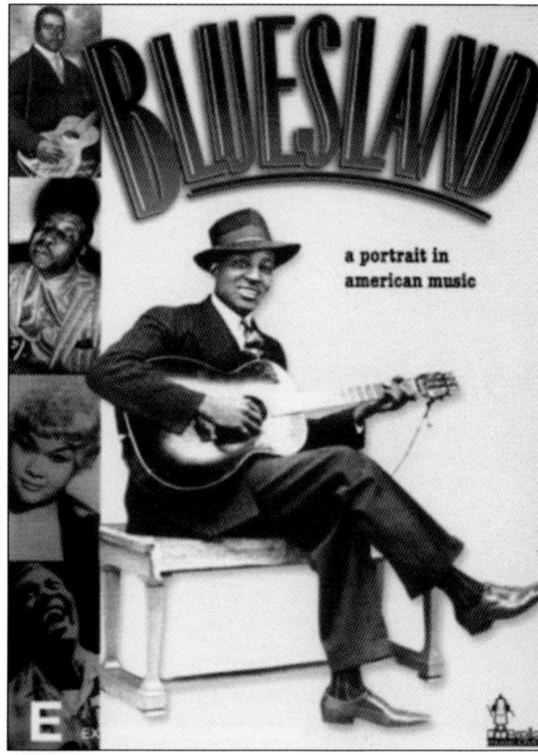

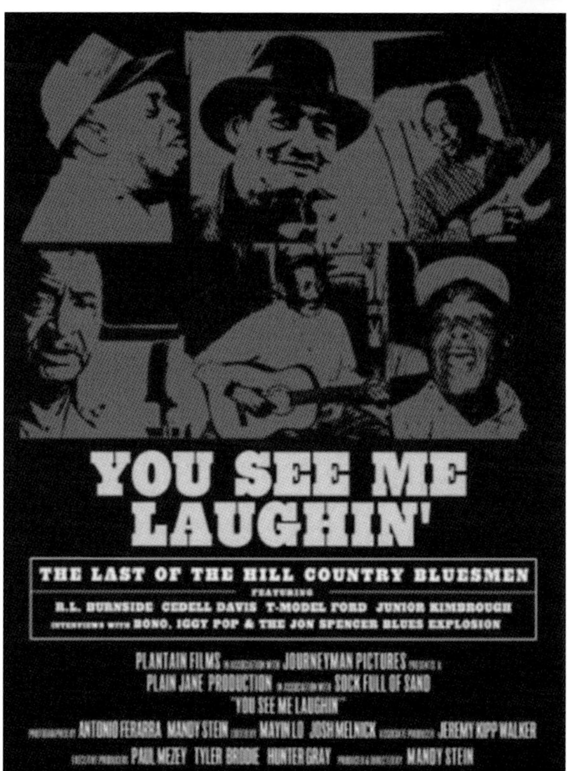

The 2003 documentary *You See Me Laughin'* explores the lives of six artists considered to be the last original pre–World War II bluesmen. Longtime Pine Bluff resident Cedell Davis, one of those highlighted, was also featured in the 1992 documentary *Deep Blues* and was the subject of the 1984 documentary *Blues Back Home*. Davis's accomplishments are underscored by his resilience. He learned to play his guitar upside-down with a butter knife because of the effects of childhood polio, and he survived a St. Louis juke joint stampede that left him in a wheelchair for life. (Courtesy of Journeyman Pictures.)

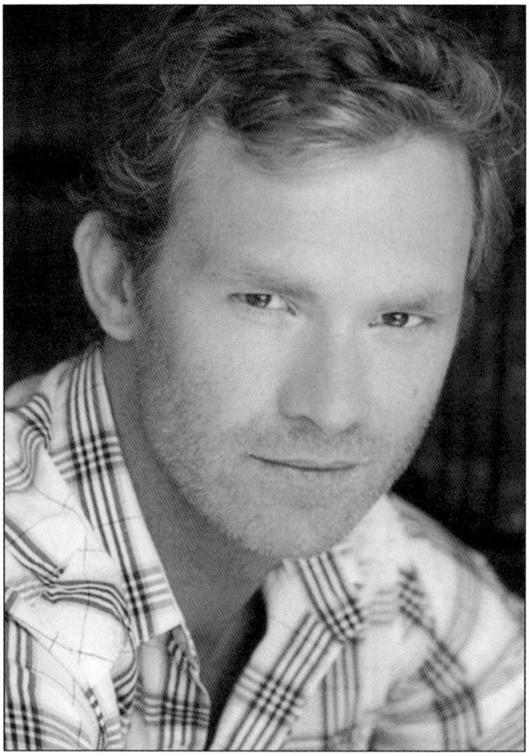

When Jason Davis of Pine Bluff appeared in the 2006 movie *Talladega Nights: The Ballad of Ricky Bobby*, he was adding to an expanding résumé. Davis has had roles in movies like *Seeking Justice* (2011) with Nicholas Cage and *Step Brothers* (2008) with Will Ferrell. He has 48 credits in film and television, including his most important work, *Lake City* (2008), in which he costarred with actress Sissy Spacek. (Courtesy of Jason Davis via IMDB.)

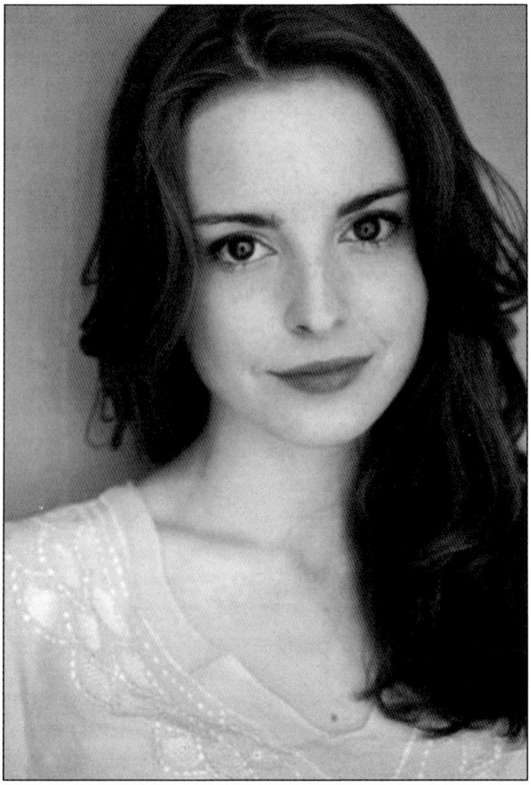

Elizabeth Rice, a recipient of the Grand Jury Award for best actress at the 2008 Solstice Film Festival for *From Within* (2008), is a native of Pine Bluff. She has acted in television, including *ER* (2001), *The Mystery of Natalie Wood* (2004), *Mad Men* (2007–2014), *CSI: Crime Scene Investigation* (2009), and *Cult* (2013). She has numerous other credits dating back to 1997. (Courtesy of Elizabeth Rice via IMDB.)

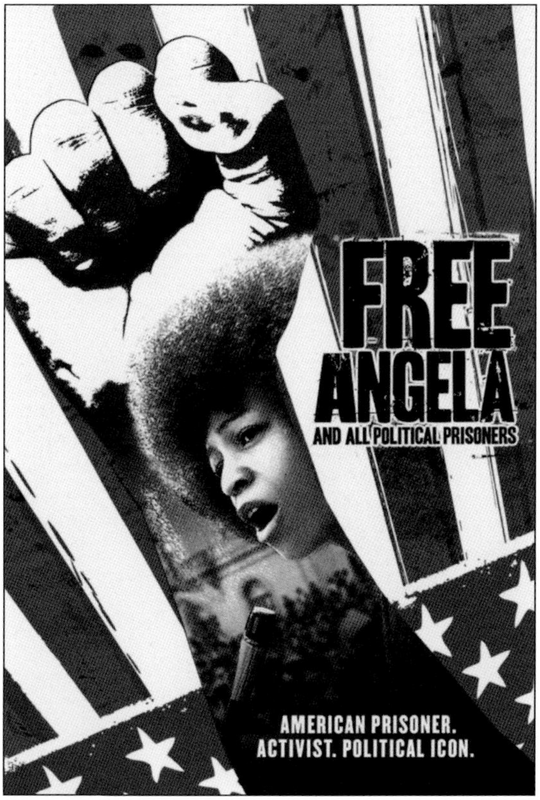

Free Angela Davis and All Political Prisoners is a 2012 documentary about former Black Panther Party member Angela Davis and the FBI murder charges that almost landed her in prison in 1972. The documentary highlights her trial, called at the time "the trial of the century," and the efforts of her lead defense attorney, Leo Branton Jr., a native of Pine Bluff. Branton's brilliant court strategy and closing arguments are cited by legal scholars as the primary reason for Davis's exoneration. Incidentally, the following year, Branton served as associate producer for the 1973 documentary *Jimi Hendrix*. (Courtesy of Shola Lynch.)

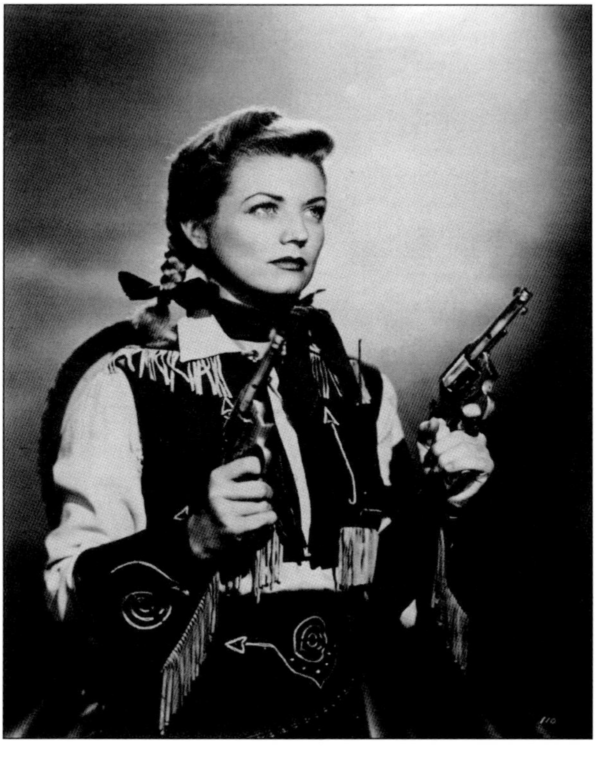

Gail Davis, raised in McGehee, compiled 32 credits in Hollywood feature films, including 14 with Gene Autry. However, she is best known for her pioneering role in the *Annie Oakley* television show. The show (1954–1957) fictionalized the experiences of the 19th-century gun-toting sharpshooter Annie Oakley. In her role, Davis became the first female to star in a television Western and was television's first female heroine. Also a singer, Davis's "I'm a Female Thru and Thru" has been cited by *The All Music Guide to Country* as one of the most popular 1950s Western songs. (Courtesy of Gene Autry Oklahoma Museum.)

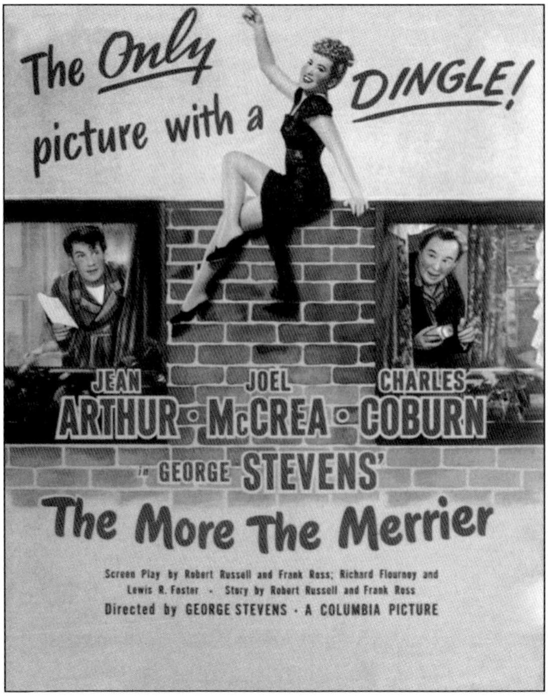

The More the Merrier is a 1943 movie about two men and a woman sharing an apartment when a romance develops. Richard Flournoy of Pine Bluff was nominated for an Oscar for his screenwriting. Flournoy wrote for 26 other films from 1934 to 1955, including several *Blondie* series movies. (Courtesy of Columbia Pictures.)

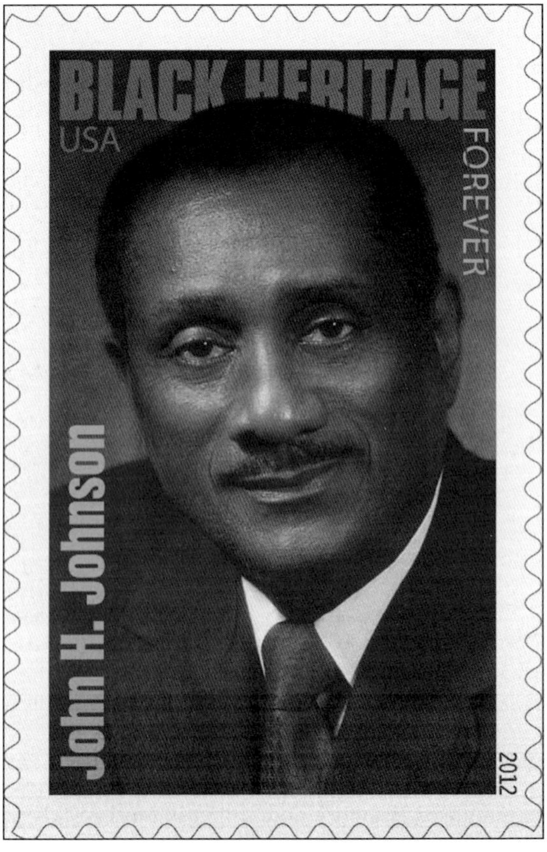

John H. Johnson of Arkansas City, the founder of *Ebony* and *Jet* magazines, was also the executive producer for the syndicated television program *Ebony/Jet Showcase*. The show highlighted African American achievers like Oprah Winfrey, Magic Johnson, and others in various professions. It aired 222 episodes and ran from 1983 to 1993. Johnson was also the subject of a 2005 television movie about his life. (Courtesy of US Postal Service.)

Byron Vaughns (at podium, left), former Pine Bluff resident and UAPB graduate, receives an award from UAPB chancellor Dr. Lawrence Davis Jr. Vaughns has directed network children's cartoon shows like *Animaniacs*, *Smurfs*, and *Alvin and the Chipmunks*, and he has produced or illustrated for *The Pink Panther*, *101 Dalmatians*, *Dumb & Dumber*, *Casper's Haunted Christmas*, *The Lionhearts*, and many others. He won an Emmy for his direction of *Steven Spielberg Presents: Tiny Toon Adventures*. (Courtesy of Thomas Vaughns.)

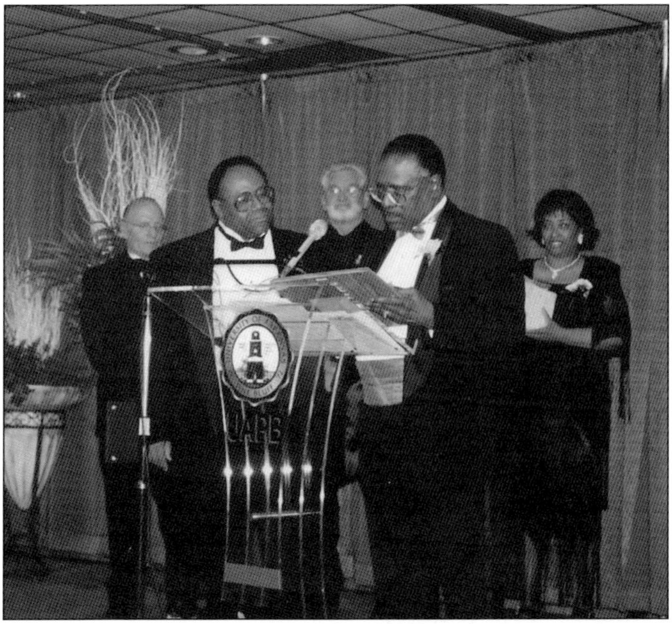

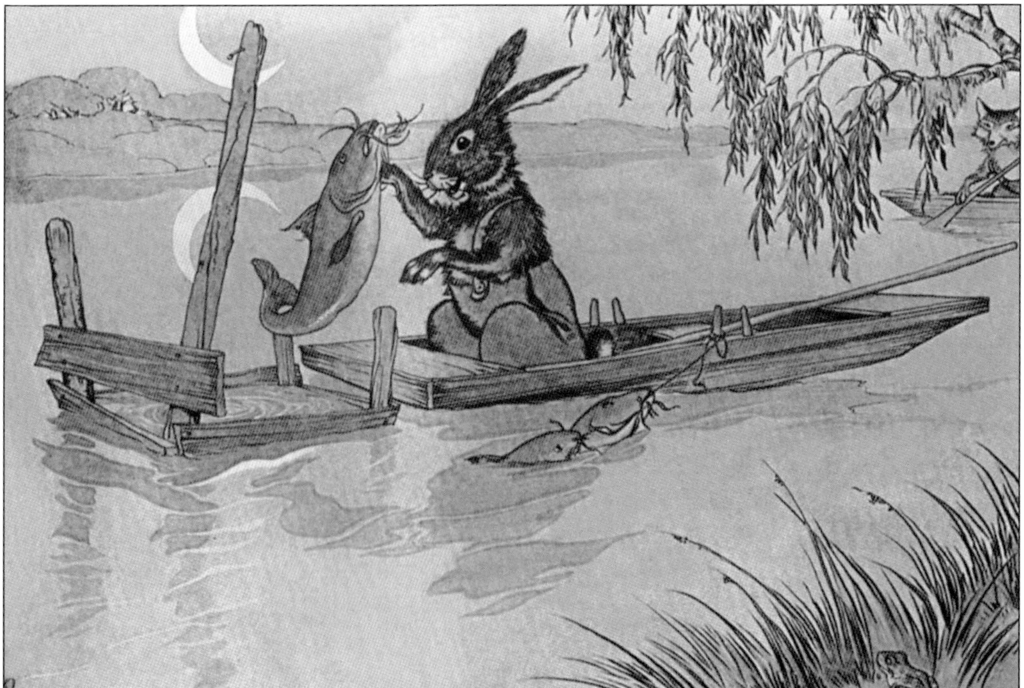

Brer Rabbit steals catfish from Brer Fox's fish trap in a 1917 illustration. In 2006, Pine Bluff's Byron Vaughns directed *The Adventures of Brer Rabbit*, a Universal Studios animated movie with voice characterizations by Danny Glover, Wanda Sykes, Nick Cannon, Wayne Brady, and D.L. Hughley. It was nominated for an Annie Award (the highest honor given in animation). The movie is based on Dr. Julius Lester's celebrated book *Uncle Remus: The Complete Tales*. Lester, an award-winning children's literature author, spent summers with his grandmother in Pine Bluff while growing up. (Courtesy of Milo Winter.)

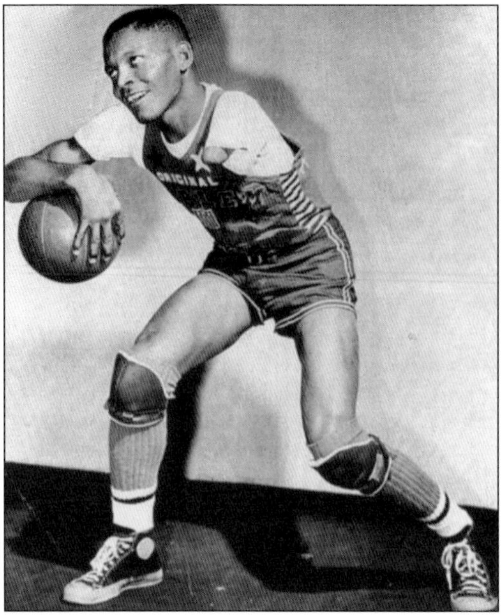

Former Pine Bluff resident and St. Peter Catholic High School basketball star Boid "One Arm" Buie was a member of the Harlem Globetrotters team highlighted in the Showtime documentary *The Team that Changed the World* (2005). It examines Buie's 1948–1951 Globetrotter squad, which actually beat the National Basketball League champions, Minneapolis Lakers, and is credited with helping to hasten integration in sports. Buie averaged 18 points a game as a nine-year Globetrotter. He is an inductee in the Tennessee State University Athletics Hall of Fame. (Courtesy of Jim Boyd.)

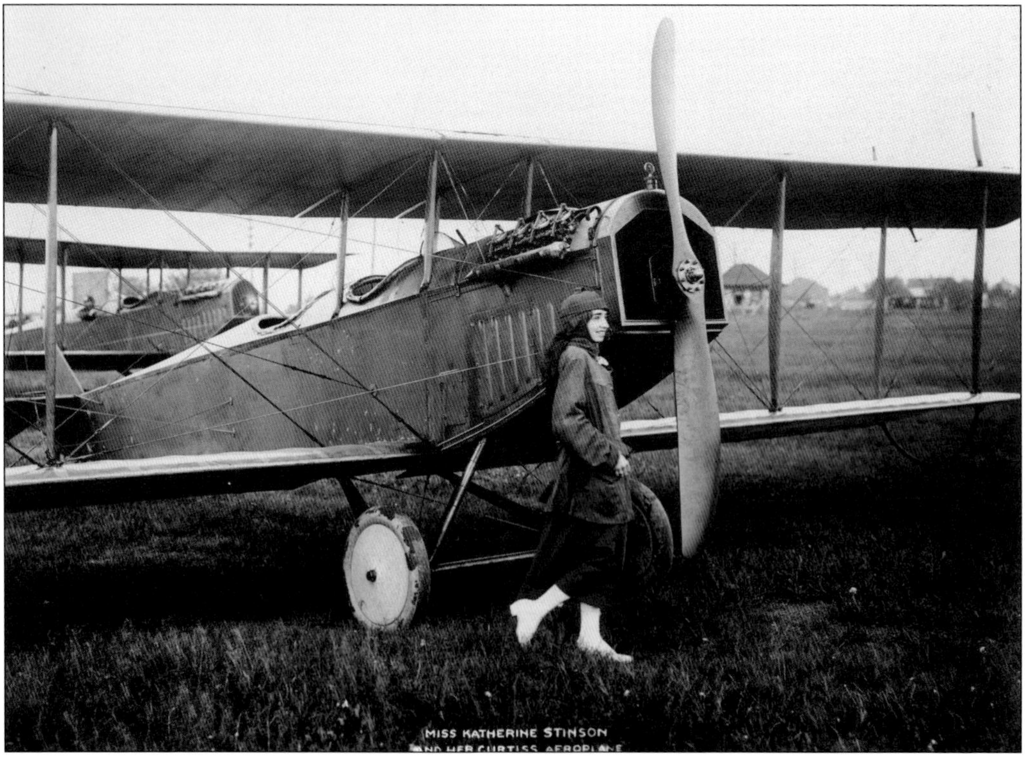

Katherine Stinson: Her Story is a PBS documentary about the former Pine Bluff resident who, in 1911, became the nation's fourth woman to acquire a pilot's license (obtained while living in Pine Bluff). She was the first woman to master the loop-the-loop maneuver, the first person ever to fly at night, and the first to undertake night skywriting. Stinson was also the first woman to fly in Asia and the first female commissioned airmail pilot in the United States. In 1917, she set a world record for the longest nonstop flight, at 610 miles. (Courtesy of Library of Congress.)

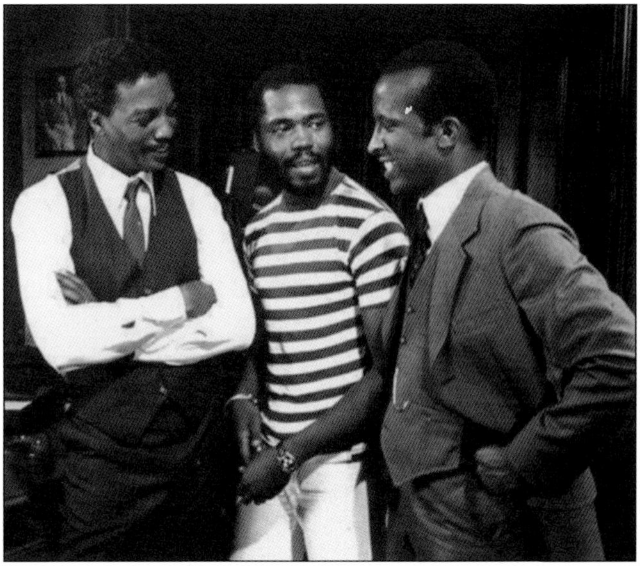

Roots: The Next Generations was the 1979 Emmy-winning television sequel to the landmark miniseries *Roots: The Saga of an American Family*. The 1979 series followed the family of author Alex Haley from 1882 to the 1960s, largely tracing the life of his father, Simon Haley, played by actor Dorian Harewood (far right), shown here in a scene from the series. Simon was a Pine Bluff resident in the 1940s and 1950s, serving as the head of the UAPB agriculture department. The music for the series was arranged and orchestrated by UAPB graduate Garnett Brown. (Courtesy of ABC Broadcasting.)

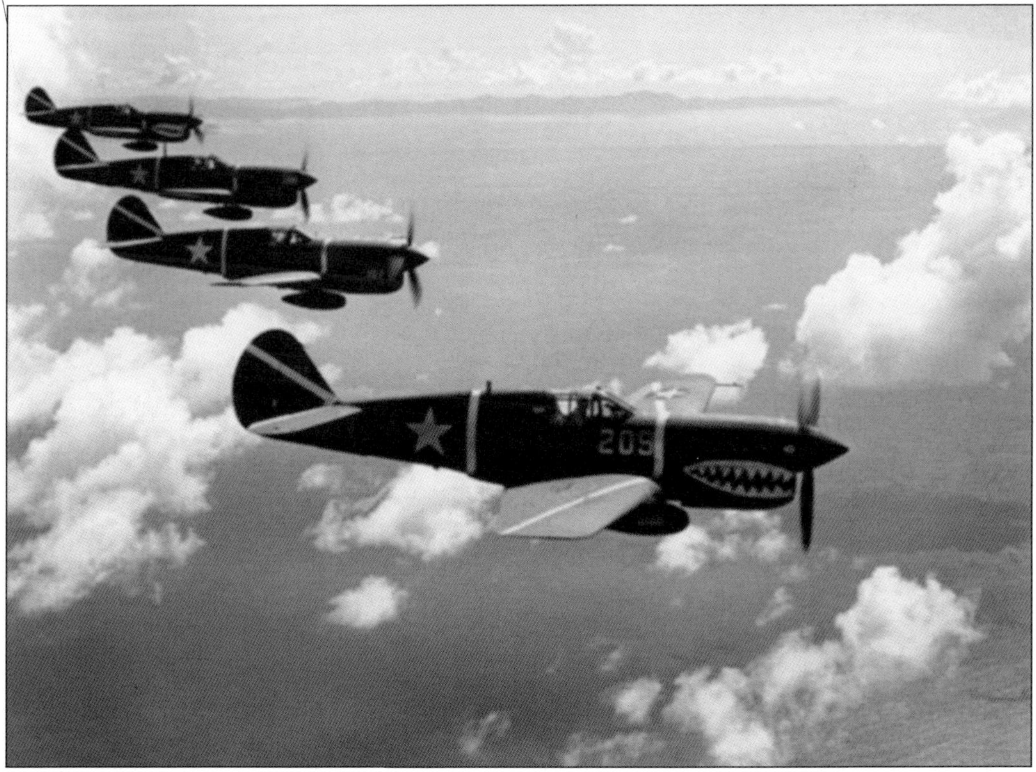

During World War II, the US Navy partnered with Walt Disney Studios to create a pilot training film, *Offensive Tactics Against Enemy Fighters*. The Navy called on a legendary aviator to produce and narrate it, Pine Bluff native John "Jimmy" Thach. A decorated combat pilot, Thatch created revolutionary aviation maneuvers like the "Thach Weave" and the "Big Blue Blanket." Before the war, he performed stunt work for Clark Gable's 1931 movie *Hell Divers*. Later, Thach became a celebrated Navy admiral, landing on the cover of *Time* magazine in 1958. (Courtesy of US Air Force.)

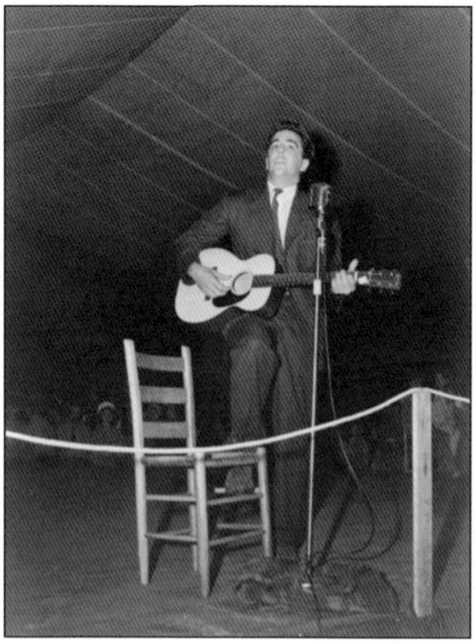

Ethnomusicologist Alan Lomax plays a guitar in 1940. *Lomax* is the 2013 award-winning short film about the legendary researcher's travels to the South (including the Delta Lowlands' Cummins and Tucker Prisons). Lomax recorded blues and folk music for the Library of Congress. It costars Altheimer-born recording artist James "Tail Dragger" Jones, who plays the role of Muddy Waters. Jones has also had roles in full-length movies like *Death and Taxis* (2007) and *Two Rivers* (1999). (Courtesy of Library of Congress.)

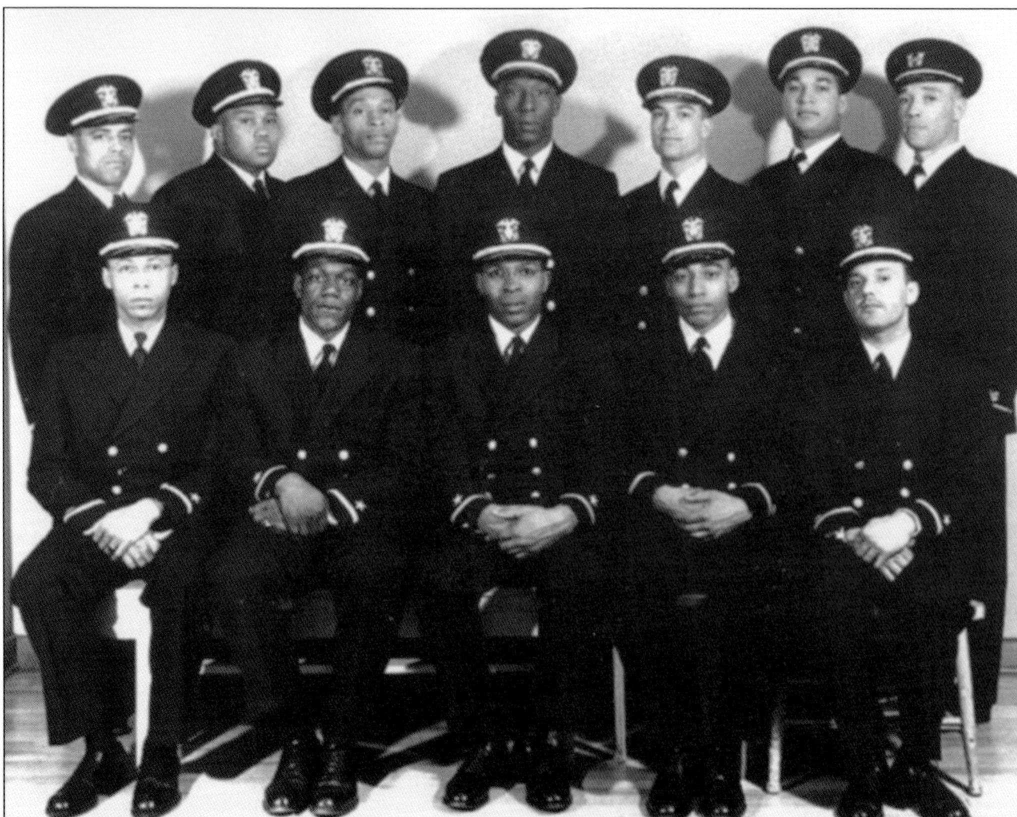

Photo # 80-G-300215 First African-American U.S. Navy officers, 1944

Ens. Jessie Arbor (seated, center) and Ens. Dalton Baugh (standing, center), both Arkansas AM&N (UAPB) graduates, pose proudly with their peers, "The Golden 13," commissioned in 1944 as the US Navy's first African American officers. After reading *The Golden Thirteen: Recollections of the First Black Naval Officers,* acting legend Sidney Poitier set out with TriStar Productions in 1994 to direct a Hollywood movie about their exploits. While a screenplay was written, funding issues prevented completion of the project. (Courtesy of US Navy.)

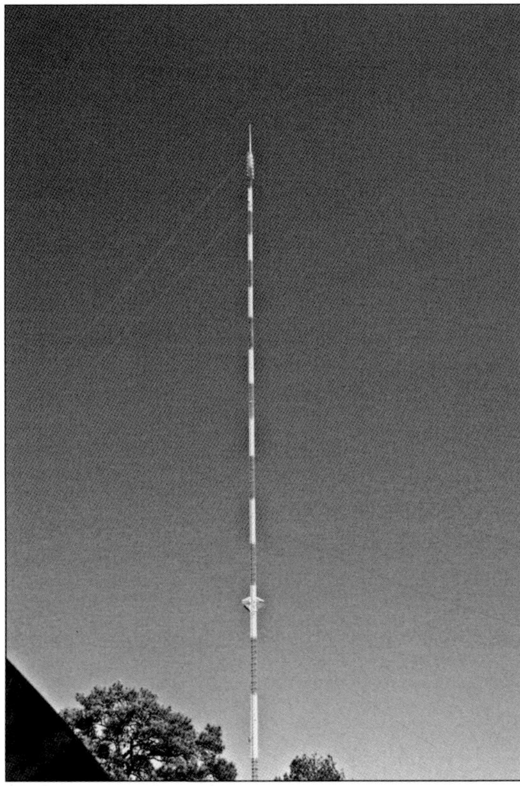

The KATV tower stands near Redfield before it collapsed in 2008. KATV was originally a Pine Bluff–based television station when it first aired in 1953. It was the first television station in Arkansas to broadcast a VHF signal. KATV's tower, when built in 1967, was the second tallest man-made structure in the world according to NBC News. The authors of this book hope to see the Delta Lowlands scale even greater heights in showcasing its majestic music and film story for the world to both admire and experience. So many possibilities exist for heritage tourism and public education with such a potent and rich narrative. With a primary roadway in US Highway 65 connecting the entire Delta Lowlands, there is no reason why the region could not become a designated music and film corridor in the same fashion as areas associated with US Highway 61 (Blues Highway) in Mississippi, Interstate 40 from Memphis to Nashville (Music Highway), a small stretch of US Highway 45 near Selmer, Tennessee (Rockabilly Highway), or US Highway 23 (Country Music Highway) in Kentucky. These aforementioned themed highways are not only cultural gems preserving history by allowing the public to creatively "experience" music and art, they are also magnets for significant economic activity because of tourism. By introducing murals, museums, historic signs, public art, conferences, galleries, and festivals in these corridors themed around their powerful music narratives, these places have seen significant economic impact from flocking tourists. In fact, heritage tourism has become a highly profitable "cash crop" for these areas when they have coordinated their regional efforts. This is why places like Clarksdale, Mississippi; Vicksburg, Mississippi; Jackson, Tennessee; and several others in "themed" regions have higher per capita rates of tourism revenue than any towns or cities in the Delta Lowlands. Given the Delta Lowlands' remarkable music and film innovations, particularly in Jefferson, Lincoln, Desha, and Chicot Counties, there is ample potential in developing a coalition designed to create new interpretive mediums promoting the region's rich artistic assets found in this Highway 65 corridor. Only time will tell if the Delta Lowlands' leadership has the vision, creativity, and wherewithal to plan and execute new ways to present its unique narrative and extol its resplendent role as a national and international leader in music and film innovation. (Courtesy of Andy King.)